READING
ISAIAH

OVERTURES TO BIBLICAL THEOLOGY

Editors

WALTER BRUEGGEMANN, Professor of Old Testament at Columbia Theological Seminary, Decatur, Georgia

JOHN R. DONAHUE, S.J., Professor of New Testament at University of Notre Dame, Notre Dame, Indiana

ELIZABETH STRUTHERS MALBON, Associate Professor of Religion, Virginia Polytechnic Institute and State University, Blacksburg, Virginia

CHRISTOPHER R. SEITZ, Associate Professor of Old Testament, Yale Divinity School, New Haven, Connecticut

READING ISAIAH

EDGAR W. CONRAD

 FORTRESS PRESS   Minneapolis

In memory of my father
AMOS K. CONRAD
with whom I talked about
this book while it was being
written, but who died before it
could be read.

READING ISAIAH

Copyright © 1991 Augsburg Fortress. All rights reserved. Except for brief quotations in critical articles or reviews, no part of this book may be reproduced in any manner without prior written permission from the publisher. Write to: Permissions, Augsburg Fortress, 426 S. Fifth St., Box 1209, Minneapolis, MN 55440.

Scripture quotations unless otherwise noted are from the Revised Standard Version of the Bible, copyright © 1946, 1952, and 1971 by the Division of Christian Education of the National Council of Churches.

Chapter 2, "The Royal Narratives and the Structure of the Book of Isaiah," originally appeared in another form in *Journal for the Study of the Old Testament* 41 (1988): 67-81 and is reprinted here by permission of Sheffield Academic Press.

Library of Congress Cataloging-in-Publication Data

Conrad, Edgar W., 1942–
    Reading Isaiah / Edgar W. Conrad.
        p.   cm. — (Overtures to biblical theology : [27])
    Includes bibliographical references and indexes.
    ISBN 0-8006-1560-3 (alk. paper)
    1. Bible. O.T. Isaiah — Criticism, interpretation, etc.
    2. Bible. O.T. Isaiah — Reading. I. Title. II. Series.
    BS1515.2.C663   1991
    224'.1066 — dc20   91-18768
                                                                   CIP

The paper used in this publication meets the minimum requirements of American National Standard for Information Sciences — Permanence of Paper for Printed Library Materials, ANSI Z329.48-1984.   ∞™

Manufactured in the U.S.A.   AF 1-1560

95   94   93   92   91   1   2   3   4   5   6   7   8   9   10

Contents

Editor's
Foreword

Edgar Conrad's book is an act of considerable methodological courage. It seeks to articulate with sustained argument and with textual specificity an interpretation of the Book of Isaiah that reflects a drastically changed interpretive situation. His argument reflects on how far we have moved in Old Testament studies in a short time. It also suggests that we may be close to a clear form of interpretation that will bring us out of the confused, formless methodological situation of the past decade.

The enormous ferment in Isaiah studies of the last decade has been more visible than that of almost any other book in the Old Testament. This is with reference to the work of Childs, Clements, Ackroyd, Rendtorff, and Sweeney, among others. Isaiah studies, however, are not unique in this regard. They simply represent a visible point at which dissatisfaction with the older historical-critical consensus has become intolerable. Conrad here brings together, takes account of, and moves beyond the considerable scholarly contribution of the past decade, providing the first synthetic presentation we have for the Book of Isaiah out of these new efforts.

Conrad's book provides a telling point from which to assess the development of the Overtures to Biblical Theology series. It is clear that Conrad has taken up a perspective and approach not heretofore utilized in the series. Indeed, his work comes the closest of any volume in the series to being an intense and intentional interface of methodological and interpretive concerns. Conrad persistently asks how new method is linked to and generative of new interpretation. In addition to Conrad's own courage and erudition, his book comes at a poignant moment in the maturing of an alternative perspective. The book accomplishes something that would not have been possible, or even conceivable, a decade ago, when the series began. His book demonstrates that we are closer to methodological clarity than we have been at any time in the brief history of the series.

Conrad's methodological focus is on the newer advances in literary theory, and he puts those advances to good advantage. The emerging importance of literary theory, however, belongs to a larger shift of categories that touches all intellectual disciplines. The larger issues he engages through literary theory are at least three. First is a reluctance, or even refusal, to continue Scripture study in the old categories of historical criticism. It can be argued that this is simply a new mode of historical criticism; such an argument, however, makes the notion of "historical criticism" so broad as to be meaningless. Quite different questions are being asked that, predictably, permit a new range of interpretive responses.

Second, the new questions reflect what is now frequently termed a postmodern or post-Enlightenment situation. It is no longer possible to imagine that the older mode of study has been "objective" or "value neutral." Indeed the older approaches (still insisted upon by some) are seen to be simply the interpretive work of a particular confessional community whose creedal standing ground is found in presumed objectivity. Such a claim increasingly carried little persuasion. We are now much more aware of our capacity to "make meaning" from a text that is open to many meanings, although not, as Conrad recognizes, open to just any chosen meaning. Such an openness to the multiple meanings of the text does not, as Conrad makes clear, open the interpretive door to unrestrained subjectivity. The contours of interpretive discipline are now of another kind, more integrally related to the text itself, rather than to scholarly constructs.

Third, Conrad shows how the shift to postmodern categories creates new openings for theological rereading. Because all such reading is interpretive, the interpreter is free to honor the claims of the text itself, claims often made in "God categories" not palatable to modernist mentality. Thus the claim of the text need not be "purified" by Enlightenment rationality but may be taken as given, as the substance of interpretation. Conrad has made only a beginning in this matter, and we have yet to see how the embrace of serious literary theory can permit and evoke a different theological interpretation. We are only at the beginning of such an enterprise, because until now, those most prepared to do literary criticism have been most reluctant to move toward theological interpretation. The importance of Conrad's work is that while he attends carefully to methodological issues, in the end he cares about the claims of the text itself.

Conrad's study is thus not about literary theory or about postmodern rationality or even about the interface of literary and theological enterprises. It is about the Book of Isaiah. Conrad shows how asking different questions of the Book of Isaiah permits our hearing afresh. His is a remarkable achievement, well written, thoughtful, irenic while daring. His is a major marker in the new season of Isaiah interpretation, sure to invite and generate more work in new directions. Such work is so crucial because in the new season of postmodern culture, biblical scholarship has a chance to be a first-class contributor to "meaning making" and "culture making." That meaning making arises in a struggle with the "otherness" of the text, which refuses to be domesticated. That chance brings with it enormous opportunity, severe responsibility, and fresh demands. While modernity has marginalized Scripture study (and historical critics have conspired in that marginality), scholarship faces opportunity, responsibility, and demand that move against such marginalization. Conrad's book reflects a new prospect for what interpretation can do and enacts a new duty. Conrad shows a way in which careful interpretive work may permit the Bible a serious hearing in a larger, more dangerous, more urgent arena. Perhaps the act of interpretation could be one as public and as significant as was the long-sounding voice of Isaiah, profoundly public and profoundly significant.

Walter Brueggemann
Columbia Theological Seminary

Preface

This study grows out of earlier work in which I attempted to show how biblical scholars could move beyond the traditional interest of form criticism in *Sitz im Leben* by considering the literary settings of literary units, or *Gattungen*. The bulk of the work was accomplished during two study leaves granted to me by the University of Queensland. The study was initiated during the northern hemisphere's fall semester of 1985, spent at the University of Heidelberg in West Germany. I wish to express my thanks to the university for the opportunity to work there and to live at the *Gästehaus*. I owe special thanks to Helga and Manfred Weippert. Although our approaches to the Old Testament text were somewhat different, the time I shared with them was both profitable and enjoyable. The bulk of the writing was completed during the northern hemisphere's spring semester of 1989, spent at Union Theological Seminary in Richmond, Virginia. I owe special thanks to Sibley Towner and William V. Arnold for helping me to arrange my stay at Union and to Mrs. B. D. Aycock, the associate librarian, for all the assistance she offered. I had many insightful conversations with Ray Jones, who was completing his dissertation on Isaiah at the time of my visit.

Special thanks should go to Han Spykerboer of Trinity Theological College in Brisbane, with whom I shared monthly luncheons in which our conversation inevitably turned to Isaiah. His perceptive comments and his patient ear have contributed much to the present venture. I am also grateful to Francis I. Andersen, an Old Testament colleague at the University of Queensland, whose office door was always open for helpful advice. Philip C. Almond, a colleague and head of the Department of Studies in Religion at the University of Queensland, kindly agreed to read the first and last chapters of the book and offered many valuable suggestions. My wife, Linda, who finished work on her doctoral dissertation in American literature while I was working on this project, was a constant partner in conversation and helped me clarify and sharpen my thinking on methodological matters. Finally, I express my thanks to Christopher Seitz and Walter Brueggemann, who have shown confidence in my work by accepting it for their series and who have offered advice as the final draft reached its completion.

Brisbane
January 1990

Abbreviations

AB	Anchor Bible
AnBib	Analecta Biblica
BCSR	*Bulletin of the Council on the Study of Religion*
BHS	*Biblia hebraica stuttgartensia*
BJRL	*Bulletin of the John Rylands University Library of Manchester*
BKAT	Biblischer Kommentar: Altes Testament
BTB	*Biblical Theology Bulletin*
BZAW	Beihefte zur Zeitschrift für die alttestamentliche Wissenschaft
CBQ	*Catholic Biblical Quarterly*
CBQMS	Catholic Biblical Quarterly – Monograph Series
ConBOT	Coniectanea biblica, Old Testament
DSB	Daily Study Bible Series
HTR	*Harvard Theological Review*
IB	*Interpreter's Bible*
IDB	*Interpreter's Dictionary of the Bible*
IDBS	*Interpreter's Dictionary of the Bible Supplement*
Int	*Interpretation*
ISBE	*International Standard Bible Encyclopedia*
JAAR	*Journal of the American Academy of Religion*
JBL	*Journal of Biblical Literature*
JES	*Journal of Ecumenical Studies*
JQR	*Jewish Quarterly Review*
JR	*Journal of Religion*
JSOT	*Journal for the Study of the Old Testament*

JSOTSup	Journal for the Study of the Old Testament — Supplement Series
MT	Masoretic Text
NCB	New Century Bible
OBT	Overtures to Biblical Theology
OTL	Old Testament Library
RSV	Revised Standard Version
SJT	*Scottish Journal of Theology*
VT	*Vetus Testamentum*
VTSup	Vetus Testamentum, Supplements
WBC	Word Biblical Commentary
WMANT	Wissenschaftliche Monographien zum Alten und Neuen Testament
ZAW	*Zeitschrift für die alttestamentliche Wissenschaft*

Introduction

The prevailing historical-critical reading of Isaiah has developed strategies focusing on the inception of the text. Since the book is seen to have originated as two or three once-independent sources, the book is read as if it were two or three Isaiahs. Even the recent redactional-critical studies of Isaiah manifest an interest in origin — that is, in how the two or three Isaiahs became one Isaiah. The meaning of the text is located in the intentions of the authors of the text, and those intentions are associated with a determination of the inception of the book.

The locus of meaning with authorial intention is at considerable variance with contemporary literary theory, which is increasingly locating meaning in the process of reading (i.e., with the reception of the text). The reader, rather than being a passive receiver of a text communicating its meaning, is an active agent in making texts speak. The author is seen to lose active control of meaning and recedes into the background.

The reading of Isaiah offered in this volume is at variance with the standard historical-critical approach to the text, since it acknowledges the primary role of the reader in the construction of a text's meaning. Although I offer a critique of the normative historical-critical reading of Isaiah because of its methodological techniques designed to explore the text's inception, I see my own reading of the book as growing out of the wealth of scholarship that the historical-critical reading of Isaiah represents. The approach I take in this study has affinities with form criticism. This is the one historical-critical technique that has shown an interest in literary convention

1

and audience reception. As it has been practiced in the study of the Old Testament, however, including the study of Isaiah, form criticism has focused on small units (*Gattungen*) rather than on complete books. Because form criticism was made to serve the primary historical-critical interest in author intention, it never developed its full potential for studying the reception of literary texts such as Isaiah.

In the following study, chapter 1 outlines in detail a critique of the prevailing historical-critical reading of Isaiah and the basis for my alternative approach to the book. Chapters 2 to 5 contain my actual reading of the Book of Isaiah. Here I make an argument for understanding the structural wholeness of the book and discuss the implied audience encoded in the text. Chapter 6 looks more broadly at the Book of Isaiah and its contemporary readers. I argue that while all interpretations of Isaiah are reader dependent, reading strategies need to recognize both its otherness and its familiarity.

CHAPTER 1

Choosing Reading Strategies

The twentieth century has witnessed a notable change in the way literary critics have understood a text to have meaning. At the beginning of the century the meaning of a text was primarily associated with authorial intentions. With the rise of the New Criticism and later of structuralism, the text itself was emphasized as an object of study detached from matters surrounding its inception. More recently the meaning of a text is increasingly being understood as emerging in the reading process itself.[1] The emergence of the reader in the establishment of meaning has radical implications for the historical-critical approach, which has predominated in the study of Bible during the twentieth century.

A central problematic assumption of historical criticism can be seen in the following comment by Brian Rice McCarthy: "One of the great scholarly and religious achievements of modern biblical studies has been . . . to allow each of the writings to speak its own distinctive word unhampered."[2] The problem with such a statement is that

1. For a discussion of reader-response criticism, see Robert C. Holub, *Reception Theory: A Critical Introduction*, New Accents (London: Methuen, 1984); Jane P. Tompkins, ed., *Reader Response Criticism: From Formalism to Post-Structuralism* (Baltimore: Johns Hopkins University Press, 1980); and Susan Suleiman and Inge Crosman, eds., *The Reader in the Text: Essays on Audience and Interpretation* (Princeton: Princeton University Press, 1980). For a study of the change of literary-critical methods and their relation to the study of the Bible, see John Barton, *Reading the Old Testament: Method in Biblical Study* (London: Darton, Longman and Todd, 1984); and Edgar V. McKnight, *The Bible and the Reader: An Introduction to Literary Criticism* (Philadelphia: Fortress Press, 1985). For a study that emphasizes the importance of reading in theological reflection on the Bible, see Werner G. Jeanrond, *Text and Interpretation as Categories of Theological Thinking*, trans. Thomas J. Wilson (New York: Crossroad, 1988).
2. Brian Rice McCarthy, "Reforming the Church's Self-Understanding: The Role of Historical-Critical Studies," *JES* 24 (1987): 232–53.

it personifies texts, speaking of them as if they did things, and fails to recognize that interpreters, not texts, actively create meaning. As Stanley Fish says,

> The text as an entity independent of interpretation and responsible for its own career . . . is replaced [in Fish's theory of interpretation] by texts that emerge as the consequence of our interpretive activities. . . . The relationship between interpretation and text is thus reversed: interpretive strategies are not put into execution after reading; they are the shape of reading, and because they are the shape of reading, they give texts their shape, making them rather than, as is usually assumed, arising from them.[3]

When historical critics claim that meaning emerges from authorial intention, they locate the origin of that meaning in the text rather than in the reading process. Fish says that it is easy

> to surrender to the bias of our critical language and begin to talk as if poems, not readers or interpreters, did things . . . it is only "natural" to assign agency first to an author's intentions and then to the forms that assumedly embody them. What really happens, I think, is something quite different: rather than intention and its formal realization producing interpretation (the "normal" picture), interpretation creates intention and its formal realization by creating the conditions in which it becomes possible to pick them out.[4]

If readers shape texts, and if readers make texts speak, then what are the interpretive strategies that historical-critical readers of the Bible bring to the text and that they confuse with the text's intention to speak for itself? These strategies are manifested in two goals: to discover the intentions of the authors of biblical books, and to read the texts against their historical backgrounds.[5] These two aims of

---

3. Stanley Fish, *Is There a Text in This Class? The Authority of Interpretive Communities* (Cambridge: Harvard University Press, 1980), 13. For a perceptive discussion of the implication of Fish's reader-response theory for biblical studies, see Stephen D. Moore, "Negative Hermeneutics, Insubstantial Texts: Stanley Fish and the Biblical Interpreter," *JAAR* 54 (1986): 707–19. For another study that emphasizes the important role of the reader in the establishment of meaning, see Wolfgang Iser, *The Act of Reading: A Theory of Aesthetic Response* (London: Routledge and Kegan Paul, 1978).
4. Fish, *Is There a Text?* 163.
5. James Barr notes the importance of this twofold emphasis on intention and background. "The biblical scholar on the whole interprets the biblical text on the basis of its *origins,* its *background,* the process which led up to it, and, above all, the *intentions* of the person or persons who produced it. In this sense we may say that biblical

historical criticism indicate an important assumption about the philosophy of language on which this interpretive enterprise rests. The assumption is that language is referential—that it designates realities external to it. This point is stated clearly by James Barr.

> Once we think of the Bible as literature, and take as units not the single words but the great literary and stylistic complexes, it becomes more and more difficult to find any use for a referential idea of meaning. The literature is its own meaning; we cannot expect to identify a set of external realities of which it is a linguistic sign, and nobody approaches other literatures in such a way. It is thus interesting that the French structuralist position seeks to avoid the reduction of the text to *a thing signified,* the expression of its meaning as the designation of something external to itself. In the theological tradition of biblical study, on the other hand, one has sought to *disengage* from the text the theological or "kerygmatic" truth, which is then taken as the essence of its mean- ing. Our survey of approaches to the Bible as literature suggests that this traditional theological treatment of the message of the Bible may be no longer possible. To say this is not to deny that the existence of any "thing signified"; it is not to maintain that the great theological entities simply are not there. It is rather that the Bible, when seen as the sort of literature that it is, is not the kind of language which can be taken as a direct representation of them.[6]

Specifically, historical critics understand the language of the Bible to signify the intentions of the author and the historical background of the text — realities that are external to it. When they say that a text should be allowed to speak for itself, they mean that it should be allowed to express authorial intentions and historical background.

scholarship is focused upon *intentionality.* Even when it goes beyond merely histori- cal assessment, it tends to look for the *theological intention,* the *kerygmatic intention* and the like, of the author or of the tradition behind him" ("Reading the Bible as Literature," *BJRL* 56 [1973]: 21).
6. Ibid., 32. Others have pointed out the problem with the historical-critical assump- tion that language is primarily referential. See David J. A. Clines, "Story and Poem: The Old Testament as Literature and as Scripture," *Int* 34 (1980): 118–19, 126. See also David Gunn, "New Directions in the Study of Hebrew Narrative," *JSOT* 39 (1987): 66. Dale Patrick (*The Rendering of God in the Old Testament,* OBT [Phila- delphia: Fortress Press, 1981]) argues that the language of the Bible describes a God who does not exist outside of language. For a discussion of the problematic use of documents in historical research because of the assumption that language is referen- tial, see Dominick LaCapra, *History and Criticism* (Ithaca: Cornell University Press, 1985), 15–44.

LOOKING FOR ISAIAH IN ISAIAH

Another important assumption has governed the reading of Isaiah and other prophetic books. The influence of nineteenth-century Romanticism on biblical studies resulted in a change in the perception of the prophet. Since then the view has persisted that the prophet is a preacher who spoke orally and not, as it was previously thought, a writer who composed written discourse. Furthermore, because it was assumed that ecstatic experience motivated the prophet to speak, it was concluded that the prophet spoke in short, poetically formed oracles rather than in longer connected discourse.[7] This assumption of the prophet as speaker of terse oracular outbursts, coupled with the interpretive strategies that aimed to discover the intentions of the author against the historical background in which the author spoke, has led historical-critical readers to shape—or better, radically to reshape—the text of Isaiah.

Since the Book of Isaiah is a written text of sixty-six chapters, the specific task of the historical-critical interpreter was to look for the prophet Isaiah in the Book of Isaiah. It was important not only to locate the short poetic oracles of the prophet but also to identify the specific historical background that occasioned them. This search for the prophet Isaiah in the Book of Isaiah has introduced complications in the reading of Isaiah and made it a highly complex undertaking. Not only have these interpretive strategies produced the prevailing view that the Book of Isaiah contains not one but three Isaiahs, they have also led to the discovery of other anonymous voices in the book. As a result, a major concern of historical criticism has been to differentiate the authentic words of the prophet from the inauthentic words of later voices.

Because the critic's search for the short oracular units of Isaiah resulted in the discovery of three Isaiahs and additional anonymous voices, the Book of Isaiah was understood to be a collection having no coherence of thought and no unity giving shape to the whole. In short, the book was seen as a collection of collections of material that grew over a period of three centuries or more. The point to be

---

7. For a more detailed discussion of the Romantic influence on the perception of the prophetic vocation, see, e.g., Bertil Wiklander, *Prophecy as Literature: A Text Linguistic and Rhetorical Approach to Isaiah 2–4*, ConB OT 22 (Stockholm: Liber Tryck, 1984): 9–16.

made here is that the reading gave this shape to the book. For the book to be otherwise would make the aims the readers brought to the text unattainable.

The reading of Isaiah by Georg Fohrer, an eminent biblical scholar whose writings typify the standard historical-critical approach to the text of Isaiah, represents a specific instance of the working out of these interpretive strategies. The assumption that the origins of the prophetic oracle originated in the ecstatic experience of the prophet is clearly evident in his description of the origin and development of the prophetic oracle.

> The development of the prophetic oracle . . . normally consists of an extended process involving at least four stages. . . . The first stage is *a moment of personal experience of God, in which God's "spirit" or "word" comes to the prophet* . . . or in which he is transported to another sphere. . . . *What he experiences or perceives he is constrained to put into words and to proclaim.* . . . Therefore, immediately after his secret experience the prophet begins to ponder over it.
>
> In the second stage come the prophet's interpretation and exposition of his unique experience according to the faith by which he lives. *The new experience is interpreted in such a way that the individual experience is incorporated into the prophet's previous total picture of God's nature and will,* enlarging it and vitalizing it. . . .
>
> Next follows, as the third stage, the process of intellectual revision. . . . This takes place so naturally that the prophet sometimes adds an appropriate motivation or appends an obvious conclusion to the word of Yahweh. *At the same time, this stage produces words spoken by the prophet in his own right, which he forms without any preceding secret experience on the basis of his certainty that he can speak as Yahweh's messenger.* This much can generally be said: *the less mediation and rational revision a prophetical oracle betrays, the more tersely and unconditionally it proclaims God's will, the more clearly it preserves as its nucleus a primitive complex of sounds . . . , the closer we are to its origin.* . . .
>
> The third stage is paralleled by a fourth, that of artistic development, to which belong the adaptation of the message to a specific, sometimes very ancient, rhetorical form and its clothing in metrical poetry.[8]

8. G. Fohrer, *Introduction to the Old Testament,* trans. David E. Green (Nashville: Abingdon, 1965), 349–50, italics mine. Fohrer discusses the formation of prophetic books on pp. 342–62 and the three Isaiahs on pp. 363–88. See also his *Das Buch Jesaja,* 3 vols., Zürcher Bibelkommentare (Stuttgart: Zwingli, 1962–64); "Entstehung, Komposition, und Überlieferung von Jesaja 1–39," *BZAW* 99 (1967): 113–47;

This elaborate understanding of the development of the prophetic oracle demonstrates the careful way in which Fohrer attempts to read the text so as to arrive at the intentions of the prophet that originated in the prophet's experience of God. Fohrer's understanding of the original prophetic word as a "primitive complex of sounds" preserves the conception of prophecy that developed in the Romantic period.

Since Fohrer, as a historical critic, is interested in the intentions of the spoken words of Isaiah understood against their historical background, and since he characterizes the original words of a prophet as terse and containing primitive complexes of sounds, his aim is to find the original words of Isaiah in the book (which is not terse and which is not a primitive complex of sounds). The aim of his reading has shaped the book. Fohrer's reading quest for the authentic words of the prophet,[9] which are in the book but are not equated with it, has resulted in his understanding of the book as a collection containing both the authentic and inauthentic words of Isaiah.

Fohrer's quest for the original words of Isaiah means that the process of collection is understood in a mechanical way.[10] The aim

and "Jesaja 1 als Zusammenfassung der Verkündigung Jesajas," *BZAW* 99 (1967): 148-67.

9. See Fohrer, *Introduction,* 358-62. That this quest of Fohrer is typical of modern historical-critical scholarship is evident in a remark of Joseph Blenkinsopp, who recently surveyed the results of critical scholarship in his book *A History of Prophecy in Israel: From the Settlement in the Land to the Hellenistic Period* (Philadelphia: Fortress Press, 1983). He notes, "Applying literary criticism to the task of identifying the actual words of the prophets, their 'authentic' message as distinct from 'secondary' editorial accretions, it [historical criticism] claimed to find in them a unique class of religious individualists with a message focused on the present rather than the distant past or distant future." Blenkinsopp adds, "One of the most significant achievements of biblical scholarship in the nineteenth century was the rediscovery of prophecy as a distinctive religious category" (p. 27). To acknowledge the important role of the reader in interpretation, however, should soften this sort of conclusion. It is more likely that the category of prophecy was constructed in a new way for the first time in the nineteenth century rather than having been lost and rediscovered.

10. Fohrer, *Introduction,* 239-40. The view that the Book of Isaiah is a collection understood as a mechanical process is reflected in the following comment: "The first part of Isaiah (1-39) is not an organically constructed work but a collection of separate little books. All these (except 36-39, which is an extract from Kings) were circulating as separate collections of oracles, repeatedly edited, before they were copied together on a single scroll of papyrus. It is only because sufficient space remained on the scroll that the final editor of the four prophetic volumes (Is., Jer., Ez., and The Twelve)—which are really a comprehensive edition of all prophetic

is to isolate the original words of the prophet. The collectors themselves cannot be understood as authors who creatively rewrote the original words of the prophet, overriding the original intentions of Isaiah with intentions of their own.[11] To attribute creative ingenuity to the collector would call into question recovery of the original words of the prophet.

Fohrer outlines his understanding of the process of collection of First Isaiah (i.e., chaps. 1–39) in his article "Entstehung, Komposition und Überlieferung von Jesaja 1–39." He understands chapters 1–39 to be a collection of seven earlier and once-independent collections (*Sammlungen*) of Isaiah's oracles.[12] He identifies the same principles of arrangement in each of the collections, which "stand out clearly from one another and are built up mostly out of three elements:

1. the body of the collection,
2. one or more fragments of Isaiah's oracles,
3. a concluding promise."[13]

Within each of the seven collections he identifies principles used by the redactors to link the individual oracles to one another. These include the principle of using a catchword (*Stichwort*).[14]

By viewing the collection as containing a core of material, followed by several fragments of oracles of Isaiah and concluding with

oracles accessible in 200 B.C. — copied Is. 40–66 (then circulating as a separate book) after Is. 1–39. Thus about 200 B.C. originated our Book of Isaiah, for which the first attestation is found in Sirach . . . , about 180 B.C. With respect to the structure of the whole, as a miniature library rather than a book, Isaiah is not essentially different from the Book of the Minor Prophets, and could nearly be regarded, like Psalms and Proverbs, as an anthology or rather a 'collection of collections'" (R. H. Pfeiffer, *Introduction to the Old Testament* [New York: Harper and Brothers, 1941], 447–48).

11. See Marvin A. Sweeney, *Isaiah 1–4 and the Post-Exilic Understanding of the Isaianic Tradition*, BZAW 171 (Berlin: de Gruyter, 1988). Sweeney, a redaction critic who sees his work moving beyond that of Fohrer and others of his generation, says: "Past scholarship viewed redactors in opposition to authors. Their basic task was not creative, like that of authors, but mechanical, merely to collect and transmit older literary works" (p. 2).

12. Fohrer, "Entstehung," 117–32.

13. Ibid., 115. (Here and throughout, translations from German sources are my own.) See also his *Introduction*, 365. Curiously, while Fohrer understands these collections to have originated independently of one another, he does not explain why each of these collections has the same structure.

14. Fohrer, "Entstehung," 131.

a promise, Fohrer's reading of the Book of Isaiah has shaped it in such a way as to enable him to carry out his interpretive goal of discovering the intentions of the prophet Isaiah. Also, by viewing the oracles as linked together by *Stichwörte*, he is shaping the text to accomplish his other goal of discovering the background of each of the oracles of Isaiah. If the oracles are strung together like links on a chain (i.e., where the last word of one oracle is linked to the one following because it contains the same or a similar word), then the oracles can be easily detached from one another and studied according to the individual and different historical backgrounds of each one.[15]

Fohrer has very little to say about the relationship of First Isaiah to the material that follows in chapters 40–66. Here he is following the convention of viewing the Book of Isaiah as not one but three books. In his *Introduction to the Old Testament,* he discusses Isaiah as if it were three independent books and sees the relationship of chapters 1–39 to 40–66 as a mechanical one. He speculates that the anonymous prophet that scholars refer to as Deutero-Isaiah could have had the same name as the Isaiah of chapters 1–39, "which would account for the association of his book with the earlier one."[16] Since he sees no evidence for this hypothesis, he gives more

15. It is interesting to compare Fohrer's understanding of the process of collection with that of C. H. Cornill, "Die Composition des Buches Jesaja," *ZAW* 4 (1884): 83–105. In "Entstheung," Fohrer began his discussion of past scholarship on the composition of the Book of Isaiah with Cornill. Cornill argued that the redactor of First Isaiah used two main principles in the arrangement of Isaiah's prophecies. "(1) The redactor had the intention to order the prophecies of the Book of Isaiah chronologically; a series of pieces, which he was not able to establish chronologically, he placed at the beginning of his collection as a kind of Prologue. (2) Within this chronological frame the order of the material is accomplished mostly according to catchwords [author trans.]" (p. 85). Cornill's understanding of the structure of Isaiah is thus much simpler than Fohrer's. It merely says that the book is arranged chronologically, often using *Stichworten.* Such a simple principle of organization, however, makes it more difficult to distinguish the oracles of Isaiah from the inauthentic oracles. Fohrer's more complex structure—of a plurality of collections, each organized around a detailed set of principles—actually makes identification of the authentic words of Isaiah easier. The more complex the structure of the collection, the simpler becomes the task of identifying the oracles of Isaiah.
16. Fohrer, *Introduction,* 375. Fohrer discusses First Isaiah on pp. 363–73, Second Isaiah on pp. 373–84, and Third Isaiah on pp. 384–88. The three are treated in separate sections of the book as if they were as unrelated as Amos, Hosea, and Micah.

credence to the view that Second Isaiah was added to First Isaiah to give it status by association to Deutero-Isaiah's preaching.[17]

Fohrer's reading of Isaiah has been presented in some detail to illustrate how the interpretive strategies of historical criticism — to let the text speak its author's intentions and to communicate information about its historical background — has resulted in the shaping of Isaiah as a collection that contains but does not equate with the words of Isaiah. Not all historical-critical readings of Isaiah using these shared interpretive strategies will arrive at the same results as Fohrer's reading. For example, Fohrer's conclusion that the eighth-century prophet Isaiah was a prophet of judgment and that all unconditional promises of salvation are to be judged as secondary has sparked debate.[18] Indeed, the secondary literature is filled with rival positions on a myriad of issues: the identification of the authentic words of Isaiah, the consistency of Isaiah's attitude toward Assyria, Isaiah's relation to the wisdom tradition, the location of his call, and so forth. Shared interpretive strategies do not guarantee shared or common results.

Here again Fish's insights concerning the reading process are important for the discussion. If, as Fish points out, the meaning of a text arises in the reading process, so that the reader is a kind of coauthor who completes a text in his or her reading of it, then theoretically there are as many texts as there are readers. This raises an important question that relates to the problem of the plurality of views on the Book of Isaiah held by historical-critical scholars. If the meaning of a text is so reader dependent, then why do the myriad of possible interpretations not result in total interpretive chaos? Or, to state the question positively, if there are ultimately as many

17. Ibid. Here Fohrer is also following Cornill, who gives the same two reasons for explaining how the two parts of the book now form one book. Cornill says, "The words of 39, 6-7, with their twice-repeated *bbl*, are the reason which united the great Babylonian address of Isaiah 40–66 to Isaiah 39. This has been used all the time as a main proof for the authenticity of Deutero-Isaiah by Apologists." Furthermore, "the simplest assumption to me, then, is that this Deutero-Isaiah was actually named Isaiah and that the identity of the name in association with the position of Isa. 39, 6-7 led the redactor to place this piece at the end of the assembled Isaiah [author trans.]," (pp. 103–4). See Pfeiffer, *Introduction,* who suggests an even more mechanical relation between these two parts of the book when he maintains that Second Isaiah was added to First Isaiah because there was room left over on the scroll.
18. See, e.g., Joseph Jensen's critique of Fohrer's position in "Weal and Woe in Isaiah: Consistency and Continuity," *CBQ* 43 (1981): 167–87.

possible meanings as there are readers, why do interpreters produce interpretations of texts that so closely approximate one another that debate and refinement of interpretation are possible?

Fish answers this question by introducing the notion of interpretive communities. He points out that the interpretation of texts has social implications, for an interpreter of a text brings to it interpretive strategies that are shared with other members of an interpretive community. These shared interpretive strategies result in approximate readings or interpretations. Because these interpretive strategies become conventional and have social support, most interpreters are unaware of them, assuming that the meaning purportedly embedded in a text gives rise to the interpretation. What really happens, Fish maintains, is just the opposite: the interpretive strategies that readers bring to a text give rise to meaning.[19] Because historical-critical scholars share interpretive strategies, a common discourse emerges in the interpretive enterprise that creates order out of a possible verbal chaos.

LOOKING FOR THE REDACTOR IN ISAIAH

Interpretive communities do not remain static. While interpretive strategies control and give shape to reading, the strategies will change over time.[20] Such a change in the reading of Isaiah has recently become evident in the interpretive strategies of historical critics. A critic such as Fohrer judged the role of the redactor to be mechanical. The redactor merely collected the words of the prophet,

---

19. Fish, *Is There a Text?* 15-17 and 167-73. He asks: "Why should two or more readers ever agree, and why should regular, that is, habitual, differences in the career of a single reader ever occur? What is the explanation on the one hand of the stability of interpretation (at least among certain groups at certain times) and on the other of the orderly variety of interpretation if it is not the stability and variety of texts? The answer to all of these questions is to be found in a notion that has been implicit in my argument, the notion of *interpretive communities.* Interpretive communities are made up of those who share interpretive strategies not for reading (in the conventional sense) but for writing texts, for constituting their properties and assigning their intentions. In other words, these strategies exist prior to the act of reading and therefore determine the shape of what is read rather than, as is usually assumed, the other way around. If it is an article of faith in a particular community that there are a variety of texts, its members will boast a repertoire of strategies for making them. And if a community believes in the existence of only one text, then the single strategy its members employ will be forever writing it" (p. 171).
20. Ibid., 171-72.

and the book was judged to be a collection or anthology, so that the whole did not have an integrated structure enabling the reader to read the book as a connected and coherent piece of literature. Recent studies indicate, however, that critics are beginning to view the redactor not simply as a collector but as a creative editor. Here the input of the redactor is more like that of an author[21] who creates and shapes and therefore gives new meaning to the original words of the prophet.[22] The Book of Isaiah is increasingly being seen not so much as a grouping of largely unrelated small units of material but, because of the creative role of the redactor, as a "redactionally unified whole."[23]

This change in the view of the redaction of the Book of Isaiah, from that of a collection to a redactionally unified whole, did not occur instantaneously. In early scholarly discussions, the unity of the book was attributed to a school of disciples who gathered, updated, and added to the words of the original prophet to meet changing needs in changing historical circumstances.[24] According to this view, the community of disciples generated new material that received its inspiration from the original prophet. The lines of continuity they saw in the book are to be understood as arising from this continuing Isaianic school.[25]

This sociological explanation of redaction still understands the process as collection, although the demarcation of the lines separating the original words of the prophet and the subsequent words generated by the Isaianic school begin to blur. More recently, redaction is being understood as the creative editing of individuals.[26] Thus Hermann Barth sees an anti-Assyrian reworking of Isaiah's oracles at the time of Assyria's decline in the days of Josiah, in the

21. Barton, *Reading the Old Testament*, 201-2, sees the redactor in redaction criticism as an author. See also his "Classifying Biblical Criticism," *JSOT* 29 (1984): 26.
22. John J. Schmitt makes this assessment of the changing role of the redactor in his book *Isaiah and His Interpreters* (New York: Paulist, 1986), 118.
23. This is the position of Sweeney, *Isaiah 1-4*, 5.
24. Isa. 8:16 is normally seen as a reference to this Isaianic school of disciples.
25. The two studies most frequently cited in this connection are D. R. Jones, "The Traditio of the Oracles of Isaiah of Jerusalem," *ZAW* 67 (1955): 226-46; and J. H. Eaton, "The Origin of the Book of Isaiah," *VT* 9 (1959): 138-57.
26. See Schmitt (*Isaiah*, 118), who also points out this change that is taking place in understanding the redaction of prophetic books.

seventh century B.C.E. This anti-Assyrian edition contrasts with the more pro-Assyrian policy of Isaiah of Jerusalem.[27] J. Vermeylen offers a more complex view of the redaction of the book. He postulates that there were seven principal stages in the formation of Isaiah over a period of five hundred years from the preaching of Isaiah to an anti-Samaritan polemic in the postexilic period. He contends that the book was updated about every five years from the time of Isaiah until it attained a sacred status that permitted only additions.[28]

More recently, scholars have begun to argue for a redactional unity based on literary observations concerning the book as a whole. Here the positions of Roland E. Clements and Rolf Rendtorff have received much attention.[29] In his two essays on the redactional unity of Isaiah, Clements argues that while it has clearly been shown that Isaiah is not the work of a single author, there are signs that the book is not simply an accidental collection put together for literary convenience. He says that "the overall structure of the book shows signs of editorial planning and that, at some stage in its growth, attempts were made to read and interpret the book as a whole."[30]

27. Hermann Barth, *Die Jesaja-Worte in der Josiazeit,* WMANT 48 (Neukirchen-Vluyn: Neukirchener Verlag, 1977). Barth has been followed by R. E. Clements in his *Isaiah 1–39,* NCB (Grand Rapids: Eerdmans; London: Marshall, Morgan and Scott, 1980), and in his *Isaiah and the Deliverance of Jerusalem,* JSOTSup 13 (Sheffield: JSOT, 1980). Barth's thesis is also reiterated and supported by Gerald T. Sheppard in his "Anti-Assyrian Redaction and the Canonical Context of Isaiah 1–39," *JBL* 104 (1985): 193–216.
28. J. Vermeylen, *Du prophète Isaïe à l'apocalyptique. Isaïe i–xxxv, miroir d'un démi-millénaire d'expérience religieuse en Israël,* 2 vols. (Paris: J. Gabalda, 1977). For a good review of literature mapping the change in interpretive conventions in Isaianic studies, see Graeme A. Auld, "Poetry, Prophecy, Hermeneutic: Recent Studies in Isaiah," *SJT* 33 (1980): 567–81.
29. R. E. Clements, "The Unity of the Book of Isaiah," *Int* 36 (1982): 117–29, and "Beyond Tradition History: Deutero-Isaianic Development of First Isaiah's Themes," *JSOT* 31 (1985): 95–113; Rolf Rendtorff, "Zur Komposition des Buches Jesaja," *VT* 34 (1984): 295–320.
30. Clements, "Unity," 121. Clements characterizes prevailing scholarship in the following way: "For the most part the Book of Isaiah has been interpreted as comprised of two separate parts which bear little real relationship to each other. Frequently it has not even been felt necessary to explain how these two parts came to be linked, and when this has been forthcoming it has taken the form of an argument based on literary convenience. It is argued that a leather scroll would be of a certain length, and it would be an economic necessity to make full use of this. Later prophecies might therefore be added in order to fill up a scroll with little concern for the mutual relationships of the various sayings, save in the broadest way" (pp. 118–19).

He argues that a correct appreciation of the book should focus on its editorial history and should not, as is usually the case, focus on individual units isolated from the larger literary contexts in a search for original meaning.[31]

While Clements understands the editorial history of the book to be complex and of longer rather than shorter duration, he argues that a relationship between First and Second Isaiah is deliberate. "From the time of their origin, the prophetic sayings of Isa. 40–55 were *intended* as a supplement and sequel to a collection of the earlier sayings of the eighth-century Isaiah of Jerusalem."[32] According to Clements, then, the words of Second Isaiah from the beginning were intentionally linked to an earlier collection of First Isaiah's sayings—not to Isaiah 1–39 in its present form but to an earlier anti-Assyrian edition of Isaiah's oracles.[33] Clements maintains that Second Isaiah consciously develops themes of Isaiah of Jerusalem. For example, the theme of blindness and deafness (42:18-20 and 43:8) is a development of the theme found in 6:9-10,[34] and the theme of the divine election of Israel in Second Isaiah, represented in such passages as 40:1; 43:6-7; and 44:1-2, is a "conscious awareness" of and response to the theme in First Isaiah that Yahweh had rejected his people (e.g., 2:6).[35] He also says that it is possible to interpret the phrase "former things" in Second Isaiah (e.g., 42:9 and 48:3) as referring to the earlier prophecies of judgment delivered by Isaiah of Jerusalem. Finally, Clements argues that the prophecies concerning Israel's salvation beginning in 40:1, which follow prophecies announcing Jerusalem's destruction in chapters 1–39, represent the intentional editorial shaping by "the scribes who have preserved and ordered the various prophetic collections . . . [and who] have sought to ensure that divine threats be

---

31. Clements, "Beyond Tradition History," 100.

32. Ibid., italics mine. In his earlier article, this point is stated a bit more cautiously. Clements says, "All of this renders it perfectly possible and feasible that the great unnamed prophet of Isaiah 40–55, who appeared with a message of hope during the latter years of the Babylonian exile, could have known and made allusion to the earlier prophetic collection now embedded in Isaiah 1–35" ("Unity," 124).

33. Clements, "Unity," 123–24, and "Beyond Tradition History," 106. Here he is following the thesis of Barth.

34. Clements, "Unity," 125–26, and "Beyond Tradition History," 101–4.

35. Clements, "Beyond Tradition History," 104–6.

followed and counterbalanced by divine promises."[36] For Clements, then, thematic relationships between the various parts of the Book of Isaiah point to an intentional unity resulting from the editorial development of the book.[37]

Rendtorff, like Clements, argues that the Book of Isaiah as a whole shows signs of intentional design related to its editorial development. Rendtorff builds his study on the earlier methodological work of R. F. Melugin and P. R. Ackroyd, who argue that the Book of Isaiah consists of collections of compositions that are not totally independent of one another, although each has its own purpose and structure. Recognizable relationships exist between these parts, "which are to be valued as pointers toward a consciously intended (*bewusste*) composition of the whole book."[38]

Rendtorff finds a number of relationships between the parts of Isaiah. First, words that appear in Isaiah 40 (the introductory chapter of Second Isaiah) such as "comfort" (*nhm*), "the glory of LORD" (*kbwd yhwh*), and "iniquity" (*'wn*) are repeated in key passages in First and Third Isaiah. Rendtorff believes that the repetition of these words represents consciously devised lines of connection joining the three major parts of the book. What is equally important for Rendtorff's argument, however, is that these key words in chapter 40 are repeated in the major collections that now

36. Clements, "Unity," 124–25, 127. See also his "Patterns in the Prophetic Canon," in *Canon and Authority,* ed. George W. Coats and Burke O. Long (Philadelphia: Fortress Press, 1977), 42–55.
37. Clements does not develop a major argument for the relationship of Third Isaiah to the rest of the book. He does say: "The relationship of chapters 56–66 of the book with its preceding parts is still a topic requiring fresh investigation and discussion. Nevertheless, it is reasonably clear that these eleven chapters, with their proto-apocalyptic character, were *intended* to be understood, not as a fresh and entirely self-contained declaration from Yahweh to the post-exilic community, but rather as a carrying forward of the divine word as it had been declared on the eve of the overthrow of Babylon by the unnamed prophet of chapters 40–55" ("Unity," 128, italics mine).
38. Rendtorff, "Komposition," 296. See Roy F. Melugin, *The Formation of Isaiah 40–55,* BZAW 141 (Berlin: de Gruyter, 1976); and Peter R. Ackroyd, "Isaiah I–XII: Presentation of a Prophet," VTSup 29 (1978): 16–48, and "Isaiah 36–39: Structure and Function," in *Von Kanaan bis Kerala: Festschrift für J. P. M. van der Ploeg,* ed. W. C. Delsman et al. (Neukirchen-Vluyn: Neukirchener Verlag, 1982), 3–21. Their methodological approach appeals to Rendtorff because, although both scholars are concerned with "the intention of the present composition of the book of Isaiah," they do not raise this question "as an alternative or in opposition to the prevailing research [author trans.]," (Rendtorff, "Komposition," 296).

constitute First Isaiah. From this he concludes that Second Isaiah was the basis for the shaping of First Isaiah in its present form.[39] Second, Rendtorff argues that there are thematic and theological relationships between the three parts of the Book of Isaiah, such as "Zion-Jerusalem," "the Holy One of Israel," and the theological concept of righteousness ($ṣdq/ṣdqh$). Without going into details, Rendtorff argues that with respect to these themes and concepts, there are certain affinities between First Isaiah and Second Isaiah and between Second Isaiah and Third Isaiah. In short, the common denominator is Second Isaiah, which plays a dominant role in the book because both First and Third Isaiah are oriented to it.[40] This leads Rendtorff to the supposition (*Vermutung*) "that chs. xl–lv form the core of the present composition from which and toward which both of the other sections have been shaped and edited."[41]

These more recent redactional-critical studies of the Book of Isaiah illustrate the change that is taking place in historical-critical interpretive strategies. Language is still understood to be referential. The redactional-critical studies retain the focus on authorial intention and historical background. Nevertheless, the aim is to recover the intentions of the redactors in the development of the book and the historical background of the redactional process, rather than the intentions of the prophet Isaiah and the prophet's historical background. The new shape of these interpretive strategies has resulted in a new shaping of Isaiah. The book is now understood to be a unified whole, not an anthology or collection, as Fohrer viewed it.

The redefinition of interpretive strategies is reflected in statements

---

39. Rendtorff, "Komposition," 305.
40. Ibid., 305–14.
41. Ibid., 318. While Clements and Rendtorff both look to the intentional design resulting from editorial development as the basis for understanding the unity in the Book of Isaiah, their respective explanations of that development have different emphases. Clements sees an earlier edition of First Isaiah as having a dominant role in presenting the themes to which Second Isaiah is a responsive development. Rendtorff, in contrast, sees Second Isaiah as having a dominant role in determining the shape of First and Third Isaiah. These positions are not mutually exclusive, however, because it is conceivable that an argument such as the following could be made: Second Isaiah was originally written as a response to an earlier edition of Isaiah of Jerusalem oracles and then became the basis on which First Isaiah in its present form was edited as well as the basis for the editorial design of the entire book. It is difficult to know, however, how one could convincingly argue for such a complicated history of editorial development.

made by the redaction critics themselves. The demotion of the original intentions of Isaiah as embedded in his "authentic" words is clearly evident in Clements's opinion that "the later, redactional stages in the formation of the book have contributed more to an understanding of what it means than can usefully be gleaned by modern attempts to reconstruct the story of the 'life and times' of Isaiah of Jerusalem in the eighth century B.C."[42]

Clements's interpretive strategies force him to this conclusion because, when redactors are allowed to rewrite creatively the prophet's words and subsequent editions of the book, the search for the prophet in the book is frustrated. It was pointed out above that Fohrer's interest in locating the authentic words of the prophet was related to his notion that the words of the prophet originated in the prophet's ecstatic experience of God. Although Clements has diminished the role of the prophet in his quest for redactional intentions, he retains an interest in the revelatory connection. He now associates revelation with the process of redaction, however, and not with the prophet's ecstatic experience.

> To trace the process of literary growth by which the Book of Isaiah came to assume its present shape is a task which cannot yet be regarded as completed. The useful essays into tracing the redactional history of such a large and primary work have not yet achieved anything approaching a consensus regarding the relative dating of each of its component parts and sayings. Nevertheless, it must be claimed that the recognition that such a redactional history was undertaken by ancient scribes and interpreters *for profound spiritual and interpretive reasons* is an important factor for us to keep in mind. *The prophetic word of God is essentially a divine message concerning his actions and intentions towards his people, and it should not be surprising for us to discover that it has been the continuity and connectedness of this divine purpose which provides the proper basis of unity in the four major prophetic collections.*[43]

Fohrer associated revelation with prophetic experience. Clements associates it with a redactional Heilsgeschichte.

In reassessing the relative importance of the roles of the prophet and redactor, redaction criticism has also increasingly seen the text

---

42. Clements, "Beyond Tradition History," 100.
43. Clements, "Unity," 129, italics mine.

as a unified whole rather than a disunified collection. After reviewing recent redactional-critical studies of Isaiah, including that of Clements and Rendtorff, Marvin A. Sweeney, in one of the most recent books to appear on the redaction of Isaiah, makes the following statement on the redactional unity of Isaiah:

> These scholars have raised a number of considerations which support the view that the book of Isaiah is a redactional unity. Not only do their studies indicate that chapters 40–66 build upon themes, concepts, and language from chapters 1–39, but that the first part of the book is presented in such a way as to anticipate the concerns of the second. In other words, the two parts of the book cannot be properly understood in isolation from each other, they must be understood as two interrelated components of a redactionally unified whole.[44]

If the Book of Isaiah is a unified whole, as redaction critics such as Sweeney maintain, then the original quest for the authentic words of Isaiah is impossible. The text, as redaction critics such as Clements acknowledge, has been reworked in such a way as to make the quest futile. In contrast, if the Book of Isaiah is understood simply as a collection of collections of material, as Fohrer understood it, then Clements's and Rendtorff's quest for redactional intention is impossible. We have here, in John Barton's phrase, "the trick of the disappearing redactor."

> The trick is simply this. The more impressive the critic makes the redactor's work appear, the more he succeeds in showing that the redactor has, by subtle and delicate artistry, produced a simple and coherent text out of the diverse materials before him; the more also he reduces the evidence on which the existence of those sources was established in the first place. No conjuror is required for this trick: the redaction critic himself causes his protege to disappear. . . . Thus, if redaction criticism plays its hand too confidently, we end up with a piece of writing so coherent that no division into sources is warranted any longer.[45]

One needs parts in order to speak about redaction, but when redaction succeeds in showing that the text is a unified whole, the original basis for the study is called into question. Disorganization and disunity of the material make a venture such as redaction criticism

44. Sweeney, *Isaiah 1–4*, 5.
45. Barton, *Reading the Old Testament*, 56–58 (quotation on 57).

necessary. When redaction criticism succeeds in demonstrating unity, however, it eliminates its reason for being.

In *Isaiah 1–4 and the Understanding of the Isaianic Tradition,* Sweeney wants to speak of redactional unity and the origins of the text along with its history of transmission. His attempt to hold together these contradictory positions highlights the quandary historical critics face and the presuppositions that have led to that quandary: the understanding of language as referential and the association of meaning with authorial intention and historical background. These presuppositions neglect the important role of the reader in the creation of meaning. Although Sweeney ignores the role of the contemporary reader or critic in shaping the text, he nevertheless acknowledges the importance of *past* readers as producers of textual meaning: namely, the redactors themselves.

> Although the final redactional understanding of Isa 1–39 may be based on the redaction's interpretation of the text, this *understanding is ultimately imposed from outside the text itself.* This is because the redaction's interpretation of the text will not necessarily correspond to the intent of the original author. Consequently, the presentation of Isa 1–39 *is determined not only by factors inherent in the text of these chapters, it is also determined by the hermeneutical viewpoint of the redaction which is actively shaping the final form of that text.*[46]

Sweeney later underscores the distinction between the authorial intention of original words and redactional intentions. "This indicates that there must be a generic distinction between the 'message' which *the original texts contain, i.e., the original meaning of the text within itself,* and the systematic conception or teaching of the book as a whole, i.e., the meaning of the text as a constitutive element of a larger system."[47] Sweeney does not acknowledge that what is true of his envisaged redactors is also true of his own reading. The redactors' intentions are no more inherent in the text than those of the prophet. His own interpretive strategies, imposed from outside the text, have shaped the text and have yielded intentions.

---

46. Sweeney, *Isaiah 1–4,* 6–7, italics mine.
47. Ibid., 199, italics mine.

THE BIBLE AND COMMUNITIES OF INTERPRETATION

I have been characterizing redactional-critical studies of Isaiah as representing a gradual change in the interpretive strategies employed by historical criticism. The increase of the creative role of the redactor has led to the view that the book is a unified whole rather than a collection. Unity, however, calls into question the critic's ability to recover the original intentions of the prophet.

The ferment associated with the study of the Bible, however, is not restricted to change within the historical-critical community itself. Rival communities of interpretation challenge the interpretive strategies of historical criticism. The strength of alternative approaches is suggested in a statement by Paul J. Achtemeier and Gene M. Tucker. "We are at a turning point concerning our fundamental methodologies for interpreting biblical texts. To call the situation a crisis may be a bit too melodramatic, but it is obvious that the historical-critical method, in various forms the dominant modus operandi since the Enlightenment, is under fire from many directions." In a later remark they imply that they view this challenge as a threat to the breakdown of the historical-critical community of readers. "From without, there is a new life from the old *enemies* of critical inquiry into the Bible: traditional, conservative, and fundamentalist theology. More decisive, however, for the future of biblical scholarship are the rumblings within the *ranks*."[48] The military language that they use to describe the critical discussion of alternative interpretive strategies suggests a threat to historical criticism so grave that it can no longer be averted by diplomatic debate. Here Fish's theory can also illumine the situation. He argues that if the primary factor in interpreting texts is the interpretive strategies of the reader shared with an interpretive community, and not anything inherent in the text, then competing and conflicting interpretations can be resolved only by power and persuasion.[49]

Achtemeier's and Tucker's remarks also indicate that for some (to extend their metaphor), this fight over conflicting interpretations is

---

48. Paul J. Achtemeier and Gene M. Tucker, "Biblical Studies: The State of the Discipline," *BCSR* 11 (1980): 73, italics mine.
49. Fish, *Is There a Text?* 15–16.

taking place on a theological battleground. Although they do not define what they mean by "the ranks," their use of theological categories to define their opponents as conservative theologians implies that historical criticism is a method employed by liberal theologians, those within the ranks.

This conflict is often seen narrowly in theological categories, rather than more broadly in literary categories embracing the study of literature generally, because the most prominent critic of historical criticism, Brevard S. Childs, describes his approach in theological terms. This is evident from the title of his well-known book *Introduction to the Old Testament as Scripture*. Here Childs maintains that his strategies are not to be confused with those of broader literary theory but are designed to deal with the Bible as a special literature, that is, as a canonical text.

> The canonical study of the Old Testament shares an interest in common with several of the newer literary critical methods in its concern to do justice to the integrity of the text itself apart from diachronistic reconstruction. One thinks of the so-called "newer criticism" of English studies, of various forms of structural analysis, and of rhetorical criticism. Yet the canonical approach differs from a strictly literary approach by interpreting the biblical text in relation to a community of faith and practice for whom it served a particular theological role as possessing divine authority.[50]

For Childs, to use a canonical approach to study an Old Testament book such as Isaiah means to call into question the strategies that govern historical-critical interpretation.[51] The canonical approach challenges the equivalence of meaning and author intention and the crucial importance of the historical background of the text, including the history of its development.[52] Childs maintains

---

50. B. S. Childs, *Introduction to the Old Testament as Scripture* (Philadelphia: Fortress Press, 1979), 74.

51. Childs does not want to refer to his approach as canonical criticism because that would imply that it is another "historical-critical technique which can take its place alongside of source criticism, form criticism, rhetorical criticism, and the like." He adds, "I do not envision the approach to canon in this light. Rather, the issue at stake in canon turns on establishing a stance from which the Bible is to be read as Sacred Scripture." ("The Canonical Shape of the Prophetic Literature," *Int* 32 [1978]: 54). For a recent study that seeks to apply Childs's approach to the Book of Isaiah, see Craig Evans, "The Unity and Parallel Structure of Isaiah," *VT* 38 (1988): 129-47.

52. The opposition that Childs has created is often evident in the asides in the secondary literature that dismiss his approach as aberrant. See, for example, Elizabeth

that, because historical-critical interpretation does not address the book in its final form, it fails to read the text as an expression of God's will. He makes this point in a comment concerned with his approach as it relates to prophetic books. Childs's approach

> begins with the recognition that a major literary and theological force was at work in shaping the present form of the Hebrew bible. This force was exerted during most of the history of the literature's formation, but increasingly in the postexilic period exercised its influence in the collecting, selecting, and ordering of the biblical traditions in such a way as to allow the material to function as authoritative Scripture for the Jewish community. In the transmission process, tradition, which once arose in a particular milieu and addressed various historical situations, was shaped in such a way as to serve as a normative expression of *God's will* to later generations of Israel who had not shared in those original events. In sum, prophetic oracles which were directed to one generation were fashioned into Sacred Scripture by a canonical process to be used by another generation.[53]

While Fohrer equated revelation with the prophet's ecstatic experience of God, and Clements equated it with the process of redaction, Childs equates it with the final form of the text.

The problem with Childs's challenge to the prevailing historical-critical approach to the study of the Bible as well as with Achtemeier's and Tucker's assessment of the present state of the discipline is that they perceive the struggle too narrowly as a theological one.[54] Historical criticism has itself attained a status as a canonical method, which is reflected in Childs's challenge. The proper way to read the text has become a matter of orthodoxy.[55]

Achtemeier, "Isaiah of Jerusalem: Themes and Preaching Possibilities," in *Reading and Preaching the Book of Isaiah,* ed. Christopher R. Seitz (Philadelphia: Fortress Press, 1988). She says, "The book must be read against its historical background, and despite Brevard Childs' more sweeping canonical views, I really do not think any portion of the Isaiah corpus can be understood apart from its historical background" (p. 26).
53. Childs, "Canonical Shape," 47, italics mine.
54. The challenge to historical criticism has come from many quarters. An important critique of prevailing methodologies has come from feminism. For a significant feminist appraisal of conventional and dominant literary methods in the humanities, see Annette Kolodny, "Dancing through the Minefield: Some Observations on the Theory, Practice, and Politics of Feminist Literary Criticism," in *Men's Studies Modified: The Impact of Feminism on the Academic Disciplines,* ed. Dale Spender, The Athene Series (Oxford: Pergamon, 1981), 11–42.
55. See Edgar W. Conrad, "Changing Context: The Bible and the Study of Religion," in *Perspectives on Language and Text: Essays in Honor of Francis I.*

Ironically, historical criticism emerged in biblical studies in the two centuries before this one as a challenge to orthodoxy in order to permit reading the Bible as any other text would be read. According to David Gunn, "The life-force of modern historical criticism was a determination to deal with the biblical text in the same way as secular texts were treated, even if that should lead to the shaking of some dearly held verities. And that assumption, ironically, is at the heart of the current challenge which historical criticism faces — a challenge to both its notion of history and its notion of text."[56]

The focal point of strategies used to interpret secular texts during this century, as indicated in the first paragraph of this chapter, has moved from author to text to reader. Historical criticism, with its retention of interest in author intention and historical background, resembles a frozen waterfall — to use a metaphor Emil Brunner once used to describe Protestant orthodoxy following the Reformation.[57]

Historical critics, as an interpretive community, have employed reading strategies so distinctive that an unbridgeable gulf has opened between them and other interpretive communities. This is certainly the view of R. M. Frye, who made the following comment on the historical-critical reading of the New Testament: "As I read certain kinds of New Testament criticism, I sometimes feel that I am observing a radically nonliterary enterprise, so different are the methods from those generally accepted in the field of the humanities."[58] Perhaps Frye's statement is a bit extreme, and perhaps it would not pertain with equal force to the study of the Old Testament. It does, however, highlight the way the historical-critical reading of the Bible has isolated itself from other readings, even other critical ones.

James Barr has discussed three gaps that historical criticism has created between itself and other communities of readers. First, historical-critical reading of the Bible by its professional practitioners

---

Andersen's Sixtieth Birthday, July 28, 1985, ed. E. W. Conrad and E. G. Newing (Winona Lake, Ind.: Eisenbrauns, 1987), 393–402.

56. Gunn, "New Directions," 66.

57. Emil Brunner, *The Divine-Human Encounter,* trans. A. W. Loos (Philadelphia: Westminster, 1943), 31. Brunner's actual words are, "The age of Orthodoxy appears like a frozen waterfall — mighty shapes of movement, but no movement."

58. The quotation is from Frye's book *Jesus and Man's Hope,* cited in Barr, "Reading the Bible," 22–23.

has created a gulf between itself and the community of lay readers. This gulf has been created because "the historical approach is a matter of training and habit, which cannot be easily acquired. . . . [It] involves an immense amount of hypothetical reconstruction . . . [and] however probable these results, they always retain a reconstructive and hypothetical element, and in this sense they differ from the reading of the biblical text as it stands."[59] To put this point in terms discussed above, the historical-critical reading of biblical books such as Isaiah has employed reading strategies that, in radically reshaping the books, make them inaccessible to the average reader. Only professional historical critics can use reading strategies that require the identification of underlying sources, the differentiation between authentic and inauthentic words, the distinction between preexilic and postexilic layers of tradition, and so forth. Even redaction criticism presupposes a book of earlier bits and pieces whose unity is understandable only when its literary history is made clear. Redaction critics understand unity diachronically ("through time") and not synchronically ("as it stands").

Second, the gulf that historical criticism has created is between itself and "the older exegetical tradition." This tradition, according to Barr, reads the Bible "as a source of true knowledge about the objects described in the Bible — about God, about the creation of the world, about his redemption of mankind, about sin and salvation, about the possibility of future life." The historical-critical mode of reading is incompatible with the traditional mode of reading because "the dominance of a historical reading of the Bible has now in effect changed the position of the religious or theological approach to it. The Bible is looked at not as a document which can be directly interpreted so as to give access to the truth about the entities mentioned in it. . . . Rather, it is looked at for the mind of the writers in their historical setting."[60]

Finally, Barr says that a gulf has been created between historical-critical appreciation of the Bible and a more literary and cultural appreciation.[61] Here Barr is suggesting the incongruity of the

59. Barr, "Reading the Bible," 19–20.
60. Ibid., 13, 17.
61. Ibid., 22.

philosophy of language presupposed by historical criticism in the current literary milieu. A theory of language and text that assumes that both language and text are meaningful because they signify realities external to them is inconsistent with contemporary theories proposing that language and text be understood as systems or structures that create meaning. According to Barr,

> Once we think of the Bible as literature, and take as units not the single words but the great literary and stylistic complexes, it becomes more and more difficult to find any use for a referential idea of meaning. The literature *is* its own meaning; we cannot expect to identify a set of external realities of which it is a linguistic sign, and nobody approaches other literatures in such a way. It is thus interesting that the French structuralist position seeks to avoid the reduction of the text to *a thing signified,* the expression of its meaning as the designation of something external to itself. In the theological tradition of biblical study, on the other hand, one has sought to *disengage* from the text the theological or "kerygmatic" truth, which is then taken as the essence of its meaning. Our survey of approaches to the Bible as literature suggests that this traditional theological treatment of the message of the Bible may be no longer possible. To say this is not to deny the existence of any "thing signified"; it is not to maintain that the great theological entities simply are not there. It is rather that the Bible, when seen as the sort of literature that it is, is not the kind of language which can be taken as a direct representation of them.[62]

This challenge being mounted against historical-critical reading strategies, then, is not a theological one. Historical-critical reading of the Bible, with its home primarily in theological communities, and even there in the more select communities of professional biblical scholars, has alienated itself from Western culture in general. Western culture has constructed a world of meaning—a kind of mythology—using the language of the Bible: its images and symbols, its forms and structures. Metaphorically speaking, to read the Bible in search for information only about its forebears is to separate it from its progeny.

In summary, then, dramatic changes have been occurring within historical criticism. Communities of interpretation outside the theological community are proposing alternative reading strategies that permit the Bible to be read as other literature is read. To continue to

62. Ibid., 32.

read the Bible using exclusively historical-critical strategies will widen the gaps that already exist between the community of historical-critical practitioners and other communities of interpretation.

INTERPRETIVE STRATEGIES USED IN THIS STUDY

In defining my own approach to reading the Book of Isaiah, I will refer to M. H. Abrams's broad classification of critical theories evoked by Barton and Wiklander.[63] In his well-known book *The Mirror and the Lamp: Romantic Theory and Critical Tradition,* Abrams maintains that theories of interpretation can be classified as mimetic, expressive, objective, and pragmatic.[64] *Mimetic* theories assume that a text mirrors the universe. In biblical studies, the mimetic approach is represented primarily by precritical readings of the text.[65] *Expressive* theories associate the meaning of the text with the intentions of the author. Historical criticism, as the previous discussion suggests, belongs in this classification. John Barton, for example, places all historical-critical methods here: not only source analysis but also form criticism, where the group is seen as the author, and redactional criticism, where the redactor is seen as a clever compiler of fragments.[66] *Objective* theories assume that the text is an object to be studied in its own right without reference to external factors such as author intention and historical background. Here the structure of the text is a central concern, that is, the relation between the parts of the text and how the parts relate to the text as a whole. This approach is represented by the New Criticism and structuralism. *Pragmatic* theories are concerned with the text in terms of its reception, that is, its readers. These theories are not necessarily or exclusively concerned with the text's actual readers, past and present.[67] In the case of the biblical text, for example, the

---

63. Both John Barton (*Reading the Old Testament,* 198–207, and "Classifying Biblical Criticism," 19–23) and Wiklander (*Prophecy as Literature,* 1–8) have utilized Abrams's classification.
64. M. H. Abrams, *The Mirror and the Lamp* (New York: Oxford University Press, 1953), see esp. pp. 3–29.
65. Barr referred to this approach as "the older exegetical tradition." See n. 60 above.
66. See Barton, *Reading the Old Testament,* 201–2, and "Classifying Biblical Criticism," 24–26.
67. For a good summary of pragmatic theories as they relate to the biblical text, see McKnight, *Bible and the Reader.* Some scholars have been interested in studying the history of the reception of texts by communities of readers (*Rezeptionsgeschichte* or

original readers of a text such as Isaiah are not available for study, "since there is no source material which testifies to the occurrence of real acts of text reception."[68] Pragmatic theories may be concerned not only with real readers but also with the audience implied by the text's structures (i.e., its rhetorical devices and techniques).

These four approaches are more heuristic than actual, for the theories may overlap.[69] For example, although historical criticism can be described as chiefly expressive because it is concerned with the intentions of "authors" in a broad sense, historical criticism as it has been practiced also reflects a mimetic dimension.[70] A number of scholars have argued recently that many reconstructions of Israelite history do not so much reconstruct the history of Israel as they mimic the general outline of history as presented in the biblical texts themselves.[71] This has certainly been true in the reconstruction of the history of the text of Isaiah. The reconstruction of the historical background of the book, which moves from an Assyrian, to a Babylonian, to a post-Babylonian background, simply mimics the progression of the book itself. The general outline of the Isaian text is therefore interpreted as if it reflects historical background. That the text is mirroring its historical background is assumed, not argued.[72]

While historical criticism has followed strategies that reflect primarily expressive theories of interpretation in combination with mimetic theories, the strategies of the present study will reflect primarily objective theories of interpretation in combination with

---

Rezeptionsästhetik). See, for example, the work of Hans Robert Jauss, "Literary History as a Challenge to Literary Theory," New Literary History 2 (1970): 7–37, and his two larger works: Toward an Aesthetic of Reception, trans. Timothy Bali, Theory and History of Literature 2 (Minneapolis: University of Minnesota Press, 1982), and Aesthetic Experience and Literary Hermeneutics, trans. Michael Shaw, History and Theory of Literature 3 (Minneapolis: University of Minnesota Press, 1982).

68. Wiklander, Prophecy as Literature, 42.

69. Abrams, Mirror and the Lamp, 6.

70. Wiklander (Prophecy as Literature, p. 14) concurs with this judgment.

71. See Giovanni Garbini, History and Ideology in Ancient Israel, trans. John Bowden (London: SCM, 1986), 1–7; and Burke O. Long, "On Finding Hidden Premises," JSOT 39 (1987): 10–14.

72. Auld argues that perhaps the book's depiction of Isaiah does not so much reflect the historical background of the book as it accommodates a poetic and intellectual tradition to prophecy ("Poetry, Prophecy, Hermeneutic," 578–81). See also Louis Brodie, "The Children and the Prince: The Structure, Nature, and Date of Isaiah 6–12," BTB 9 (1979): 30–31, who argues for a postexilic dating and against an attempt to find an eighth-century dating for any of the material.

pragmatic ones. I should first emphasize that "objective" here in no way denotes detachment or claims an ersatz nonsubjectivity. My reading, like every reading of every text, will produce meaning only because of my active participation in creating meaning in the reading process. Every reading is of necessity a reading *into,* or eisegesis. Indeed, the worst kind of eisegesis may be readings in which interpreters remain unaware of their involvement because they think they are reading meaning *out of* the text, or doing exegesis. My approach more closely fits contemporary theories of language and text. Both language and text create meaning. Literature such as the Book of Isaiah "*is* its own meaning."[73] To continue to read biblical texts primarily as the signification of external realities of author intention and historical background is to isolate one's study from the larger practice of literary interpretation. My study is intended to do what historical criticism started out to do: to treat the biblical text as other texts are treated rather than to give it special treatment as a special kind of text. By considering the objective and pragmatic dimensions of the text, I am identifying with a growing community of biblical scholars who want to move biblical inquiry beyond its preoccupation with issues that were crucial at the turn of the century. I will follow the route taken in the study of secular literature, which has profited from the changing focus from author to text and reader. To do this is to help close the gaps that have grown between the professional critical biblical scholar and the Bible's other readers as outlined by Barr.

Having placed my approach within the larger framework of literary study, it is necessary to say something about the specific interpretive strategies employed. My primary aim is to understand the text as a whole by paying special attention to its structure. My understanding of the structure of the book differs from that of redaction criticism in that I will be concerned with the text's aesthetic momentum, not its historical development.

My reading does not assume the genre of the text, but it assumes the text is something as a whole and seeks to discover what that whole is. I am therefore interested in relating parts of the text not to a world external to it (its historical background or its history of

73. Barr, "Reading the Bible," 32.

literary development) but to the literary world of the text itself. I will be dealing with the so-called final form of the text, but I will be focusing on the form itself, not on the process by which it became final.

The structural unity of a text such as Isaiah is not obvious to contemporary readers of the text. This is because the text has been read customarily by biblical critics as a largely disunified collection of material of disparate origin. It is possible, however, in a close reading of Isaiah to identify recurring rhetorical techniques and patterns that suggest its unity. In the following chapters I look at repetition in the text of Isaiah as a clue to its structural unity.

The Book of Isaiah contains repetition in vocabulary, motif, theme, narrative sequence, and rhetorical devices such as rhetorical questions, pronominal shifts, and forms of address. This repetition creates cohesion in the text. The repetition in the book, however, is not literal; repetition is always repetition with a difference. Variation in the recurrence of repeated elements in the text suggests movement and progression.[74]

The attention to these elements of repetition in the text will alert my reading to the function of its narratives, the interaction of narration and poetry, the interplay of narrative voices, and the relation between the narrators and poetic personae. My study will concern the book's presentation of the prophet, not the prophet's presentation of the book.[75]

My approach will also show a peripheral interest in the pragmatic dimension of the text, that is, with reader and audience. I will be concerned not only with narrators and poetic personae but with their relation with an implied audience and reader. Shlomith

74. Literary critics have pointed out that the techniques of repetition are a feature of Hebrew narrative. Repetition is not only a unifying device but also a key to the narrative's development. See Robert Alter, *The Art of Biblical Narrative* (London: George Allen and Unwin, 1981), 88–113, and his "Biblical Type-scenes and the Uses of Convention," *Critical Inquiry* 5 (1978): 355–68. See also Meir Sternberg, *The Poetics of Biblical Narrative: Ideological Literature and the Drama of Reading*, Indiana Studies in Biblical Literature (Bloomington: Indiana University Press, 1985), 365–440. What appears to be a key to the unity and structure of narrative is akin to what I am suggesting indicates the unity of the largely poetic Book of Isaiah. To point out this commonality, however, is not to suggest the significant differences separating narrative and poetry.

75. In this sense I extend the insights of Peter R. Ackroyd in his article "Isaiah I–XII." Ackroyd's methodological approach, however, is that of a redaction critic.

Rimmon-Kenan has summarized the various concepts of the reader by saying that they represent "two diametrically opposed views and various nuances between them. At one extreme the concept is of a real reader, whether a specific individual or the collective readership of a period. At the other, it is a theoretical construct, implied or encoded in the text, representing the integration of data and the interpretive process 'invited by the text.' "[76]

I view the implied reader and the implied audience as theoretical constructs encoded in the text. In this way my view differs from the historical-critical approach, which, because of its interest in a real world external to the text, is interested in real past communities who were the recipients of prophets' or redactors' words. Although I am not interested in reconstructing the original "real audiences" of Isaiah, subsequent Isaiahs, or redactors, I have been keenly aware of my own involvement as a "real reader" of the book and the role played by my own reading strategies in my construction of the text and their relation to what the text implies about how it is to be read. Literary conventions available to the book's first readers are no longer obvious. Contemporary readers can no longer bring to the Book of Isaiah reading conventions shared with its "author."[77] To read an ancient and alien text such as Isaiah means that we must be more consciously reflective in our reading endeavor. Although we readily know, because of shared literary conventions, what gives unity and wholeness to contemporary genres, this immediate and largely unreflective understanding of wholeness and unity is lacking in our reading today of Isaiah. Hence it is important to consider information in the text concerning reader and audience reception.

In studying the book's structure, with its implications for the encoded audience, I am following strategies that have clear links to

---

76. Shlomith Rimmon-Kenan, *Narrative Fiction: Contemporary Poetics,* New Accents (London: Methuen, 1983), 119. Rimmon-Kenan summarizes the various ways of identifying the reader in the following series of questions: "Who is the reader I am talking about? Is he the 'Actual Reader' (Van Dijk, Jauss), the 'Superreader' (Riffaterre), the 'Informed Reader' (Fish), the 'Ideal Reader' (Culler), the 'Model Reader' (Eco) the 'Implied Reader' (Booth, Iser, Chatman, Perry), or the 'Encoded Reader' (Brooke-Rose)?" (pp. 118–19).
77. I have placed the word "author" in quotation marks because it is no longer clear that contemporary notions of authorship equate with the original production of the Book of Isaiah. See Barton, "Reading the Bible as Literature: Two Questions for Biblical Critics," *Literature and Theology* 1 (1987): 135–53.

Formgeschichte as it has been practiced by historical critics since Gunkel. This is the one technique that historical critics have employed in which they have paid some attention to the objective and pragmatic dimensions of the text. The implementation of form criticism, however, was made subordinate to the primary theories that governed historical-critical inquiry.[78] Form criticism was used as a technique only insofar as it contributed to the major goals of uncovering authorial intention and historical background. Form and setting were deemed important only for the information about realities external to the text. Form was thought to have little inherent importance and was valued because it supplied information about prophecy, cultic festivals, and other institutions. Many forms discovered by form critics were thus seen to have secondary settings in their present literary contexts. A *Heilsorakel* in Second Isaiah was important because of what it said about the cultic background and not because of what it implied about the structure of the text of Isaiah.[79] Covenant lawsuits, disputations, confessions, and hymnic elements were not understood in terms of their function within the larger text but were primarily important for uncovering information from the text about a world external to it.[80] Hence form criticism

---

78. The failure of form criticism to attain its full literary potential has been pointed out by Robert Morgan and John Barton. See their *Biblical Interpretation,* Oxford Bible Series (Oxford: Oxford University Press, 1988), 211.
79. That Second Isaiah was imitating a cultic form in his use of the *Heilsorakel* was argued by Joachim Begrich in the article in which he first propounded the thesis that the "fear not" oracles in Second Isaiah should be understood as *Heilsorakeln.* See his "Das priesterliche Heilsorakel," *ZAW* 52 (1934): 91–92, reprinted in *Gesammelte Studien zum Alten Testament,* Theologische Bücherei 21 (Munich: Chr. Kaiser, 1964), 229–31. My critique of this approach was that it failed to consider seriously the literary setting of this form in Second Isaiah and other places in the Old Testament. See my "Second Isaiah and the Priestly Oracle of Salvation," *ZAW* 93 (1981): 234–46; "The Fear Not Oracles in Second Isaiah," *VT* 34 (1984): 126–52; and *Fear Not Warrior: A Study of 'al tira' Pericopes in the Hebrew Scriptures,* Brown Judaic Studies 75 (Chico, Calif.: Scholars, 1985), esp. 1–6. See also Werner Grimm, *Fürchte dich nicht: Ein exegetischer Zugang zum Seelsorgepotential einer deuterojesajanischen Gattung,* European University Studies 23 (Frankfurt: Peter Lang, 1986).
80. In his review of form-critical scholarship on Second Isaiah, Antoon Schoors sees that the major issue in form-critical scholarship is the relationship of *Gattungen* to their proper *Sitz im Leben.* "The attempts of form criticism to define the setting of the texts from Dt.-Is. must be on two levels: (1) the real and to Dt.-Is. himself existing *Sitz im Leben;* (2) the *Sitz im Leben* which originally forms the background of the genres used by him. Both may coincide but they do not necessarily do so" (*I Am God Your Saviour: A Form Critical Study of the Main Genres in Is. XL–LV,* VTSup 24 [Leiden: Brill, 1973]: 29).

could be applied to small units (*Gattungen*) but nearly never to large structures such as the Book of Isaiah.[81] Because the present study does not assume that Isaiah is a collection, it is possible to do a form-critical study of Isaiah as a whole.

There is another major distinction between my strategies and those of form criticism. Form criticism never really focused on the pragmatic dimension (audience reception) in its discussion of forms. The identification of forms was important for understanding the intentions of an author's peculiar use of a form. Again this starting point accounts for the reason that so many forms are said to be imitations (as Gunkel understood was the case with the Psalms)[82] or to have secondary settings in the literature. Or formal structure was understood to be indicative of the community as author. For this reason Barton classifies form criticism as an expressive theory concerned with author intention.[83] Forms were studied not so much for understanding their implications for reception as for the purpose or intentions of the community evinced in the structure.[84]

My making the structure of the Book of Isaiah the object of critical inquiry is due to my interest in understanding the text as text and not as something else (e.g., as a source of information external to it). This focus may have significance for historical-critical reading because it calls into question the assumption that Isaiah can be understood only as a collection, even an organized collection. Although my interest in the audience is limited to the interaction between text and audience implied by the structure of the text, I will suggest how this kind of study can contribute to future studies of the interaction of the text and audiences both real and implied. This approach may also help bridge the gulf between biblical studies and the larger communities of readers of Isaiah.

81. See Wiklander (*Prophecy as Literature,* 16), who also notes the odd procedure of restricting form-critical analysis to small units of texts of Isaiah and not to the entire book.
82. Hermann Gunkel, *The Psalms: A Form-Critical Introduction,* trans. Thomas Horner, Facet Books Biblical Series 19 (Philadelphia: Fortress Press, 1967), 26–29.
83. Barton, *Reading the Old Testament,* 201; and "Classifying Biblical Criticism," 26.
84. See Klaus Koch, *The Growth of the Biblical Tradition: The Form-Critical Method,* trans. S. M. Cupitt (New York: Charles Scribner's Sons, 1969), 26–34.

CHAPTER 2

The Royal Narratives
and the Structure of
the Book of Isaiah

The name "Isaiah" occurs just 16 times in the Book of Isaiah. In contrast, the name "Jeremiah" occurs 131 times in the book that bears his name.[1] This difference is even more striking because, whereas the name "Jeremiah" is distributed throughout the book, the name "Isaiah" is restricted to the three so-called superscriptions (1:1, 2:1, and 13:1) and to three third person narratives (chaps. 7, 20, and 36–39). But even in these three narratives the name is concentrated primarily in chapters 36–39, where it occurs 10 times;[2] it occurs only once in chapter 7 (v. 3) and twice in chapter 20 (vv. 2, 3). These figures alone indicate that whereas the persona of Jeremiah is a central focus of attention in the Book of Jeremiah, as past critics have observed,[3] this is not the case in the Book of Isaiah. Isaiah only briefly appears "onstage" as a character, and even in those appearances his character does not dominate in the way Jeremiah's character does.[4]

---

1. The name in 52:1 refers to Zedekiah's grandfather and not to the prophet Jeremiah.
2. It is lacking in chap. 36 but occurs in 37:2, 5, 6, 21; 38:1, 4, 21; 39:3, 5, 8.
3. See Christopher R. Seitz, "Isaiah 1–66: Making Sense of the Whole," in *Reading and Preaching the Book of Isaiah*, ed. C. R. Seitz (Philadelphia: Fortress Press, 1988), who says, "Here is the major point where Jeremiah and Isaiah are so different: All three levels of Jeremiah tradition are concerned with the figure of the prophet Jeremiah . . . Jeremiah remains the main character in the fifty-two chapter story," (p. 120). For studies that concentrate on the person of Jeremiah as a product of the literary imagination, see Walter Brueggemann, "The Book of Jeremiah: The Portrait of the Prophet," *Int* 37 (1983): 130–45; and Timothy Polk, *The Prophetic Persona: Jeremiah and the Language of the Self*, JSOTSup 32 (Sheffield: JSOT, 1984).
4. The substance of this discussion was published in an earlier article, "The Royal Narratives and the Structure of the Book of Isaiah," *JSOT* 41 (1988): 67–81.

A different contrast emerges with reference to the occurrences of prophets' names when the Book of Isaiah is compared with the Book of Ezekiel. In the latter, Ezekiel's name occurs only two times (Ezek. 1:3 and 24:24)—significantly fewer than the sixteen times Isaiah's name occurs in the Book of Isaiah. The prophet Ezekiel, however, also dominates the book that bears his name, but in a different way than does the prophet Jeremiah. The appearance of the name at the beginning of the Book of Ezekiel identifies the narrative voice, speaking in the first person singular throughout the book. (When Ezekiel does refer to himself in the third person, usually indicating how the *Lord* addressed him, he employs the phrase "son of man" rather than the proper name "Ezekiel.") Isaiah also speaks in a first person singular voice, but this voice is primarily found in chapters 6 and 8, two chapters that frame the third person account in chapter 7 (cf. also the first person speaking voice in chap. 21 following the third person narrative in chap. 20). Isaiah speaks only briefly in a narrative first person singular voice—a striking contrast to the sustained first person narration of Ezekiel. In fact, as one critic has observed, "in the Book of Isaiah God does most of the talking."[5]

While the characters of Ezekiel and Jeremiah, each in his own way, dominate the prophetic books associated with their names, the prophet Isaiah appears in Isaiah only as a supporting character. Christopher R. Seitz, in an article entitled "Isaiah 1–66: Making Sense of the Whole," makes a similar observation when he says, "Isaiah is startlingly absent not just from 2 and 3 Isaiah collections—he does not put in much of an appearance in First Isaiah, the collection attributed to him."[6] As a character, then, Isaiah plays an insignificant background role throughout the Book of Isaiah. His portrayal as a character is restricted to the three superscriptions and to the three narratives (chaps. 6–8, 20, and 36–39).[7]

5. Seitz, "Isaiah 1–66," 121.
6. Ibid., 176.
7. Most critics interested in historical background have understood these narratives in a mimetic sense, i.e., seeing them as mirroring events in Isaiah's life. To be sure, critics attempt to discern more about setting (e.g., the locale of Isaiah's vision). Yet without these narratives and their counterparts in Kings and Chronicles, we would know nothing about Isaiah. He would remain as anonymous as the so-called Second Isaiah. The presence of only meager references to Isaiah in the narratives has suggested to some critics that the prophet Isaiah was secondarily related to the poetry of the book at a late stage and was not associated with it at its inception. See

Isaiah's general absence from the book makes those places where he does appear even more conspicuous—particularly because he appears in prose, which is distinctive in a book that is primarily poetry.[8] The presence of these prose narratives in a book of poetry suggests that their location may be strategic and significant for the book's overall structure. The book neither begins nor ends with a narrative, however; the narratives appear in the midst of the poetry. This placement of the narratives within the book has generated a number of questions in Isaian studies. The most prominent is, Why does the call narrative come only in chapter 6 and not at the beginning of the book, as in the Books of Jeremiah and Ezekiel?[9] In due course, I will deal with all these observations concerning the narrative settings, arguing that they provide the structural framework for the poetry.

The present chapter, however, will deal only with the relationship between what I will call the royal narratives in the Book of Isaiah: chapter 7 and chapters 36–39. Both of these narratives portray Isaiah in the third person, and both concern Isaiah's interactions with Judean kings—first with Ahaz, and then with Hezekiah. The two narratives follow the same fixed sequence of motifs and are similar to what Robert Alter identifies as a recurring "type-scene," a technique of repetition in Hebrew narrative that is a major indication of structural unity in the Book of Isaiah.[10]

THE ROYAL NARRATIVES IN THE BOOK OF ISAIAH

In each of the royal narratives Isaiah comforts the king with an oracle containing the formula "fear not." He comforts Ahaz with

especially Graeme A. Auld, "Poetry, Prophecy, Hermeneutic: Recent Studies in Isaiah," *SJT* 33 (1980): 567–81. See also Louis Brodie, "The Children and the Prince: The Structure, Nature, and Date of Isaiah 6–12," *BTB* 9 (1979): 27-31. He argues that the narratives should be understood as a literary projection back into the past and not taken as supplying reliable historical data.

8. Auld notes, "With *very* few exceptions: beyond the prosaic structures of chapters 6–8 and 36–9 . . . the most extended prose sections are chapters 20—the famous symbolic act of the prophet going naked three years—and the second half of chapter 22; the rest of the prose is in the form of short snippets or editorial addition" ("Poetry, Prophecy, Hermeneutic," 578).

9. See Seitz, "Isaiah 1–66," 121.

10. Robert Alter, *The Art of Biblical Narrative* (London: George Allen and Unwin, 1981), 96. See also his "Biblical Type-scenes and the Uses of Convention," *Critical Inquiry* 5 (1978): 355–68.

such an oracle in 7:4-9 and Hezekiah in 37:6-7. In an earlier book, *Fear Not Warrior: A Study of 'al tira' Pericopes in the Hebrew Scriptures,* I argued that these two "fear not" oracles follow conventions used in oracles, which I called war oracles, to encourage a king faced with military threat. In such literary settings, I maintained that a king, unlike a conventional warrior, was given either orders not to fight or a promise that the LORD would fight for him.[11] Significantly, in the Book of Isaiah the war oracle is not used just to comfort kings. It is also used by the LORD to address the community directly, providing them with comfort in contexts of military threat (10:24-27; 41:8-13, 14-16; 43:1-4, 5-6; 44:1-5). This use of the language stereotypical of royalty suggests that the LORD is addressing the community as king.[12]

In this chapter I build on this argument concerning the stereotypical use of "fear not" language in the Book of Isaiah, arguing that it represents a clue to understanding the structure of the book as a whole. The argument utilizes the important observations of Peter R. Ackroyd, who has pointed out the relationship between the two royal narratives in the Book of Isaiah and has made the methodological suggestion that scholars take note of the function the narratives have in their present position in the book.[13] I maintain that

11. Edgar W. Conrad, *Fear Not Warrior,* Brown Judaic Studies 75 (Chico, Calif.: Scholars, 1985). See esp. pp. 52–62. The entire book is a study of stereotypical language in the Old Testament using the formula "fear not." It was my purpose in that study to identify the literary setting of war oracles in the Old Testament, what I called their *Sitz im Text,* and not an institutional setting (what form critics call *Sitz im Leben*). On a similar use of conventional language in Assyrian inscriptions, which I also alluded to in my study, see Manfred Weippert, "Assyrische Propheten der Zeit Asarhaddons und Assurbanipals," in *Assyrian Royal Inscriptions: New Horizons in Literary, Ideological, and Historical Analysis,* ed. F. M. Fales, Orientis Antiqui Collectio 17 (Rome: Istituto per l'Oriente, 1981), 78–79 and 96–98. He argues that "fear not," used in what he calls *das Königsorakel,* occurs in situations of war and that it is the deity and not the king and his army who will fight.
12. Conrad, *Fear Not Warrior.* See pp. 120–23 for a discussion of Isa. 10:24-27 and pp. 79–107 for the other community war oracles. On addressing the community as king, see pp. 52–62. See also my "Community as King in Second Isaiah," in *Understanding the Word: Essays in Honor of Bernhard W. Anderson,* ed. James T. Butler, Edgar W. Conrad, and Ben C. Ollenburger, JSOTSup 37 (Sheffield: JSOT, 1985), 99–111.
13. Peter R. Ackroyd, "Isaiah 36–39: Structure and Function," in *Von Kanaan bis Kerala: Festschrift für Prof. Mag. Dr. Dr. J. P. M. van der Ploeg O. P. zur Vollendung des siebzigsten Lebenjahres am 4 Juli 1979,* ed. W. C. Delsman et al., Alter Orient und Altes Testament 211 (Neukirchen-Vluyn: Neukirchener Verlag, 1982), 16–20, reprinted in *Studies in the Religious Tradition of the Old Testament*

the use of "fear not" oracles in both the Ahaz (chap. 7) and Hezekiah (chaps. 36–39) narratives is only one of a number of structural similarities in the narratives. The close relationship between these two narratives extends to the larger contexts in which they occur, for each royal narrative is followed by a "fear not" oracle addressed to the community: the Ahaz narrative is followed by the community war oracle of 10:24-27, and the Hezekiah narrative is followed by the five community war oracles in 41:8-13, 14-16; 43:1-4, 5-6; 44:1-5. Furthermore, when these two narratives are read in light of one another, a certain movement or progression can be observed in the book; the Hezekiah narrative is not simply a structural clone of the Ahaz narrative. The community war oracle in 10:24-27 helps explain the movement or development between the Ahaz and Hezekiah narratives, just as the community war oracles in 41:8-13, 14-16; 43:1-4, 5-6, and 44:1-5 help explain the development beyond the Hezekiah narrative.

An examination of the similarities between the two narratives in the following paragraphs can serve as a starting point for a discussion of how these two narratives provide a functional framework to the poetry in the Book of Isaiah. Each narrative reflects the same type-scene and contains the same sequence of motifs.

1. Each narrative begins by indicating that an invading army has entered the territory and represents a threat to the city of Jerusalem. In the Ahaz narrative the city is threatened by two kings working in alliance with one another: Rezin king of Syria and Pekah king of Israel. They "came up to Jerusalem to wage war against it, but they could not conquer it" (7:1). In the Hezekiah narrative the Assyrian king Sennacherib poses a threat to the city. "And the king of Assyria [i.e., Sennacherib] sent the Rabshakeh from Lachish to King Hezekiah at Jerusalem, with a great army" (36:2).

2. The locus of activity for the threat to Jerusalem is the same in both narratives: "the conduit of the upper pool on the highway to the Fuller's Field" (7:3; 36:2). The detail suggests that this place represented a strategic location for the defense of the city.[14]

(London: SCM, 1987). See also Joseph Blenkinsopp, *A History of Prophecy in Israel* (Philadelphia: Westminster, 1983), 109–10.
14. Isaiah 7 adds the further detail that this place was at the end (*qṣh*) of the conduit.

3. The narratives indicate that when the respective kings were informed of the invading army, they were greatly distressed. The Ahaz narrative notes, "When the house of David was told, 'Syria is in league with Ephraim,' his heart and the heart of his people shook as the trees of the forest shake before the wind" (7:2). The Hezekiah narrative reports, "When King Hezekiah heard it, he rent his clothes, and covered himself with sackcloth, and went into the house of the LORD" (37:1).

4. In response to this military threat to Jerusalem and the panic of the king, Isaiah delivers a comforting oracle containing the words "fear not" to both kings.[15] In the Ahaz narrative Isaiah speaks directly to the king (7:4-9), and in the Hezekiah narrative the oracle is communicated through Hezekiah's servants (37:6-7).

5. In each narrative the king is offered a sign ('wt) as a confirmation that the LORD's word will come to pass, so that the present threat will end (7:10-16; 37:30-32). Hezekiah is given an additional sign (38:7) and requests a sign (38:22).[16]

6. Although in both narratives the king and the city are spared, each passage ends on an ominous note. Isaiah predicts at the end of each narrative that a far greater catastrophe is to be expected from another invading king. In the Ahaz section of the book, the king of Assyria poses the future threat. He is mentioned in the explanation of the sign Immanuel (7:15-17) and in one of the four pericopes beginning "in that day" (7:20) which close the narrative and suggest the future ravaging of the country by the Assyrians and their king. The Hezekiah narrative ends with Isaiah's oracle concerning the coming catastrophe for Jerusalem and its kings from the king of Babylon, when Hezekiah's treasures will be carried to Babylon and some of his sons will be made eunuchs in the palace of Babylon (39:6-7).

See Ackroyd, "Isaiah 36-39," 17. See also Otto Kaiser, *Isaiah 1-12,* 2d ed., trans. John Bowden, OTL (Philadelphia: Westminster, 1983), 146.

15. Blenkinsopp points out that "an oracle of assurance" containing the phrase "fear not" appears in both narratives (*History,* 110).

16. Ackroyd points out that the vocabulary in 7:11, "go deep" (h'mq) and "on high" (lm'lh), is closely related to the vocabulary in 38:8, where the roots 'lh and yrd occur and where m'lwt occurs five times ("Isaiah 36-39," 17). This similarity suggests to Ackroyd, who understands the relationship between the narratives diachronically, that 38:8 may have been revised in light of 7:11 when it was placed in its present position in the Book of Isaiah.

The similarities between these two third person narratives suggest that they have similar structural functions. As will be shown later, however, these two passages are not merely repetitious. Between them there are significant differences. Before focusing on these differences, however, it will be necessary to consider the first war oracle addressed to the community. This oracle stands between the Ahaz narrative and the Hezekiah narrative and is suggestive of movement or development as one moves between the two episodes concerning Judean kings.

A WAR ORACLE TO THE PEOPLE

I have shown elsewhere that this oracle uses the language that is conventional in the Hebrew Scriptures for encouragement of a king faced with a military threat.[17] The people are strengthened with "fear not" language like that in the war oracles addressed to Ahaz and Hezekiah. My purpose here is not to deal with the structure of this specific oracle but to consider the significance of this oracle for understanding the larger structure of the Book of Isaiah.

This royal war oracle to the people comes after the narrative account of the war oracle addressed to King Ahaz indicating that the two kings Rezin and Pekah will not succeed in their threat to Jerusalem but warning that the king of Assyria will pose an even greater threat to Judah in the future. The material following the Ahaz narrative continues to develop the notion of this coming peril. Isaiah's first person narrative warns of the threat that the king of Assyria poses for Judah (8:7-8). After the passage concerning a future ideal ruler (9:2-7), the text turns again to the coming catastrophe for Judah (9:8-21),[18] and it becomes clear in 10:5-6 that the LORD will use the king of Assyria as "the rod of my anger." In 10:7-14 the text takes up the arrogant boasting of the king of Assyria. In verses 15-19

---

17. Conrad, *Fear Not Warrior,* 120–23.
18. In citing biblical references, I follow throughout the versification of the RSV, not the Hebrew. In Isaiah, differences between the two involve only two passages, which correlate as follows:

RSV	MT
9:1	8:23
9:2-21	9:1-20
64:1	63:19b
64:2-12	64:1-11

a future judgment is announced for the Assyrian king, and a promise given of a future deliverance of the people (vv. 20-23), followed by the war oracle (vv. 24-27) addressed to the people as king, offering additional assurance of deliverance in the near future. The people, then, are addressed as if they were a king and are promised deliverance from the Assyrian threat with which the Ahaz narrative closes.

This war oracle is significant in that the promise of future deliverance from Assyria actually is fulfilled in the book. The record is found in the account of the eventual overthrow of the Assyrian king later in the Hezekiah narrative. The occurrence of this war oracle addressed to the people between the Ahaz narrative and the Hezekiah narrative signals movement or development in the text from promise to fulfillment.

THE AHAZ AND HEZEKIAH NARRATIVES:
THE DIFFERENCES

The single most significant difference between the Ahaz and Hezekiah narratives concerns the portrayal of kings—both the Judean kings and the foreign kings. Sennacherib the king of Assyria and Hezekiah the king of Judah in the Hezekiah narrative are more fully developed characters than their counterparts in the Ahaz narrative.[19] In the Ahaz narrative Rezin and Pekah hardly make it "onstage." They are not given a chance to speak. They are portrayed as a toothless threat. Their powerlessness is made explicit at the very beginning of the narrative: "Rezin the king of Syria and Pekah the son of Remaliah the king of Israel came up to Jerusalem to wage war against it, *but they could not conquer it*" (7:1).

The picture of these two kings is in contrast to that of Sennacherib, the king of Assyria in the Hezekiah narrative, who takes center stage through the person of the Rabshakeh and who at the beginning of the narrative dominates the conversation. He shows both authority

---

19. On characterization in the Bible, see Adele Berlin, *Poetics and Interpretation of Biblical Narrative*, Bible and Literature Series 9 (Sheffield: Almond, 1983): "The purpose of character description in the Bible is not to enable the reader to visualize the character, but to enable him to situate the character in terms of his place in society, his own particular situation, and his outstanding traits—in other words, to tell what kind of person he is" (p. 36).

and arrogance by speaking in the language of Judah rather than the diplomatic language of Aramaic. Likewise, Hezekiah is a more active figure than Ahaz. Ahaz speaks one sentence, "I will not ask, and I will not put the LORD to the test" (7:12). In contrast, Hezekiah, on hearing of the Assyrian threat, goes immediately into the temple of the LORD (37:1), sends a message to Isaiah (37:2-4), goes again into the temple after receiving Isaiah's response, prays at the renewed threat of the Assyrian king (37:16-20), talks with the LORD about his imminent death (38:1-6), and after his illness writes words of praise concerning the LORD (38:10-20). Indeed, as the narrative progresses, the character of Hezekiah dominates; at the end he is showing the king of Babylon his treasures. Unlike Ahaz, who dropped out of the scene, Hezekiah has the last word when he says in response to Isaiah about the coming Babylonian catastrophe, "'The Word of the LORD which you have spoken is good.' For he thought, 'There will be peace and security in my day'" (39:8). In the literary world of the book, then, both Sennacherib and Hezekiah are portrayed as more significant kings than Pekah, Rezin, and Ahaz. Because of the attention given to Sennacherib and Hezekiah, the Assyrian deliverance appears to be of greater importance than the deliverance from the alliance of the Syrian and Israelite kings.

The significance of Sennacherib and Hezekiah, however, is emphasized in another way in the world of the book. Their appearances are foreshadowed in the material leading up to the narrative in which they dominate. It has already been suggested that the promise in the war oracle delivered to the people in 10:24-27 was fulfilled in the Hezekiah narrative. In a similar way, material preceding the Hezekiah narrative concerning these two kings is echoed in the narrative. Things did not just happen in the Hezekiah narrative; they were foretold in the oracles of Isaiah.

THE KING OF ASSYRIA, SENNACHERIB

While there are references to the "king of Assyria" (e.g., 7:17; 10:12) in the earlier part of the book, he is not mentioned specifically by name until he appears in the Hezekiah narrative. What he does and what he says in that narrative, however, are anticipated in the following ways before chapters 36–39. First, destruction by the

Assyrian king, described in the Hezekiah narrative ("Sennacherib king of Assyria came up against all the fortified cities of Judah and took them" [36:1]), has been predicted not only in the conclusion of the Ahaz narrative (7:14-25) but also in the autobiographical account in a personal message from the LORD to Isaiah (8:6-8). Second, the speech of the Rabshakeh, designed to instill fear into the people by its claim that the LORD had commanded the Assyrian king to attack Judah (36:10), was anticipated when the LORD had said that he would send the boastful Assyrian king as the "rod of my anger" to destroy and plunder Judah, "a godless nation" (10:5-6). Third, the Assyrian king's arrogant boasts, through the Rabshakeh, that neither any god of other nations nor the LORD could deliver Jerusalem out of his hand (36:18-20; 37:10-13) are anticipated (10:8-11, 13-14) before Sennacherib speaks them in the time of Hezekiah. Fourth, the LORD's words of judgment (37:22-29) spoken against the arrogant king of Assyria are also foreshadowed earlier in the book, in the context of the Ahaz narrative (10:15-19). Finally, the words of the LORD in 10:15-19 (see esp. v. 16) anticipate the eventual downfall of the king (37:36-38).

For those reading or hearing the book—traveling through the chronological world of the book, so to speak—everything about the invading Assyrian king is known. As was mentioned earlier, even a war oracle promising deliverance from this king was spoken to the people before the Assyrian invasion of Judah appears in the book.

THE KING OF JUDAH, HEZEKIAH

If the words of Isaiah and the LORD spoken in the context of the Syro-Israelite crisis about the king of Assyria find fulfillment in Sennacherib, are there any words about a future king of Judah that find fulfillment in Hezekiah? Yes; as in the case of Sennacherib, however, his name is not mentioned until he appears in the Hezekiah narrative. Just as the king of Assyria is alluded to in the Ahaz narrative in conjunction with the giving of the sign, so—not surprisingly—Hezekiah is alluded to in the sign itself, Immanuel.[20]

20. The arguments presented here concern the identification of Hezekiah with Immanuel in the present literary structure of the book and are not meant to identify what a historical Isaiah might have meant by Immanuel if he had uttered the name

As has been argued earlier in this chapter, the outcome of the Syro-Israelite crisis gave rise to the announcement by Isaiah, both in the Ahaz narrative and after it, of a greater crisis to be precipitated by the Assyrians. As one moves through the book and arrives at the Hezekiah narrative, the Assyrian crisis does come, the Assyrian king does come in the person of Sennacherib, and the promise of the deliverance of the people made in the war oracle is fulfilled. It should not be startling, then, that the prediction of the birth of one with the name Immanuel, "God with us," also finds its fulfillment in the Hezekiah narrative. Just as the extended portrayal of Sennacherib fulfills the announcement concerning the future Assyrian king, so the appearance of Hezekiah fulfills the announcement of one who bears the name "God with us." Hezekiah's actions, in contrast to the actions of Ahaz, illustrate how he fulfills this symbolic name.[21]

First, in the Syro-Israelite crisis Ahaz's actions belie the notion that God is with him; he does not even bother to ask the LORD for a sign. Hezekiah not only accepts signs (37:30; 38:7) but also requests a sign (38:22).[22]

Second, the Ahaz passage gives the impression that Isaiah's appearance on the scene is an unwanted intrusion. In contrast, when Hezekiah first hears of the Assyrian invasion, he sends a message directly to Isaiah requesting that the LORD intervene to rebuke the words of the Rabshakeh (37:4). In response to this request Isaiah gives the war oracle (vv. 6-7) to Hezekiah promising the downfall of the Assyrian king, implying "God with us." Even the words of the Rabshakeh, suggesting on the one hand that Hezekiah is misleading the people by saying "the LORD will deliver us" (36:18), and on the

at the time of Ahaz. Even so, the identification of Hezekiah with Immanuel has often been made. See Christopher R. North, "Immanuel," *IDB,* vol. 2 (New York: Abingdon, 1962), 687-88. Both Ackroyd ("Isaiah 36-39," 20) and Blenkinsopp (*History,* 110) suggest the strong possibility that Hezekiah is the fulfillment of the promised sign Immanuel.

21. Both Ackroyd ("Isaiah 36-39," 18) and Blenkinsopp (*History,* 109-10) point out that these two narratives in Isaiah are intended to present a contrast between faithful Hezekiah and unfaithful Ahaz.

22. Ackroyd ("Isaiah 36-39," 19) has pointed out that the reference to the sundial of Ahaz in the sign given to Hezekiah in 38:7-8 functions to contrast Ahaz, who rejects the LORD's signs, with Hezekiah, who not only accepts but also seeks signs from the LORD.

other hand that Hezekiah is deceiving himself by relying on the LORD (37:10), portray Hezekiah as believing in God's presence.

Finally, in Hezekiah's petition to be healed from his sickness, he speaks about how he has walked before the LORD in faithfulness (*b'mt,* 38:3). Here Hezekiah is in sharp contrast with Ahaz, who, the account implies, did not follow the orders in the war oracle stated conditionally, "If you will not believe (*t'mynw*), surely you shall not be established (*t'mnw*)" (7:9b). The repetition of the same word root implies a contrast between Ahaz and Hezekiah, portraying Hezekiah as a king with whom God is present.

After the Ahaz narrative, words of Isaiah and the LORD concerning the king of Assyria find fulfillment in Sennacherib as he is portrayed in the Hezekiah narrative. It should be expected, therefore, that words about a future Judean king that occur after the Ahaz narrative will find fulfillment in Hezekiah. This is the case in 9:2-7, which contains the promise of a future Davidic king. Ackroyd has argued that, in the book, Hezekiah is portrayed as the idealized king of 9:2-7. This is evident, he suggests, in the phrase "the zeal of the LORD of hosts will do [or accomplish] this," which comes both at the climax of the promise of the ideal king (9:7) and in connection with the granting of a sign to Hezekiah (37:32).[23] Yet there is a difference between the promised ideal king (9:2-7) and his realization in Hezekiah. When Hezekiah petitions the LORD to prolong his life (38:2-3), he speaks about his reign in terms that have features as idealized as those in 9:2-7. Yet, Hezekiah was given only fifteen years of further life, and the Hezekiah narrative ends with the prediction that his sons will be taken into exile. The promise in chapter 9 states that the government will be established "from this time forth and evermore" (*m'th w'd 'wlm,* 9:7). This is an important observation that will be treated later in this chapter.

The links between 9:2-7 and Hezekiah as the king who fulfills these expectations are further strengthened by a consideration of verse 4, which speaks of the deliverance of the future ideal king. Here the promise of deliverance of the future king is expressed, using a perfect verb as if the deliverance has already been completed.

23. Ibid.

For the yoke (*'l*) of his burden (*sblw*),
and the staff for his shoulder (*škmw*),
the rod of his oppressor,
thou has broken (*hḥtt*) as on the day of Midian (*mdyn*).

This promise of deliverance of the future ideal king has striking parallels to the war oracle given to the people in 10:24-27 regarding their deliverance from the Assyrians, a deliverance that we have already argued has its fulfillment in the Hezekiah narrative. The war oracle contained this promise to the people: "And the LORD of hosts will wield against them a scourge, as when he smote Midian (*mdyn*) at the rock of Oreb; and his rod will be over the sea, and he will lift it as he did in Egypt. And in that day his burden (*sblw*) will depart from your shoulder (*škmk*), and his yoke (*'lw*) will be destroyed from your neck" (10:26-27). Both the deliverance of the future ideal king and the deliverance of the people are likened to the deliverance from Midian; and both passages speak of the oppression as a yoke (*'l*) and a burden (*sbl*) on the shoulder (*škm*). The similar ways in which 9:4 and 10:24-27 speak about the deliverance from Assyrian oppression reinforce the suggestion that the Hezekiah narrative fulfills the promise of the king who is announced in 9:2-7, just as it fulfills the promise of the deliverance of the people announced in 10:24-27.

THE WAR ORACLES TO THE COMMUNITY

The discussion has concentrated primarily on how the Hezekiah narrative fulfills announcements about the future in chapters 7–10. It has said nothing about the relationship of the Hezekiah narrative to what occurs in chapters 11–35 and to the larger structure of the book. This relationship deserves full treatment and will be dealt with in subsequent chapters. It can be said broadly, however, that what is said in chapters 11–35 falls into three categories. Some of the material concerns the Assyrian crisis and finds its fulfillment in the Hezekiah narrative: for example, the promise of the deliverance of the people from the Assyrians (14:24-27), the promise of the defeat of the Assyrians (31:8-9), the promise of the Judean king who will reign in righteousness (32:1; cf. 16:5), and possibly an allusion to the end of the treacherous rule of the Assyrian king (33:1).[24]

Second, some of the material concerns the judgment against foreign nations other than Assyria and does not find fulfillment in the Hezekiah narrative. It is possible to understand these oracles against foreign nations as demonstrating the LORD's case against the Assyrian king (cf. 10:13-19): that it was the LORD and not the Assyrian king who was responsible for the destruction of the nations. This material, however, points beyond a clear and narrow association with the Hezekiah narrative. For example, a great deal of attention is given to judgment against Babylon and its king, who is mentioned as a future threat at the end of the Hezekiah narrative. Indeed, Babylon is mentioned first in the series of oracles against the nations beginning in chapter 13 (see also 14:4-23; cf. 21:1-10).

Finally, some of the material concerns a future deliverance of Judah and its people that goes far beyond the limited deliverance from the Assyrian crisis reported in the Hezekiah narrative. The vision is universal, concerning all creation and all nations. See, for example, the vision of universal peace in 11:6-9, the vision of the Egyptians and the Assyrians who will worship the LORD (19:18-24), and the restoration of the people in a more magnificent way than depicted in the Assyrian deliverance (see chaps. 24-27; 34-35).

The point here is that not all that is said in the book between the Ahaz and Hezekiah narratives finds its fulfillment in the Hezekiah narrative. The fact that some things remain unfulfilled is a clue to the function of the war oracles to the community found in chapters 41, 43, and 44. Just as the war oracle to the community in 10:24-27 announces the deliverance of the people from the Assyrian crisis, so these later war oracles in the book announce the deliverance of the community from the Babylonian crisis.

The war oracles in chapters 41, 43, and 44 differ in one significant way from the one in 10:24-27. There is no narrative in the book depicting the fulfillment of these oracles. No complete narrative of the Babylonian oppression and deliverance is appended to the end

---

24. The allusion here is not clear. See Otto Kaiser, *Isaiah 13–39*, trans. R. A. Wilson, OTL (Philadelphia: Westminster, 1974), 339–40.

of the book. The war oracles in chapters 41, 43, and 44 precede only the promises of judgment on Babylon and the restoration of the people.

This is the time of waiting, as a voice of exhortation makes clear before the first war oracle to Jacob-Israel in Isaiah 41. The voice challenges those who have lost faith in the power of the LORD to wait (*qwh*) for the LORD, who will renew their strength (40:27-31). But this time of waiting has had parallels in the earlier part of the book. Before the war oracle spoken to the people concerning the deliverance from Assyrian oppression, Isaiah speaks of that time as a time of waiting. "Bind up the testimony, seal the teaching among my disciples. I will wait (*ḥkh*) for the LORD, who is hiding his face from the house of Jacob, and I will hope (*qwh*) in him" (8:16-17). The book, then, suggests that its implied audience is waiting for the fulfillment of the LORD's promise of deliverance from Babylonian oppression. That their waiting will be rewarded is implied by the fact that the first community waited—and was delivered from Assyrian oppression. To read the book this way, however, does not require inferences about a real community experiencing Babylonian oppression in the sixth century. Who the original audience was and what it might have understood as Babylonian oppression is not clear and probably never will be.[25]

It will be recalled that one of the significant differences between the Ahaz and Hezekiah narratives was in their respective portrayals of the Judean kings. Hezekiah's character was more fully developed than Ahaz's character. Unlike Ahaz, Hezekiah spoke to God. When one reads the Book of Isaiah, the same kind of development takes place in the portrayal of the community. At the beginning of the

---

25. What is clear is that many subsequent readers of the book understood Babylonian oppression metaphorically and did not restrict its meaning to the sixth century B.C.E. See, e.g., the Book of Revelation (14:8; 18:2), Ibn Ezra (M. Friedländer, ed., *The Commentary of Ibn Ezra on Isaiah: Edited from MSS. and Translated, with Notes, Introductions, and Indexes* [London, 1873; reprint, New York: Philip Feldheim, 1948], 169-70), and Martin Luther ("The Babylonian Captivity of the Church," in *Three Treatises*, trans. A. T. W. Steinhäuser and rev. F. C. Ahrens and A. R. Wentz [Philadelphia: Fortress Press, 1960], 115-260). For a contemporary reader who emphasizes the metaphorical import of the Babylonian oppression in Isaiah, see Walter Brueggemann, *Hopeful Imagination: Prophetic Voices in Exile* (Philadelphia: Fortress Press, 1986), 94. For a more detailed discussion of my understanding of the metaphorical sense of Babylon in the Book of Isaiah, see the final paragraphs of chapter 3 below.

book the community is addressed or spoken about, but it does not directly speak to the LORD. At the end of the book the community speaks to the LORD. Furthermore, this community is not a community that needs to be exhorted to wait for the LORD as the earlier community in the book had been. Rather, the community proclaims its faith in the LORD as a God who acts for those who wait (64:3-4, *ḥkh* and *qwh*) for him. Just as the faithless and essentially voiceless Ahaz gives way to the faithful Hezekiah, who speaks to the LORD, so the voiceless community becomes at the end of the book a community that speaks to the LORD (see chaps. 63-64). This development in the character of the people suggests why the people are addressed with royal war oracles in chapters 10, 41, 43, and 44. As the book looks forward to the future deliverance of the people, it is looking beyond the time of Davidic kingship to a time when the people will be king.[26]

SUMMARY AND CONCLUSION

I have argued that the royal narrative in chapters 36-39 and its accompanying war oracles in chapters 41, 43, and 44 echo the royal narrative in chapter 7 and its accompanying war oracle in 10:24-27. This repetitive device creates cohesiveness and is a key to the structural unity of the book as a whole. Specifically, I have argued that the war oracle addressed to the people in 10:24-27, following the announcement of Assyrian devastation at the end of the Ahaz narrative and promising deliverance from the Assyrians, is fulfilled in the Hezekiah narrative. The fulfillment of this promise provides the basis for the hope in the fulfillment of the war oracles addressed to the people following the announcement of Babylonian devastation at the end of the Hezekiah narrative.[27] The Hezekiah narrative is strategically located in the book because it provides the persuasive basis on which the implied audience can look forward to salvation

26. See my "Community as King," 99-111.
27. Although I am arguing synchronically rather than diachronically, my study adds weight to existing scholarship, for example, the studies of Ackroyd and Melugin, who have already argued convincingly that Isaiah 36-39 provides the narrative context for the message of hope beginning in chapter 40. See Ackroyd, "Isaiah 36-39," 20-21; and Roy F. Melugin, *The Formation of Isaiah 40-55*, BZAW 141 (Berlin: de Gruyter, 1976): 176-78.

from the Babylonians. Indeed, Isaiah's words of judgment on the Assyrian king Sennacherib (37:22-29) suggest that the LORD is bringing to fruition what he planned long ago. He challenges the king,

Have you not heard
that I determined (*'śyty*) it long ago?
I planned (*wysrtyh*) from days of old
what I now bring to pass. (37:26)

Just as the LORD brought to pass what he determined long ago concerning the Assyrians, so the implied audience can assume that the LORD will bring to pass what he determined long ago in Isaiah's pronouncements of judgment and salvation regarding the Babylonians. On the basis of the precedent seen in the Hezekiah narrative, those looking to deliverance from Babylonian captivity can have faith in the LORD's word that he will bring to pass what he proclaimed long ago. The Book of Isaiah, then, is presenting the poetry of Isaiah in the context of a structured and predetermined pattern of history in a way not dissimilar to the way in which apocalyptic visions such as those in the Book of Daniel forecast a predetermined history.[28] It is significant, then, that the superscription of the Book of Isaiah invites the audience to receive the book as the "vision of Isaiah" (*ḥzwn yš'yhw*).[29] The narrative structure of the book suggests that it is providing Isaiah's vision of world history, which has already received partial fulfillment in the judgment of Assyria and the deliverance of Jerusalem at the time of Hezekiah.

This chapter has offered an initial insight into the structure of the Book of Isaiah. The Hezekiah narrative has a transitional function

28. See Peter R. Ackroyd, "The Biblical Interpretation of the Reigns of Ahaz and Hezekiah," in *In the Shelter of Elyon: Essays on Ancient Palestinian Life and Literature in Honor of G. W. Ahlström,* ed. W. Boyd Barrick and John R. Spencer, JSOTSup 31 (Sheffield: JSOT, 1984): 257. He observes that the alternating pattern of a bad king followed by a good king seems to be typical of the final structuring of books.
29. It is quite possible that in its present form the book is structured in such a way as to provide clues to its readers to read it according to what John Barton terms "prophetic foreknowledge of the present day," one of four modes of reading prophetic literature in the postexilic period. He notes that this and other modes of reading prophetic literature may have influenced the final structuring of prophetic books (*Oracles of God: Perceptions of Ancient Prophecy in Israel after the Exile* [London: Darton, Longman and Todd, 1986], 179-213 and 270-73).

in the book.[30] It points back to the Ahaz narrative and forward to a yet-undetermined narrative of deliverance from Babylonian captivity. The missing narrative anticipated by the end of the book makes sense in terms of the book's design. Just as the Hezekiah narrative mirrors the same sequence of motifs as the Ahaz narrative, so the narrative still to be determined will mirror a similar sequence of motifs. But just as the Hezekiah narrative presented Hezekiah as a different sort of king than Ahaz, so the missing narrative will portray the community as a different sort of king than Hezekiah. The book, then, is constructed to challenge its audience to envision an unwritten and yet-to-be-experienced narrative of deliverance from Babylonian oppression, a deliverance that will entail world peace such as that proclaimed, for example, in chapters 24–27.

Problems still need to be resolved. Structural issues still to be settled concern the beginning of the book. Why does the call narrative of Isaiah come only in chapter 6 and not at the beginning of the book? More needs to be said about the appearance of Isaiah's name in the narrative in chapter 20 and also the three so-called superscriptions. The discussion of the Hezekiah narrative needs to be expanded, for very little has been said about the episode in which Hezekiah, suffering from a grave illness, is given fifteen more years of life (chap. 38). Finally, the notion of an implied audience that has been introduced in this chapter needs further explanation. Who is that audience? What else does the book tell us about it? Before moving on to these issues, however, in the next chapter, I discuss the motif of the LORD's plan—his military strategy—for all the earth. This motif adds weight to the hypothesis presented in this chapter concerning the royal narratives, namely, that they perform the literary function of providing a historical framework that presents events as part of a predetermined plan.

30. According to my analysis, the Hezekiah narrative is structurally linked to what follows. This assessment is in conflict with the traditional historical-critical argument that it represents the conclusion to a document that was once independent and is only secondarily related to what follows it in the present Book of Isaiah.

CHAPTER 3

The LORD's Military Strategy concerning All the Earth

The analysis of the royal narratives of the Book of Isaiah, outlined in the last chapter, suggests that the narratives function to provide a pylon of the book's structure, namely, the presentation of history as moving in a predetermined way in specific historical situations. This element of the book's structure supports a recurring motif in the poetry as well as the prose: the LORD planned long ago what has happened and what will come to pass. Repetition of motif is coupled with the repetition of type-scene, with both rhetorical techniques indicating the book's structural unity.

This chapter broadens the conclusions reached in the last chapter in two ways. It shows that the LORD's plan to liberate his people from the Assyrians and the Babylonians is only part of a larger plan to conduct warfare against all the nations of the world, who will be brought under his judgment. The LORD's universal judgment will lead to an unprecedented world peace. The chapter also clarifies the function of chapters 13–27 — chapters that scholars have traditionally understood as oracles of judgment against the nations (13–23) and the "little apocalypse" (24–27).[1] These chapters, which concern universal judgment against the nations (13–23) and universal salvation and world peace (24–27), also receive partial fulfillment in the Hezekiah narrative. The narrative functions as evidence of the inevitability of God's plan. As the book approaches its end, the implied audience is therefore called on to envision a narrative of deliverance that goes beyond a mere deliverance from Babylonian

---

1. See, e.g., the consensus view stated in Bernhard W. Anderson, *Understanding the Old Testament,* 4th ed. (Englewood Cliffs, N.J.: Prentice-Hall, 1986), 322.

captivity. Deliverance and salvation will be for those who survive the LORD's strategy of war against all the nations.

THE LORD'S PLAN: A STRATEGY FOR WAR

The motif concerning the LORD's military planning is primarily associated with the noun *'ṣh* and its related verb root *y'ṣ*. But other words are used in association with these to express the notion of what the LORD is planning and doing (e.g., *'śh, m'śh, 'bd, 'bdh, p'l, ḥpṣ, yṣr, dmh*). This vocabulary is used to convey the idea that the LORD has a military strategy against "all the nations of the earth." He has "planned" (*y'ṣ, dmh*), "purposed" (*ḥpṣ*) or "formed" (*yṣr*) this strategy long ago. History is therefore moving in a predetermined way to accomplish the LORD's "plan" (*'ṣh*) or "work" (*m'śh, 'bdh*) that he is "doing" (*'śh, p'l, 'bd*).

In the past, historical-critical scholars have drawn attention to the LORD's plan in Isaiah.[2] While they have understood the LORD's plan to involve his control of history, they have not stressed the military connotations of this plan, as I do in this chapter. Furthermore, they have interpreted this motif in light of their strategies to identify the authentic words of Isaiah, not in terms of the book's structure. That this motif is pervasive and is a unique feature of the Book of Isaiah is reflected in the remarks of Joseph Jensen: "In general there is little that resembles Isaiah's use of this terminology [i.e., the terminology surrounding the motif of the LORD's plan] to designate the LORD's control of history, except in Deutero-Isaiah and some other later sections of the Isaiah collection."[3] Even when historical critics have found one motif to be unique and pervasive in a book, their diachronic understanding of a text has prevented a full understanding of the motif's significance. Metaphorically speaking, the text is seen as scraps of cloth rather than as a garment. My study of this motif differs from these previous historical-critical studies because I am interested in how the motif functions in the text as a literary object

2. See J. Fichtner, "Jahves Plan in der Botschaft des Jesaja," *ZAW* 63 (1951): 16–33; Joseph Jensen, "Yahweh's Plan in Isaiah and in the Rest of the Old Testament," *CBQ* 48 (1986): 443–55; and Hans Wildberger, "Jesajas Verständnis der Geschichte," VTSup 9 (1962): 83–117.
3. Jensen, "Yahweh's Plan," 455.

rather than how the motif illustrates the intentions of an authentic Isaiah, subsequent Isaiahs, or editors.

As I have suggested, the noun *'ṣh* and the verb *y'ṣ* often have military connotations and concern the plans or strategies for warfare. They have these connotations in the so-called historical books in the Old Testament (see Judg. 20:7; 2 Kings 6:8, and 2 Chron. 25:17).[4] Of more immediate importance, the verb and the noun occur in both the Ahaz and Hezekiah narratives in the Book of Isaiah, and in both narratives they concern military planning. In the Ahaz narrative the verb occurs in the war oracle that Isaiah speaks to Ahaz. Isaiah says that Ahaz is not to be afraid, "because Syria, with Ephraim and the son of Remaliah, has devised (*y'ṣ*) evil against you, saying, 'Let us go up against Judah and terrify it, and let us conquer it for ourselves, and set up the son of Tabeel as king in the midst of it'" (7:5-6). Ahaz is not to be afraid of the plan by Syria and Ephraim to terrify and conquer Judah and set a puppet king on the throne. The LORD will not allow this military plan to succeed (vv. 7-8). He has the power to undo the military strategy devised by the nations.

In the Hezekiah narrative the noun occurs with military connotations in the initial speech of the Rabshakeh, who says, "Say to Hezekiah, 'Thus says the great king, the king of Assyria: On what do you rest this confidence of yours? Do you think that mere words are strategy (*'ṣh*) and power for war? On whom do you now rely, that you have rebelled against me?'" (36:4-5). Here the Rabshakeh is saying that successful military planning requires more than words of rebellion. It requires the aid of superpowers such as Egypt, although Egypt is only a "broken reed of a staff" (v. 6).

The language of the royal narratives, including the war oracles to the Kings Ahaz and Hezekiah along with the subsequent war oracles delivered to the people, provides a military backdrop for the book's poetry. The words *'ṣh* and *y'ṣ* and associated words elsewhere in the book have military connotations as well. As I will show below, the LORD's plan is a strategy for war against his own people, against Assyria, against Babylonia, and eventually against all the world.

4. See ibid., 453.

THE LORD'S STRATEGY AND THE ASSYRIANS

A survey of the motif of the LORD's plan to conduct a war against the world can begin with the Ahaz narrative of chapter 7 and the material that follows it. I have already noted that the LORD will not allow the Syro-Ephraimite military strategy, mentioned in 7:5-6, to succeed. The reason that this strategy will not succeed is given in the autobiographical narrative in chapter 8; the LORD is raising up the king of Assyria against them (vv. 5-8). But the emergence of the king of Assyria will not bring safety. As is clear in verses 8-9, the Assyrian, like the "waters of the River," "will sweep on into Judah" and "will overflow" and fill the entire land. The same motif occurs here in chapter 8 as was found at the end of the Ahaz narrative of chapter 7: there will be deliverance from Israel and Syria, but a far greater catastrophe will follow in the person of the invading Assyrian king. Chapter 8 introduces a new motif that was not made explicit in either the Ahaz or Hezekiah narrative material. Invading armies such as Assyria will affect all the world. All the peoples, even those of the far countries (*mrḥqy 'rṣ*), will be terrified by this invading army (8:9-10). These countries, near and far, can make war plans or strategies for defense, but they will come to nought. "Make a plan together (*'ṣw 'ṣh*), but it will come to nought; / speak a word, but it will not stand" (v. 10).[5] The strategies of other nations have no more chance of success than those of Syria and Ephraim.

The Ahaz narrative (chap. 7), which ended on the ominous note of the impending Assyrian invasion, was followed by a war oracle delivered to the people (10:24-27) promising them deliverance from the Assyrians, who themselves will eventually be defeated. It should not be surprising, therefore, to read later in the book that it is part of the LORD's plan to overthrow the Assyrians.

The LORD of hosts has sworn:
"As I have planned (*dmyty*),
    so shall it be,
and as I have purposed (*y'ṣty*),
    so shall it stand,

---

5. For "make a plan together" the RSV has "take counsel together," a perfectly acceptable translation. For consistency in the presentation of my argument, I have altered the RSV translation of *'ṣh* and *y'ṣ*, in most instances, to "plan" and "to plan" where it has an alternative translation.

that I will break the Assyrian in my land,
and upon my mountains trample him under foot;
and his yoke shall depart from them,
and his burden from their shoulder."
This is the plan (*h'sh*) that is planned (*hy'wsh*)
concerning the whole earth;
and this is the hand that is stretched out
over all the nations.
For the LORD of hosts has planned (*y's*),
and who will annul it?
His hand is stretched out
and who will turn it back? (14:24-27)[6]

The plan here for the LORD to defeat the Assyrians uses similar vocabulary to that used in the war oracle promising the people deliverance from the Assyrians (10:24-27) and to that used in the promise of the deliverance of the future ideal king (Hezekiah) in 9:4. In all three passages the Assyrian oppression is described as a "yoke" (*'l*) and a "burden" (*sbl*) on the "shoulder" (*škm*). The LORD's plan is to defeat the Assyrians, just as it was his plan to use the Assyrians to thwart the strategies of the Syro-Ephraimite alliance. Here again, however, as in 8:9-10, the theme emerges (one not made explicit in either the Ahaz or Hezekiah narratives) that the LORD's plan for war is a plan concerning "the whole earth," for his hand "is stretched out over all the nations" (14:26).

The announcement concerning the LORD's plan to defeat the Assyrians contains rhetorical questions—a feature that recurs in subsequent passages that announce the LORD's plan. Just as war oracles are rhetorical features associated with the narratives, so rhetorical questions are associated with the theme of the LORD's plan to destroy the nations. In 14:24-27 cited above, the rhetorical questions "Who will annul it?" and "Who will turn it back?" have an implied answer: no one can overturn the LORD's plan. He can annul the plan of the Syro-Israelite alliance. He can use the Assyrians in his plan. But no one can interfere with the LORD's plan. These rhetorical questions with their implied answer are a persuasive device directed at the book's implied audience.

The rhetorical question is also part of the LORD's taunt of the

6. The RSV translates *h'sh* as "purpose" and *hy'wsh* and *y's* as "purposed."

arrogant Assyrian king in the Hezekiah narrative. The LORD says to the Assyrian king,

Have you not heard
   that I determined (*'śyty*) it long ago?
I planned (*wysrtyh*) from days of old
   what now I bring to pass. (37:26)

The implied answer to the question is no. The Assyrian king could not have heard or known that. The situation is different for the book's implied audience, however, because the plan was announced earlier in the text, in 14:24-27, before the narration of the downfall of the Assyrian king in chapter 37 of the Hezekiah narrative. The rhetorical question, purportedly directed at the Assyrian king in association with the LORD's announcement of a military plan involving this king, is actually a rhetorical device directed at an implied audience that is "in the know," enabling that audience to envision with confidence the final narrative fulfillment of the LORD's victory. The narrative, then, containing a poetic taunt of the king and accented by a rhetorical question, gives support to the inevitability of the LORD's plan reaching fruition and the view of the LORD's final victory over the other nations and over all the world. The Hezekiah narrative functions as a specific instance of the outworking of the LORD's plan.

THE LORD'S STRATEGY AS IT AFFECTS EGYPT

The motif of the LORD's strategy or plan appears not only in 14:24-27 but also elsewhere in chapters 13–27. It appears in the oracle of judgment against Egypt in chapter 19. The LORD will foil the plan of Egypt as he did the strategy of the Syro-Israelite alliance by causing the Egyptians to fight against one another, assuring their self-destruction (19:2-4). Significantly, the LORD's action will incorporate an assault on Egypt's *plans:* "I will confound their plans" (*w'stw 'bl'*, v. 3). The LORD will empty out the "spirit" (*rwḥ*, v. 3) of the Egyptians and replace it with a "spirit of confusion" (*rwḥ 'w'ym*, v. 14). The result will be that "the wise counselors [or planners] of Pharaoh" (*ḥkmy y'śy pr'h*) will give "stupid counsel [or plans] (*'śh nb'rh*, v. 11). An association of the "spirit" with good and sound planning occurs in other passages to be discussed shortly.

The Egyptian plans will be confused because they are counter to the plan of the LORD (*'ṣt yhwh*) that he planned (*hw' yw'ṣ*) against them (19:17). The plan of the LORD will be carried out "in that day" when "Judah will become a terror to the Egyptians" (vv. 16-17).

This chapter, like the chapter announcing the LORD's planned destruction of Assyria, raises rhetorical questions. After describing the "wise planners" of Egypt as giving "stupid plans" (19:11), the LORD asks the "princes of Zoan" and the "wise counselors of Pharaoh,"

> How can you say to Pharaoh,
> "I am a son of the wise,
> a son of ancient kings"?
> Where then are your wise men?
> Let them tell you and make known
> what the LORD of hosts has planned (*y'ṣ*) against Egypt. (19:11b-12)[7]

Here, as elsewhere, the LORD's plan frustrates the plans of the nations. The Egyptians cannot answer questions about what the LORD of hosts has planned, and they are deemed to be fools and deluded. They can consult the idols, the sorcerers, the mediums, and the wizards (v. 3), but to no avail. Here rhetorical questions have the effect of persuading the audience of the inevitability of the LORD's plan and the folly of any alternative plan.

THE LORD'S PLAN AGAINST TYRE

The motif of the LORD's military plan of judgment against the nations also appears in the oracle against Tyre. After announcing the judgment of Tyre, the oracle says,

> Is this your exultant city
> whose origin is from days of old,
> whose feet carried her
> to settle afar?
> Who has planned (*y'ṣ*) this
> against Tyre, the bestower of crowns
> whose merchants were princes,
> whose traders were the honored of the earth?

---

7. The RSV translates *y'ṣ* as "purposed."

The LORD of hosts has planned it (y'ṣh),
to defile the pride of all glory,
to dishonor all the honored of the earth. (23:7-9)[8]

Here a rhetorical question addressed to the inhabitants of Tyre ("inhabitants of the coast") draws attention to the dramatic fall from greatness. This rhetorical question is followed by a question raised in connection with the LORD's plan of judgment against Tyre, but it is not addressed to Tyre. It serves to make more emphatic the announcement to the implied audience, which is a direct response to the question: It is the LORD who planned (y'ṣ) this. The text is supplying the reader with both a question and an articulated answer. The earlier questions were answered by implication, but here the answer to the question is explicit.

The answer to this question also states the purpose of the LORD's plan of destruction. The LORD's planned warfare against the nations is against the proud—not just the proud of Tyre, but the proud in all the earth. The theme of the LORD's campaign against the haughty is reiterated later in the book in relation to the arrogant boasting of the Assyrian king. The words of the Assyrian king, like the words of the LORD, are spoken by a messenger; the Assyrian king speaks through the Rabshakeh, the LORD through the prophet Isaiah. The Assyrian king demonstrates his arrogance by using (as does the LORD) not only the prophetic messenger formula ("thus says . . .") but also rhetorical questions.

> And the Rabshakeh said to them, "Say to Hezekiah, 'Thus says the great king, the king of Assyria: On what do you rest this confidence of yours? Do you think that mere words are strategy ('ṣh) and power for war? On whom do you now rely, that you have rebelled against me? Behold, you are relying on Egypt, that broken reed of a staff, which will pierce the hand of any man who leans on it. Such is Pharaoh king of Egypt to all who rely on him. But if you say to me, "We rely on the LORD our God," is it not he whose high places and altars Hezekiah has removed, saying to Judah and Jerusalem, "You shall worship before this altar"? Come now, make a wager with my master the king of Assyria: I will give you two thousand horses, if you are able on your part to set riders upon them. How then can you repulse a single captain among the least of my master's servants, when you rely

8. The RSV translates y'ṣ and y'ṣh as "purposed."

on Egypt for chariots and for horsemen? Moreover, is it without the LORD that I have come up against this land to destroy it? The LORD said to me, Go up against this land, and destroy it.'" (36:4-10)

Here the Assyrian king announces his plan to overthrow Jerusalem, whose plan for war he considers to be useless (36:5). He, like the LORD, does this by asking rhetorical questions that are persuasive in force. That rhetorical questions characterize the speech of the Assyrian king, as they do the LORD's speech in his announcement of his military strategy, is evident in the second speech of the Rabshakeh.

> Thus says the king: "Do not let Hezekiah deceive you, for he will not be able to deliver you. . . . Beware lest Hezekiah mislead you by saying, 'The LORD will deliver us.' Has any of the gods of the nations delivered his land out of the hand of the king of Assyria? Where are the gods of Hamath and Arpad? Where are the gods of Sepharvaim? Have they delivered Samaria out of my hand? Who among all the gods of these countries have delivered their countries out of my hand, that the LORD should deliver Jerusalem out of my hand?" (36:14-20)

Later in the narrative the Assyrian king, after hearing that the Ethiopians had engaged him in battle, again sends messengers to Hezekiah announcing his plans concerning Jerusalem and using rhetorical questions as a persuasive device.

> Do not let your God on whom you rely deceive you by promising that Jerusalem will not be given into the hand of the king of Assyria. Behold, you have heard what the kings of Assyria have done to all lands, destroying them utterly. And shall you be delivered? Have the gods of the nations delivered them, the nations which my fathers destroyed, Gozan, Haran, Rezeph, and the people of Eden who were in Telassar? Where is the king of Hamath, the king of Arpad, the king of the city of Sepharvaim, the king of Hena, or the king of Ivvah? (37:10b-13)[9]

9. The references to the cities are meaningful because they are so insignificant that no one has heard of them. See John D. W. Watts, *Isaiah 34–66*, WBC 25 (Waco, Tex.: Word Books, 1987): "No cities by these names are known" (p. 33). To suggest as he does, however, that attempts should be made to identify the cities is to miss the point. Here the Assyrian king is bragging about his victory over cities of which no one has ever heard. The bragging of the Assyrian king pales in significance in the context of the LORD's announced plan to defeat all those

The Assyrian king, like the LORD, announces his plans for warfare with rhetorical questions. Nevertheless, the arrogance of the Assyrian king, who mimics the LORD's speech, is subverted by the rhetorical strategies of the book itself. The answers to the Assyrian king's questions are not as obvious to the book's implied audience as the character of the king appears to think. The implied audience knows what the character of Sennacherib does not know, namely, that the LORD plans to overthrow the Assyrian king and that this plan was announced long ago (at least in terms of the book's chronology). The implied audience knows that the LORD is about to break the Assyrian in his land (14:24-27). This end is reflected in the rhetorical question that the LORD poses for this arrogant king—a question the audience can answer. The implied audience knows that the king's ignorance will lead to his downfall. The LORD challenges the king with the question:

> Have you not heard
> that I determined (*'śyty*) it long ago?
> I planned (*wysrtyh*) from days of old
> what now I bring to pass,
> that you should make fortified cities
> crash into heaps of ruins. (37:26)

The LORD's long-established plan presents unanswerable questions to the proud of the earth such as the Assyrian king, the wise counselors and princes of Egypt, and the merchants, princes, and traders of Tyre who "were the honored of the earth" (23:8). The LORD will foil the plan of the Assyrian king and deliver the city of Jerusalem. In the book, the Hezekiah narrative represents the fulfillment of that part of the LORD's plan.

THE LORD'S PLAN AND JERUSALEM'S FATE

As the reader follows the motif of the LORD's plan through the oracles of judgment against the nations, the rhetorical questions increase the persuasiveness of the promises that the LORD's plan will come to fruition. The language of the book is establishing the certainty of the LORD's plan about the future course of world events.

nations about which everyone has heard, including Assyria, Babylon, Egypt, and Tyre.

As the audience reaches the end of this section of the book (chaps. 13–27), the LORD's military punishment is reiterated; this time its consequences are stated universally:

> On that day the LORD will punish
> the host of heaven, in heaven
> and the kings of the earth, on the earth.
> They will be gathered together
> as prisoners in a pit;
> they will be shut up in a prison,
> and after many days they will be punished.
> Then the moon will be confounded,
> and the sun ashamed;
> for the LORD of hosts will reign
> on Mount Zion and in Jerusalem
> and before his elders he will manifest his glory. (24:21-23)

In response to this universal judgment and victory over heaven and earth, a first person voice praises the LORD for his plan to destroy the whole earth. Significantly, the praise is for a universal destruction that includes even the city of Jerusalem:

> O LORD, thou art my God;
> I will exalt thee, I will praise thy name;
> for thou hast done ('śyt) wonderful things,
> plans ('swt) formed of old, faithful and sure.
> For thou hast made the city a heap,
> the fortified city a ruin;
> the palace of aliens is a city no more,
> it will not be rebuilt for a long time (l'wlm). (25:1-2)[10]

These verses contain two new items concerning the LORD's plan. One is the first person voice that speaks here, the significance of which will be treated in later chapters. The other is that the LORD's bellicose plans for heaven and earth have implications even for the city of Jerusalem. Like the other nations, it will eventually be destroyed.[11] The deliverance of the city at the time of Hezekiah will be temporary. This destruction, even of Jerusalem, will cause the LORD to be glorified by "strong peoples" and feared by "ruthless

---

10. The RSV translates l'wlm as "never," but the following context, esp. chapter 26, suggests the translation "not for a long time." The book clearly looks forward to the restoration of Jerusalem.

11. The LORD's planned destruction of Jerusalem is also made explicit in Isa. 22:11.

nations" (25:3). This will not be a time of despair, however, for the LORD is a stronghold to the poor and needy (v. 4), and the LORD's plan for the restoration of Jerusalem will involve a new time of peace and salvation for all peoples, described eschatologically:

> On this mountain the LORD of hosts will make for all peoples a feast of fat things, a feast of wine on the lees, of fat things full of marrow, of wine on the lees well refined. And he will destroy on this mountain the covering that is cast over all peoples, the veil that is spread over all nations. He will swallow up death forever, and the Lord GOD will wipe away tears from all faces, and the reproach of his people he will take away from all the earth; for the LORD has spoken. (25:6-8)

The underlying picture in Isaiah, however, is not one in which judgment on the proud will simply and finally be ignored. In 25:10-12, which follows the description of joyful salvation, the text describes Moab, which seems to be an exemplar of all proud peoples,[12] as being "trodden down in his place, as straw is trodden down in a dung-pit. And he will spread out his hands in the midst of it as a swimmer spreads his hands out to swim; but the LORD will lay low his pride together with the skill of his hands" (vv. 10b-11). This and other similar verses of judgment in Isaiah (e.g., the judgment on Babylon that envisions the slaughter of infants and the ravishing of women [13:15-16]) use images that in horror and gruesomeness compete with images of twentieth-century military atrocities.[13]

THE LORD'S PLAN AGAINST BABYLON:
CHAPTER 40

I have argued in this chapter that, between the Ahaz and Hezekiah narratives in chapters 13–27, the LORD announces his military strategy to defeat all the nations of the earth, including Judah and its city of Jerusalem. The Hezekiah narrative represents an instance

---

12. My reading of the book does not assume the book's referentiality to history. Moab is probably better understood as illustrating the fate that is in store for the proud among the nations. Other texts in the Old Testament exclude Moab from entering the assembly of the LORD (e.g., Deut. 23:3 and 13:12). For a similar interpretation of this text about Moab, see John E. A. Sawyer, *Isaiah*, 2 vols., DSB (Philadelphia: Westminster, 1984–86), 1:212–15.

13. See also the last verse in the book, 66:24, where the judgment of those who rebelled against the LORD is described as gruesome and enduring.

of the partial fulfillment of that plan as it relates to the Assyrian king. What happened concerning the Assyrian king was planned by the LORD long ago—a point made in the rhetorical question (37:26) used to taunt the Assyrian king just prior to his downfall. The LORD is bringing to fruition, in the Hezekiah narrative, what he declared earlier in the book about Assyria in the oracles of judgment against the nations. As was pointed out in the previous chapter, however, not all the pronouncements of the LORD are fulfilled in that narrative. Significantly, from the perspective of the Hezekiah narrative, the oracle of judgment against Babylon, which begins the oracles of judgment against the nations (13:1–14:23), is not fulfilled. The rise of Babylon as an arrogant military power has yet to occur.

This emergence is imminent, however, for Hezekiah has only fifteen more years to live. The transition from the end of the Hezekiah narrative to chapter 40 represents a dramatic change of scene. The judgment against Jerusalem has already occurred. It is a heap of ruins. It is now time for the LORD's judgment against Babylon to reach fruition. In fact, in the verses that follow Isaiah's announcement that Judah would be defeated by Babylon (39:5-8), the announcement is made that the LORD's people are to be comforted and their warfare to be ended. The LORD's hand was outstretched against them as it was against all nations (14:27), but they received more than their share:

> Comfort, comfort, my people,
>   says your God.
> Speak tenderly to Jerusalem,
>   and cry to her
> that her warfare is ended,
>   that her iniquity is pardoned,
> that she has received from the LORD's hand
>   double for all her sins. (40:1-2)

The swiftness with which the text moves in these matters is one of its notable features. Throughout the text, as others have pointed out,[14] there is quick and abrupt movement from judgment to salvation. The text is characterized by recurring promises of salvation

---

14. See, e.g., Roland E. Clements, "Patterns in the Prophetic Canon," in *Canon and Authority,* ed. G. W. Coats and B. O. Long (Philadelphia: Fortress Press, 1977), 42-55; and William J. Dumbrell, "The Purpose of the Book of Isaiah," *Tyndale Bulletin* 36 (1985): 111-28.

rather than detailed descriptions of events. Even in the Ahaz and Hezekiah narratives, where there is narrative description, the focus is on the salvation of the LORD. Description of the campaigns of Syria and Israel and of Assyria against Judah are all but lacking.

In the last chapter it was argued that the war oracles in Isaiah 41, 43, and 44 were used as a rhetorical device directed to the implied audience to persuade them that the LORD was about to conclude his campaign against the Babylonians. The book is structured to create in its implied audience a vision of deliverance from Babylonian exile. Rhetorical questions associated with the LORD's plan in his pronouncements of judgment against the nations in chapters 40–47 have a similar rhetorical function to the war oracles in these same chapters. Both rhetorical questions and war oracles function to persuade the implied audience of the imminent and inevitable overthrow of Babylon. In light of the oracles against the nations, however, the envisioned Babylonian deliverance takes on worldwide proportions. The LORD's judgments against the Assyrians and the Babylonians are only instances of a universal judgment that will result in a new era of peace and salvation.

The rhetorical questions occur for the first time in 40:12-31, in the chapter immediately after the Hezekiah narrative ends. Unlike the questions in the oracles of judgment against the nations, where the questions occur singly and in pairs, the questions here are numerous and occur in rapid-fire succession. The implied audience, like Job, who heard the voice of incessant questions from the whirlwind, is overwhelmed. The effect of the questions is to give persuasive weight to the argument that the LORD is incomparable and the accomplishment of his plan inevitable.

The five sets of questions in 40:12-31, like the question in the oracle of judgment against Tyre (23:8-9), are each followed by an articulated answer.

Questions	Answer
40:12-14	40:15-17
40:18	40:19-20
40:21	40:22-24
40:25	40:26
40:27-28a	40:28b-31

These questions and answers in succession function as an argument supporting the inevitability of the LORD's plan.[15] Furthermore, these questions and answers reiterate points made in the articulation of the LORD's military plan against the nations (chaps. 13–27) and its partial fulfillment in the Hezekiah narrative (chaps. 36–39).

40:12-17. The first set of questions concerns the incomparability of the LORD as a military planner:

> Who has measured the waters in the hollow of his hand
>   and marked off the heavens with a span,
> enclosed the dust of the earth in a measure
>   and weighed the mountains in scales
>   and the hills in a balance?
> Who has directed the Spirit (*rwḥ*) of the LORD,
>   or as his planner ('*ṣtw*) has instructed him?
> Whom did he consult (*nw'ṣ*) for his enlightenment,
>   and who taught him the path of justice,
> and taught him knowledge,
>   and showed him the way of understanding? (40:12-14)[16]

These rhetorical questions indicate that the LORD as planner and military strategist is incomparable. As a planner, he stands in sharp contrast with the planners of Egypt referred to earlier in the book (chap. 19). In 19:3 the LORD says that he will empty out the spirit (*rwḥ*) of the Egyptians so that their plans will be confounded. In fact the Egyptian planners will give stupid advice (v. 11). In contrast, no one can empty out the "spirit" (*rwḥ*) of the LORD and send his plans into confusion (chap. 40). Furthermore, the LORD does not need to consult anyone as the Egyptians did. In fact, as has just been learned from the Hezekiah narrative, Hezekiah's success came about because he consulted the LORD for his military strategy (36:5). The LORD does not consult; rather, he is consulted by those who are successful in military adversity.

When nations such as Egypt and Assyria are compared with the LORD, they are nothing. And that is exactly what is said in the answer that is given to the rhetorical questions in 40:12-14:

---

15. For a recent study that discusses the rhetorical techniques utilized in these chapters, see Bruce D. Naidoff, "The Rhetoric of Encouragement in Isaiah 40:12-31: A Form Critical Study," *ZAW* 93 (1981): 62–76.
16. The RSV translates '*ṣtw* as "his counselor."

Behold, the nations are like a drop from a bucket,
and are accounted as the dust on the scales;
behold, he takes up the isles like fine dust.
Lebanon would not suffice for fuel,
nor are its beasts enough for a burnt offering.
All the nations are as nothing before him,
they are accounted by him as less than nothing and emptiness.
(40:15-17)

40:18-20. The Egyptians in their confusion consulted idols
(19:3). If the nations are nothing to the LORD, who can empty out
their spirit and send their plans into confusion, then how does the
LORD compare with idols such as those the Egyptians consulted?
"To whom will you liken God, / or what likeness compare to him?"
(40:18). For the implied audience the answer is "no one" because the
implied audience has just heard Hezekiah's prayer of confidence and
has heard the LORD's deliverance of Hezekiah. "Of a truth, O LORD,
the kings of Assyria have laid waste all the nations and their lands,
and have cast their gods into the fire; for they were no gods, but
the work of men's hands, wood and stone; therefore they were
destroyed" (37:18-19).

The answer to the question in 40:18 reiterates what the Hezekiah
narrative demonstrates, namely, that unlike the LORD, who is
successful in warfare, idols of wood and stone have no power.

The idol! a workman casts it,
and a goldsmith overlays it with gold,
and casts for it silver chains.
He who is impoverished chooses for an offering
wood that will not rot;
he seeks out a skillful craftsman
to set up an image that will not move. (40:19-20)

40:21-24. The next set of questions poses the central motif concerning the LORD's plan: because the LORD is unlike the nations and
their idols, he can announce his plans beforehand and bring them
to fruition. The questions ask:

Have you not known? Have you not heard (*hlw' tšm'w*)?
Has it not been told you from the beginning?
Have you not understood from the foundations of the earth? (40:21)

For the implied audience these questions are an echo of the rhetorical question posed for the Assyrian king:

> Have you not heard (*hlw' šm't*)
>   that I determined it long ago?
> I planned from days of old
>   what now I bring to pass. (37:26ab)

Not only has the implied audience known and heard that the LORD's plan is invincible, they have also heard what happened to the Assyrian king, who was deaf to the question of the LORD. He fell victim to the LORD, mistaking the LORD's success with his own. The answer given to the rhetorical questions in 40:21 suggests that the LORD blows away earthly princes and rulers as if they were nothing, recalling the LORD's easy victory over the Assyrian king just described in the Hezekiah narrative:

> It is he who sits above the circle of the earth,
>   and its inhabitants are like grasshoppers;
> who stretches out the heavens like a curtain,
>   and spreads them like a tent to dwell in;
> who brings princes to nought,
>   and makes the rulers of the earth as nothing.
> Scarcely are they planted, scarcely sown,
>   scarcely has their stem taken root in the earth,
> When he blows upon them, and they wither,
>   and the tempest carries them off like stubble. (40:22-24)

What the Assyrian king has not heard, the audience of the book has heard. The LORD has announced his plan long ago and is bringing that plan to fruition. No king can stand in his way.

40:25-26. The first three sets of questions function to convince the implied audience that the LORD is not like nations or their idols and kings. This incomparability of the LORD is demonstrated in his predetermined plan against all the nations of the earth, a plan that has reached partial fulfillment in the Hezekiah narrative. Answers to these questions reassure the implied audience and function to assuage any doubts. If the LORD is not like nations and their idols and kings, then who is like the LORD?

> To whom then will you compare me,
>   that I should be like him?
> says the Holy One.

Lift up your eyes on high and see:
who created these? (40:25-26a)

These questions and their answer suggest that the LORD is incomparable because, unlike the others with whom he has been compared, he has created (*br'*) the heavens.

He who brings out their host by number,
calling them all by name;
by the greatness of his might,
and because he is strong in power
not one is missing. (40:26bc)

The LORD as creator of the heavens echoes the theme of the LORD's announced victory "over the host of heaven, in heaven / and the kings of the earth, on the earth" (24:21). The LORD is incomparable not only to earthly things (nations, idols, and kings) but also to heavenly things.

40:27-31. This last set of questions is directed to Jacob-Israel. The question posed earlier to the king of Assyria ("Have you not heard [*hlw' šm't*]?") and echoed in the third set of rhetorical questions (40:21) is echoed again in this final series of questions.

Why do you say, O Jacob,
and speak, O Israel,
"My way is hid from the LORD,
and my right is disregarded by my God?"
Have you not known? Have you not heard (*l' šm't*)? (40:27-28a)

The accent on hearing in the recurring rhetorical question "Have you not heard?" recalls the emphasis on hearing in the Hezekiah narrative.[17] In the interaction between the Assyrian king, Hezekiah, and the LORD (chaps. 36-37), they repeatedly refer to hearing. In response to the Rabshakeh's initial speech (36:4-10), the servants of Hezekiah ask him not to speak in the language of Judah when he is in the "hearing" (*b'zny*, lit. "in the ears") of the people (v. 11). In a defiant retort the Rabshakeh stood and called out in the language of Judah, "Hear . . ." (v. 13). In this second speech he tells the audience, "Do not listen to Hezekiah" (v. 16). Then "when King

---

17. For a discussion of the emphasis on hearing in this narrative as it appears in 2 Kings, see Donna Nolan Fewell, "Sennacherib's Defeat: Words at War in 2 Kings 18:13-19:37," *JSOT* 34 (1986): 84.

Hezekiah heard" (37:1), he sent a message to the prophet Isaiah, saying, "It may be that the LORD your God heard the words of the
Rabshakeh" (v. 4). The text implies that the LORD has heard; in the
comforting war oracle the LORD says, "Do not be afraid because of
the words that you have heard" (v. 6).

At this point in the narrative one begins to get the sense that
something is going wrong for the Assyrians. The Rabshakeh "had
heard that the king [of Assyria] had left Lachish" (37:8). This happened because the king of Assyria "heard" that "Tirhakah king of
Ethiopia" had set out to fight against him, and "when he heard it,
he sent messengers to Hezekiah" (v. 9). The messengers say to Hezekiah, "Behold, you have heard what the kings of Assyria have done
to all lands, destroying them utterly" (v. 11). Hezekiah then prays
to God, petitioning the LORD, "Incline thy ear, O LORD, and hear;
open thy eyes, O LORD, and see; and hear all the words of Sennacherib, which he has sent to mock the living God" (v. 17). The
LORD does hear and answer Hezekiah with a taunt against the
Assyrian king in which he questions the king, "Have you not
heard?" (v. 26) because "your arrogance has come to my ears" (v.
29). The king who had challenged the power of the LORD because
he had overcome the gods of the other nations is slain worshiping
in the temple of Nisroch his god (v. 37). The emphasis on hearing
is used to represent a strategy of war; boasting before the city walls
is a strategy of war to persuade a besieged city to surrender without
fighting.[18] Given the military connotations of the LORD's plan, his
rhetorical questions concerning his incomparability are an enact-
ment of this strategy of war. The emphasis on hearing has another
significance in the book. Earlier in the text, the LORD has announced
his defeat of the Assyrian king. The correctness of that announcement is now proved: he has been slain. That he was slain in the
temple of his god further strengthens the case the text is making as
it develops the theme that the LORD is not like the nations and their
gods and kings. He has announced his plans long ago, and his plans
prevail. Those who "hear" the book have been given a demonstration

---

18. See Joshua 2:10-11 and 5:1, where the emphasis is placed on the psychological
consequences of *hearing* about the exploits of the invading army. Robert G. Boling
refers to this as "psychological warfare" (*Joshua: A New Translation with Notes and
Commentary,* AB [Garden City, N.Y.: Doubleday, 1982], 187).

of the LORD's ability to accomplish all his plan: what the LORD has previously announced he has done.

Naming Jacob-Israel in 40:27-28 has an important consequence for the development of thought in the book. The implication is that for Jacob-Israel, unlike the king of Assyria and unlike the nations to whom questions were posed in the announcement of the LORD's plan, the questions can be and are answered. Jacob-Israel has heard and does know what the king of Assyria did not hear and did not know. The LORD has announced his plan long ago and is bringing it to fruition. This matter of having heard and having known the LORD's plan confers special status on Israel among the world's nations, on whom the LORD is planning a global warfare.

The questions in chapter 40, however, indicate that Jacob-Israel is not entirely persuaded of the LORD's ability to accomplish his plan and that some within Jacob-Israel may not be persuadable. The text intimates that the LORD's plan may not be clearly manifest to everyone, for Jacob-Israel is portrayed as contending an opposite case, namely, that the LORD has hidden himself from Jacob-Israel. To counter this contention the following answer is given:

> The LORD is the everlasting God,
>   The Creator of the ends of the earth.
> He does not faint or grow weary,
>   his understanding is unsearchable.
> He gives power to the faint,
>   and to him who has no might he increases strength.
> Even youths shall faint and be weary,
>   and young men shall fall exhausted;
> but they who wait for the LORD shall renew their strength,
>   they shall mount up with wings like eagles,
> they shall run and not be weary,
>   they shall walk and not faint. (40:28b-31)

This answer emphasizes the LORD as creator, reinforcing the theme of 40:26b that the LORD is creator of the heaven and the earth. With its references to the LORD's giving of "power to the faint" and increasing strength "to him who has no might," it also alludes to the final announcement about the LORD's plan in 25:1-5 to provide strength to the poor and needy. The answer to the claim that the LORD has hidden his face is that this is a time of waiting; the weak and powerless will receive strength in the future (40:31). These last questions and their answer suggest that there may be a division within Jacob-Israel—between those who are prepared to wait for the LORD and those who are not. While Jacob-Israel is the community addressed in 40:27-31, the picture that is beginning to emerge is that the implied audience is not all of Jacob-Israel but a smaller group within it. The use of rhetorical questions as a literary device of persuasion functions in the text not so much to sway the unconvinced within Jacob-Israel as to reassure the implied audience— those within Jacob-Israel already convinced of the inevitability of the LORD's plan reaching its fruition. The identification of the implied audience as a smaller group within Jacob-Israel will be more clearly developed in the next chapter.

THE LORD'S PLAN AGAINST BABYLON:
CHAPTERS 41–47

The rhetorical questions in chapter 40 are used to build a persuasive argument concerning the LORD's plan for Babylonia and its implications for the implied audience. The imminent demise of Babylon is announced in chapters 41–47, where the motif of the LORD's plan appears for the last time in the text (46:8-11). Rhetorical questions appear in chapters 41–47 interspersed with other material. When read together and in succession, these questions establish the following case. The LORD is about to fulfill his announced plan to defeat the Babylonians (13:1 — 14:23). The nations, including Babylon, are as uninformed about the meaning of the LORD's plan as was the Assyrian king in 37:26, to whom the LORD posed questions about his plan. When questions are posed to the nations in chapters 41–47 about what is happening, they do not answer, and the implication is that they cannot answer. But the LORD has witnesses — Jacob-Israel, to whom the LORD's plan has been made known. The community also knows that in the days of Hezekiah the LORD fulfilled that part of his plan concerning the Assyrians.

In the following section I summarize the material in chapters 41–47 in order to highlight the significance of the rhetorical questions. The first rhetorical questions after chapter 40 are found in 41:2-4. Here the coastlands and the peoples are summoned to come together as if they are being brought to trial,[19] and the LORD interrogates them with the following questions:

Who stirred up one from the east,
   whom victory meets at every step?
He gives up nations before him,
   so that he tramples kings under foot;
he makes them like dust with his sword,
   like driven stubble with his bow.
He pursues them and passes on safely,
   by paths his feet have not trod.
Who has performed (*p'l*) and done (*'śh*) this,
   calling the generations from the beginning?

The LORD answers this question himself, implying that the nations are unable to respond. "I, the LORD, the first, / and with the last; I am He."

The new military event that will be the undoing of the Babylonians is about to occur, and it is the LORD who has planned it. In response to this new military threat, the uncomprehending scurry around making idols for their protection (41:5-7),[20] apparently in order to consult them, as it was said the Egyptians would do (19:3). The implied audience, however, knows that idols are of no protection. This was indicated in the prayer of Hezekiah (37:18-19). They also know that the LORD is not like an idol (40:18-20) and was therefore able to deliver Hezekiah from the Assyrian king, who defeated only nations whose gods were made of wood and stone. When the LORD delivered Hezekiah from the Assyrians, he addressed him with a war oracle. In this new situation, with a new conqueror on the scene, he comforts Jacob-Israel with royal war oracles (41:8-13, 14-16). When Jacob-Israel is threatened by military attack, the LORD, unlike the idols, will deliver his people, who are not like the other nations with their kings.

19. For a discussion of the traditional form-critical analysis of the disputation *Gattungen* in Second Isaiah, including the trial speeches, see Anton Schoors, *I Am God Your Saviour: A Form Critical Study of the Main Genres in Is. XL-LV,* VTSup 24 (Leiden: Brill, 1973): 176–295.
20. For a study of the idol passages in their present literary context in so-called Second Isaiah, see H. C. Spykerboer, *The Structure and Composition of Deutero-Isaiah: With Special Reference to the Polemics against Idolatry,* Rijksuniversiteit te Groningen (Franeker, Netherlands: T. Wever, 1976); and Richard J. Clifford, "The Function of Idol Passages in Second Isaiah," *CBQ* 42 (1980): 450–64.

There follow additional words of comfort (41:17-20), a new trial scene in which the gods this time are to tell what is to happen but are not able to because they are nothing (vv. 21-24), and an announcement that the LORD had proclaimed and declared to Zion-Jerusalem what was about to happen (vv. 25-29). At this time the image of the servant is introduced (42:1-4), and the way the servant is described picks up key motifs associated with the LORD's military planning. The LORD, whose spirit cannot be directed (40:13) and who had emptied out the spirit of the Egyptians and sent them into confusion (19:3), will put his spirit in his servant (42:1), who, like the LORD (40:14), will bring justice to the nations (42:1). This servant, who will have the LORD's spirit, will be a "wonderful planner," as was Hezekiah (9:6). The vocation of this royal servant, to whom the LORD will give his spirit (42:1), is further described in 42:5-9. A song is given in praise of the LORD (vv. 10-13) because of his actions as "a man of war" (v. 13). The LORD reiterates his plan to conduct his global warfare (vv. 14-17), and then a new set of rhetorical questions is raised. These questions, like the questions in 40:27-28, are addressed to a community that appears to be a reluctant servant:

> Hear you deaf;
>   and look, you blind, that you may see!
> Who is blind but my servant,
>   or deaf as my messenger whom I send?
> Who is blind as my dedicated one,
>   or blind as the servant of the LORD? (42:18-19)

The response to these questions is significant not only because it also contains questions but because it is spoken in a first person plural voice, the voice of the implied community:

> Who among you will give ear to this,
>   will attend and listen for the time to come?
> Who gave up Jacob to the spoiler,
>   and Israel to the robbers?
> Was it not the LORD, against whom *we* have sinned,
>   in whose ways *they* would not walk,
>   and whose law they would not obey? (42:23-24)

This questioning first person plural voice is important because it undergirds the movement I have been pointing out in the design of the text. The text is shaped so as to present the case persuasively that the LORD is about to fulfill his plans for the world announced long ago. This first person plural voice, the voice of the implied audience, now invites the larger community (Jacob-Israel) to "give ear," "attend," and "listen" (*wyšm‘*). The LORD's question "have you not heard?" addressed to the Assyrian king (37:26) and repeated twice in the rhetorical questions in chapter 40 (vv. 21 and 28) is now a question that the implied audience asks of Jacob-Israel itself. The emphatic nature of this question is underscored by the use of the word *šm‘* with two of its synonyms, *’zn* and *qšb*. The passage 42:18-25 offers another perspective on the last rhetorical questions addressed to the implied community, Jacob-Israel, in 40:27-28. There the questions suggested that Jacob-Israel thought that the LORD had hidden his face from them. This passage suggests otherwise. It is Jacob-Israel who is blind and deaf (42:18-20) and therefore cannot see and hear what the LORD is doing in this new phase of his plan.

This verse confirms my earlier observation that the implied audience, which speaks here in a first person plural voice, is part of a divided community—a "we" and a "they." The implied audience is emerging as a character with a speaking voice in the Babylonian section of the text, just as Hezekiah emerged with a speaking voice in the Babylonia section of the text. We explore this observation further in the next chapter.

These questions of the implied audience, challenging the larger community of Jacob-Israel to hear, are followed by royal war oracles (43:1-4, 5-7) that give comfort to that community as the servant of the LORD. The war oracles are followed by another trial scene (vv. 8-13) involving the blind and deaf servant of the LORD (v. 8) and all the nations (v. 9). The nations are not able to bring any witnesses to testify for them because they are not able to speak about the former things or the things to come. They do not know the LORD's plan. But the LORD has witnesses to what he planned long ago and to what he is now bringing to pass:

"You are my witnesses," says the LORD,
  "and my servant whom I have chosen,
that you may know and believe me
  and understand that I am He.

> Before me no god was formed,
>   nor shall there be any after me.
> I, I am the LORD,
>   and besides me there is no savior.
> I declared and saved and proclaimed (*wh̆šm'ty*)
>   when there was no strange god among you;
>   and you are my witnesses," says the LORD. (43:10-12)

This passage clarifies why it is important for Jacob-Israel, the royal servant, to hear the LORD. They are to keep their ears open so that they can witness to what is happening as the fulfillment of the LORD's plan for the nations.

Following this passage, in which the servant of the LORD is designated as his witnesses, the LORD says that he is about to defeat the Babylonians (43:14-24). Even though his people have transgressed (vv. 25-28), he comforts them as if they were a king, uttering a royal war oracle in which he promises to pour his spirit on their descendants, assuring sound counsel and planning (44:1-5). This last war oracle is followed by another set of rhetorical questions in which the LORD reiterates the point that characterizes the argumentation: the LORD planned, proclaimed, and announced long ago what he is now bringing to pass and, unlike the gods of the other nations, has witnesses to prove it:

> Who is like me? Let him proclaim it,
>   let him declare and set it forth before me.
> Who has announced from of old the things to come?
>   Let them tell us what is yet to be.
> Fear not, nor be afraid;
>   have I not told you from of old and declared it?
>   And you are my witnesses!
> Is there a God besides me?
>   There is no Rock; I know not any. (44:7-8)

The text then reiterates the main points already raised. There is another attack on the idols, who are nothing and whose witnesses neither see nor know (44:9-20); a call for Jacob-Israel, the LORD's servant, to remember (vv. 21-22); a responsive praise to the LORD (v. 23); and a final passage (vv. 24-28) that says the LORD will confirm "the plan of his messengers" (*'ṣt ml'kyw*). In this passage the conqueror who is to carry out the LORD's plan is mentioned by name (v. 28). He is Cyrus. The LORD says of him that he is "my shepherd" and that he will fulfill "my purpose" (*ḥpṣy*). Just as Hezekiah and Sennacherib were not mentioned in the book by name until the LORD was about to fulfill his plan concerning Assyria, so Cyrus, the king who is to carry out the LORD's plan against Babylon, is mentioned by name for the first time here as the book moves toward the final announcement of the fall of Babylon (chaps. 46–47). Before 44:28 there are only veiled references to Cyrus ˙e.g., in 41:2).

In chapter 45 the LORD again mentions Cyrus by name ˍn an extended passage where the LORD argues that he is responsib˙e for what Cyrus does (vv. 1-8). At that point a woe oracle is pronounced on these who doubt (cf. 40:27-28). They are challenged with the following questions, again used to persuade rather than to discover answers:

> Woe to him who strives with his Maker (*yṣrw*),
>   an earthen vessel with the potter!
> Does the clay say to him who fashions it, "What are you making (*tʿśh*)?"
>   or [to a woman] "Your work (*pʿlk*) has no handles?"
> Woe to him who says to a father, "What are you begetting?"
>   or to a woman, "With what are you in travail?"
> Thus says the LORD,
>   the Holy One of Israel, and his Maker (*wyṣrw*):
> "Will you question me about my children,
>   or command me concerning the work (*pʿl*) of my hands?" (45:9-13)

Here the images of the potter and of parents use a variety of the words (*yṣr, pʿl, ʿśh*) associated with the announcement of the LORD's plan and its accomplishment.

In 45:14-17 the makers of idols are again condemned as confused. This is followed by a passage saying that the LORD did not speak in secret (vv. 18-20). At this point another trial scene appears. The survivors of the nations are asked to make their case and to answer questions after consulting with one another:

> Declare and present your case;
>   let them make plans (*ywʿṣw*) together!
> Who told this long ago?
>   Who declared it of old?
> Was it not I, the LORD?
>   And there is no other god besides me,

a righteous God and a Savior;
   there is none besides me. (45:21)[21]

The nations again cannot answer this question and are invited to come to the LORD and be saved (45:22-25).

Chapter 46 is another attack on the idols, but this time the idols are mentioned by name as Babylonian gods, as the text moves toward the climax of announcing the LORD's victory over Babylon. The ineffectiveness of the idols Bel and Nebo is suggested in the images of beasts struggling to carry them (vv. 1-2). These idols are borne by beasts, but it is the LORD who has borne Jacob-Israel (vv. 3-4). Again the point is made that the LORD is incomparable and that for this reason his plan cannot be averted. Here the LORD mentions for the last time his plan to use a new conqueror to defeat Babylon:

Remember this and consider,
   recall it to mind, you transgressors,
   remember the former things of old;
for I am God, and there is no other;
   I am God, and there is none like me,
declaring the end from the beginning
   and from ancient times things not yet done,
saying, "My plan (*'şty*) shall stand,
   and I will accomplish (*' 'śh*) all my purpose (*ḥpşy*)
calling a bird of prey from the east,
   the man of my plan (*'ştw*) from a far country.
I have spoken, and I will bring it to pass;
   I have purposed (*yṣrty*), and I will do it (*' 'śnh*). (46:8-11)[22]

Chapter 47 concerns the imminent downfall of Babylon. It makes the point that Babylon's planners cannot save it:

You are wearied with your many planners (*'ştyk*);
   let them stand forth and save you,
those who divide the heavens,
   who gaze at the stars,
who at the new moons predict
   what shall befall you. (47:13)[23]

21. The RSV translates *yw'şw* as "take counsel."
22. The RSV translates *'şty* and *'ştw* as "my counsel."
23. The RSV translates *'ştyk* as "counsels."

Babylon's planners, like those of the Syro-Israelite alliance, the Egyptians, and the Assyrians, cannot prevail against the LORD's plan.

Chapter 47 is a fitting climax to the section of the book that began in chapter 13, containing the major theme of the LORD's military plan to conduct a warfare against all the nations. The oracle containing the LORD's intention to overthrow Babylon (13:1 – 14:23) is followed immediately by the announcement of the LORD's plan to overthrow the Assyrians and their king (14:24-27). The fulfillment of the plan to overthrow the Assyrians in the Hezekiah narrative (chaps. 36–39) provides a persuasive setting for the imminent overthrow of the Babylonians and their king in chapters 40–47. Here in chapter 47 the LORD announces specifically his plan to overthrow the Babylonians. The development of the theme concerning the overthrow of the Babylonians and its relation to the Assyrians thus has four parts:

1. Announcement of judgment on the Babylonians and their king (13:1 – 14:23).
2. Announcement of the LORD's plan to overthrow the Assyrian king, a plan that "is purposed concerning the whole earth" (14:24-27).
3. The fulfillment of the LORD's plan concerning the Assyrians in the Hezekiah narrative (chaps. 36–39).
4. The imminent fulfillment of the LORD's plan to overthrow the Babylonians (chaps. 40–47).

In the development of the theme of the LORD's plan, the Hezekiah narrative is a pivotal element. It is clearly related to the material that both precedes and follows it. This is a radically different assessment of the narrative from that usually given by historical critics who see it as a narrative borrowed from the Deuteronomistic history and attached to the sayings of Isaiah as a suitable conclusion. The narrative as seen by historical critics acts as a kind of moat prohibiting any crossing of shared motifs to the material that follows.

SUMMARY AND CONCLUSION

In this chapter I have argued that the development of the motif concerning the LORD's plan to conduct warfare against all the nations of the world supports the conclusion reached in the last chapter that the royal narratives represent essential elements in the structure of the book. The Hezekiah narrative represents the partial fulfillment of the LORD's plan as that relates to Assyria and in that way provides a persuasive basis for the implied audience to believe that the LORD will fulfill his military strategy to conduct a global war against all the nations of the earth.

This plan is announced in the book with rhetorical questions that also have a persuasive function. They provide reassurance to the implied community, waiting, like a besieging army before a city wall, the final triumph of the LORD over Babylon and all the nations of the world. The LORD will fulfill his plan. The LORD is not like the gods made of wood and stone, who are accounted as nothing. The plans of the other nations therefore cannot prevail over the LORD's plan. Also, unlike the other nations, the LORD has witnesses to the fulfillment of his plan: Jacob-Israel, his royal servant, who has heard and who knows what the other nations and their gods do not. The LORD is responsible for the rise of military conquerors and their downfall, as is manifestly evident in the rise and fall of the king of Assyria. The LORD's witnesses know the LORD's plan and can look forward with hope to the final deliverance of the LORD.

The discussion of this theme in Isaiah has led to additional information about the implied audience. It is an audience that is part of a larger community that is not homogeneous — a divided "we-they" community. Some in Jacob-Israel have not heard and have not seen the LORD's work to fulfill his plan and mistakenly claim that the LORD has hidden his face and has totally given up on his people. The implied community that has begun to emerge as a character in the text with a first person plural speaking voice will be the subject of the next chapter.

Before moving on, however, another point needs to be made in the conclusion to this chapter. In both this chapter and the last I have indicated that the book is arranged in such a way as to encourage its implied audience to imagine deliverance from Babylonian captivity. It is important to make clear here that I am not understanding either the implied community or the Babylonian captivity mimetically. Throughout the discussion of the LORD's plans, the nations are exemplars of the LORD's judgment against all the nations of the world. The Syro-Ephraimite alliance exemplifies the inability of the military strategies of the nations to succeed. Egypt exemplifies the confusion of the plans of the nations. Tyre exemplifies pride, which is the undoing of nations. Moab illustrates the inescapability of judgment, even during world peace. Assyria exemplifies the relative powerlessness of kings, compared with the LORD's power to save Zion-Jerusalem. In the same way Babylon is to exemplify the LORD's final victory over all the nations. To attempt to read deliverance from Babylonian captivity as having a historical referent is to fail to appreciate the symbolism of the book. The language of the text of Isaiah creates a vision and a hope for the future; it does not supply source information reflecting the past.

My reading of Isaiah helps to close a gap that has emerged between contemporary readings of Isaiah and traditional ones. For example, the rabbi Ibn Ezra (twelfth century c.e.) is often cited as a nascent historical critic because he concluded that chapters 40–66 could not have been written by Isaiah of Jerusalem.[24] But it is important to see that Ibn Ezra did not read these chapters simply as a reflection of Babylonian captivity, as historical critics do when they attempt to understand Babylon solely in terms of historical context. Ibn Ezra reads Babylonian captivity as exemplar:

> This chapter [Isa. 40] has been placed here for the following reason: in the preceding chapter it is predicted that all the treasures of the King, and even his sons will be carried away to Babylon; this sad prediction is properly followed by the words of comfort. These first comforting promises, with which the second part of the Book of Isaiah begins, refer, as R. Moses Hakkohen believes, to the restoration of the temple by Zerubbabel; *according to my opinion to the coming redemption from our present exile; prophecies concerning the Babylonian exile are introduced only as an illustration,* showing how Cyrus, who allowed the captive to return to Jerusalem . . . (TEXT DEFECTIVE AT THIS POINT). About the last section of the book there is no doubt, that it refers to a period yet to come, as I shall explain.[25]

24. For example, Otto Eissfeldt says, "Following on hints made by Ibn Ezra (1167), it was first explicitly recognized by Eichhorn (1783) and Döderlein (1789) that xl–lxvi . . . could not derive from the prophet Isaiah who was active in the eighth century, but must be attributed to a prophet who appeared in the sixth century" (*The Old Testament: An Introduction,* trans. P. Ackroyd [New York: Harper and Row, 1965], 304).
25. M. Friedländer, ed., *The Commentary of Ibn Ezra on Isaiah: Edited from MSS.*

In citing Ibn Ezra here, I am not implying that our respective readings of Isaiah are in agreement, for Ibn Ezra, like all precritical readers, understands texts mimetically.[26] I am saying, however, that my reading of Isaiah merges with his because both understand Babylon to function as exemplar of future deliverance. I see this future in terms of the literary imagination; Ibn Ezra sees it as a reflection of the messianic period yet to come.[27]

To read Isaiah and analyze it for information about the past is to fail to appreciate its structure. The text is designed to persuade its implied audience to envision a future world conquered by the LORD. In such a universal defeat of all the earth, the LORD will establish a new world peace.

and Translated, with Notes, Introductions, and Indexes (London, 1873; reprint, New York: Philip Feldheim, 1948), 169–70, italics mine. For a detailed discussion of Ibn Ezra's interpretive strategies, see Uriel Simon, "Ibn Ezra between Medievalism and Modernism: The Case of Isaiah XL–LXVI," VTSup 36 (1985): 257–71.

26. See Simon, "Ibn Ezra," esp. pp. 264–65.
27. Friedländer, *Commentary,* 171. Other traditional readings of Isaiah have also seen Babylonian captivity as exemplar. See n. 25 in chapter 2 above.

CHAPTER 4

Who Are "We"
in Isaiah?

In the last chapter I argued that questions were used as persuasive rhetorical techniques to reassure the implied audience that history was unfolding in such a way as to demonstrate the inevitability of the LORD's plan to wage war against all the nations of the earth. In the course of that discussion I suggested that the implied audience itself emerged as a character with a first person plural speaking voice, also raising questions. In 42:23-24, in response to questions the LORD raises about his servant who is deaf and blind, a first person plural voice asks,

> Who among you will give ear to this,
>   will attend and listen for the time to come?
> Who gave up Jacob to the spoiler,
>   and Israel to the robbers?
> Was it not the LORD, against whom we have sinned,
>   in whose ways they would not walk,
>   and whose law they would not obey?

I also pointed out in the last chapter that this first person plural voice suggests that the implied audience is part of a community divided into a "we" (the implied community) and a "they" (a rival faction). In this chapter, I want to explore in more detail this first person plural voice in Isaiah. Like the war oracle and the rhetorical question, it represents a rhetorical technique in the book and is a clue to the text's structure.

I have so far said nothing of any significance about the beginning and end of the Book of Isaiah, other than that it neither opens nor closes with a narrative. As I will show in this chapter, however, a first person plural voice, which occurs at the beginning and near the end of the book, is a key to understanding the relationship between them.

ISAIAH AND ORALITY

Before discussing the specific texts involving the first person plural, a few preliminary words need to be said about the first person plural as a rhetorical device. To the reader, the first person plural language in the Book of Isaiah sometimes appears to be abrupt and can be disconcerting, as, for example, the sudden appearance of the first person plural in 42:23-24 just cited. How is the reader to understand the sudden appearance of the first person plural here, which just as quickly turns to a third person plural? I suggest that the answer to this question, and others raised by the similarly sudden appearance of the first person plural in other passages in the book (e.g., 1:9-10), becomes less problematic for the reader if the text is understood in terms of oral delivery, that is, as something originally read aloud to an audience rather than silently by an individual. Such an understanding, however, requires a change in the conventions that have informed the usual academic readings of Isaiah. As was pointed out in chapter 1, to emphasize the role of the implied audience when reading the text was an approach considerably different from the prevailing historical-critical reading of Isaiah, which stresses the role of the actual, if not entirely accessible, author.

Most academic study of the Book of Isaiah has equated the meaning of the text with authorial intentions and has sought to understand those intentions in terms of the historical situations in which the author wrote. The text has therefore been understood to be composite. Reading strategies have developed to analyze the text into its component parts in order to identify the plurality of contributing authors and their respective historical backgrounds.[1] These reading strategies have two major consequences for understanding the meaning of the text: (1) they devalue the role of the implied audience in the text by stressing the primary importance of authorial intention,[2] and (2) they devalue the final form of the text

1. For an overview of the reading conventions presupposed by the historical-critical approach, see John Barton, *Reading the Old Testament: Method in Biblical Study* (London: Darton, Longman and Todd, 1984), 20–76.
2. The implied audience to which I refer is the audience that can be inferred from

as a focus of attention by stressing the primary importance of recovering earlier components of the text. To assume the essential orality of the text, as I do in this study, necessitates a change in these two areas by stressing both the importance of the implied audience in the text and the final form of the text in the determination of meaning.

An increasing number of scholars have pointed out that biblical texts, like other ancient texts, were composed to be read aloud.[3] An appreciation of biblical texts therefore needs to be alert to the fact that books like Isaiah were written in order to be performed to an audience. The reception of ancient texts was a social activity, not a private one.[4] In order to avoid anachronistic readings, contemporary readers of those texts should be attentive to the rhetorical features having to do with their orality.[5] The orality of Isaiah accounts for the use of devices such as the rhetorical question and the first person plural, persuasive techniques that imply a listening audience in a social gathering who, as the receivers of the text, are participants in its presentation.

In a recent article, John Barton has suggested that ancient texts such as biblical texts are distinct from contemporary texts in terms

the text itself. There are other audiences whose reception of the text is important, because the text has had a history of reception since the time of its inception, but I am not concerned with those audiences in this study. For a discussion of the history of text reception, see Edgar V. McKnight, *The Bible and the Reader: An Introduction to Literary Criticism* (Philadelphia: Fortress Press, 1985), 75–82. For a discussion of the variety of ways in which the reader or audience has been used in reader-response criticism, see Robert M. Fowler, "Who Is 'the Reader' in Reader Response Criticism?" in *Reader Response Approaches to Biblical and Secular Texts,* Semeia 31 (Decatur, Ga.: Scholars, 1985), 5–23.

3. For example, Yehoshua Gitay, *Prophecy and Persuasion: A Study of Isaiah 40–48,* Forum Theologiae Linguisticae 14 (Bonn: Linguistica Biblica, 1981), 45, and "Deutero-Isaiah: Oral or Written?" *JBL* 99 (1980): 190–94; Willem S. Vorster, "Readings, Readers, and the Succession Narrative: An Essay on Reception," *ZAW* 98 (1986): 353; Thomas E. Boomershine, "Peter's Denial as Polemic or Confession: The Implications of Media Criticism for Biblical Hermeneutics," in *Orality, Aurality, and Biblical Narrative,* ed. Lou H. Silberman, Semeia 39 (Decatur, Ga.: Scholars, 1987), 51–55.

4. On Isaiah as performance literature, see the recent two-volume commentary by D. W. Watts, who reads the book as a drama that he calls the "Vision of Isaiah" (*Isaiah 1–33* and *Isaiah 34–66,* WBC 24 and 25 [Waco, Tex.: Word Books, 1985 and 1987]).

5. See J. Goody, "Introduction," in *Literacy in Traditional Societies,* ed. J. Goody (Cambridge: Cambridge University Press, 1968), 1–26. He says that scholars have focused on content and style of literature in traditional societies and not on the means and methods of communications.

also of their inception.[6] Authorship in the contemporary world is understood primarily to be a private matter: an individual writes to communicate private ideas.[7] To understand the inception of ancient texts in terms of private authorship, however, may be as anachronistic as to understand the reception of those texts as a private activity.[8] In short, the author of ancient texts should be understood not so much as an individual doing his or her own thing but as a representative of a community assembling traditional texts for community performance.[9] The social dimension of authorship in the ancient world is another reason that the reading of Isaiah should not concentrate on authorial intention, as historical critics tend to do. To search for author intentions downplays the social dimension of the text by putting the stress on individuals, such as prophets and redactors. Ancient texts such as Isaiah are better understood in terms of how they function in the reading process understood as a social and oral activity.

The text itself provides the only evidence for that social and oral activity. A close reading of Isaiah can disclose the implied audience created by the literary world of the text, an audience that appears as a speaker to itself in a first person plural voice. In this sense the

6. John Barton, "Reading the Bible as Literature: Two Questions for Biblical Critics," *Journal of Literature and Theology* 1 (1987): 142–45. He was prompted to raise this issue about biblical texts after reading J. A. Burrow, *Medieval Writers and Their Work: Middle English Literature and Its Background, 1100–1500* (Oxford: Oxford University Press, 1982).

7. In such a situation one might attempt to justify the interest of literary critics in an author's intention. The ability to uncover the intentions of a contemporary author, however, has been contested since the rise of the New Criticism. For a rejoinder to those who would dispense with authorial intention, see E. D. Hirsch, *The Aims of Interpretation* (Chicago: University of Chicago Press, 1976) and *Validity in Interpretation* (New Haven: Yale University Press, 1967).

8. In this sense Barton argues that biblical texts may be "intentionless" because their composition cannot be easily equated with a contemporary understanding of authorship ("Reading the Bible," 145). Noting that biblical scholarship has recognized the composite nature of many biblical texts, Barton has suggested that it may be necessary to think of the composer of biblical texts not as an author with individual intentions but as an assembler of traditional texts.

9. On this point Barton says, "The historical criterion of authorial intention as the key to a text's meaning runs into as great difficulties here as it does with modern literature in which intertextuality is a conscious ploy. To ask about the detailed intentions of authors who understood themselves to be producing for public performance texts that were primarily a compilation and re-ordering of older texts, is to ask an anachronistic question" (ibid., 143).

present study reverses the traditional historical-critical approach. An interest in the reception of the text causes one to read the text as literature, with possible implications for historical speculation, rather than to do historical inquiry, with possible implications for understanding the literature.[10] Here the text is not read mimetically, as precritical scholars read it; nor is it read as a source of historical information about its literary past, as historical-critical readers read it. Rather, the text is read as literature to see how it functions as a created world of meaning that through its very structure lays bare the imagination of the community: that is, the interaction between the production and reception of the text, a process in which we, as contemporary readers, are active participants.

"WE" IN ISAIAH: PRELIMINARY OBSERVATIONS

The implied audience as "we" appears briefly in the initial chapter of the book (1:9-10) but does not take center stage with extended discourses until close to the end of the book (59:9-15 and 63:7—64:12). In most of the book it makes only brief and abrupt appearances, as in 2:5; 16:6; 17:14; 32:15; 33:2, 21-22; 42:24, and 47:4. Throughout the book other groups are quoted as speaking in the first person plural. Some of these quotations have positive connotations and mostly concern what some group will say in the future.[11] The other quotations are attributed to groups who tend to be presented negatively.[12] In a few places also the LORD speaks in the first person plural.[13]

For two closely linked reasons, this chapter concentrates on the passages in which the "we" speaks at the beginning and the end of the book. What the "we" implies about itself in the first chapter of the book parallels what the LORD says about the community in the last chapter of the book. What the "we" implies about itself in the

10. For a study that challenges the traditional reconstructions of Israelite history and that argues instead for a study of the ideology of the literature, see Giovanni Garbini, *History and Ideology in Ancient Israel,* trans. John Bowden (London: SCM, 1986).
11. Those that will speak in the future are found in 2:3-4; 9:6; 20:6; 24:16; 25:9; chap. 26; 35:2; 40:3, 8; 53:1-6; 55:7, and 61:2, 6. Two times the voice is of one who spoke in the past: 36:7 and 37:20.
12. Those with negative connotations are 4:1; 5:19; 14:8, 10-11; 22:13; 28:15; 29:15; 30:10-11, 16; 33:14; 42:17; 51:23; 56:12, and 58:3.
13. The LORD speaks in the first person plural in 6:8; 41:21-24; 43:9, 26, and 44:7.

two passages toward the end of the book parallels what the LORD says about the community toward the beginning of the book. The self-description of the "we" at the beginning and end of the book, with its counterpoint in the LORD's description of the community, provides further evidence about the structure of the book as a whole. It also provides the basis for assessing other first person plural speech in the book, often making abrupt and brief appearances.

A COMMUNITY OF SURVIVORS

The first person plural voice occurs for the first time in the text in 1:9-10.

> If the LORD of hosts
>   had not left us (*lnw*) a few survivors,
> we should have been (*hyynw*) like Sodom,
>   and become like (*dmynw*) Gomorrah.
> Hear the word of the LORD,
>   you rulers of Sodom!
> Give ear to the teaching of our God (*'lhynw*),
>   you people of Gomorrah!

This passage appears unexpectedly[14] following a section of the text where the nation (v. 4) is condemned in second person plural address (vv. 5-8).[15] The passage itself in verse 10 combines the first person plural ("our God") with imperative plural verbs addressed to the "rulers of Sodom" and the "people of Gomorrah." The text following the passage continues the second person plural address (vv. 11-20). This awkward change of person and number, the first person plural interruption of an essentially second person plural form of address, while somewhat disconcerting to the silent reader, gains

14. Many historical critics have handled the awkwardness of this verse by understanding it as a late addition to an earlier oracle. See, e.g., R. E. Clements, who understands this to be the case, "since it introduces an alleviating factor in the prophet's condemnation" (*Isaiah 1–39*, NCB [Grand Rapids: Eerdmans; London: Marshall, Morgan and Scott, 1980], 32). Otto Kaiser comments that "a last hand added the comforting and yet demanding notion that survival itself is a sign of the grace of Yahweh (Ps. 94.17)" (*Isaiah 1–12*, 2d ed., trans. J. Bowden, OTL [Philadelphia: Westminster, 1983], 23). Most critics also see a secondary relationship between vv. 9-10 on the basis of the catchwords "Sodom and Gomorrah." See, e.g., Clements, *Isaiah 1–39*, 32.
15. In v. 8 "the daughter of Zion" is not qualified by a second person plural pronominal suffix; the context makes it quite clear, however, that the second person plural is to be understood here.

clarity if one thinks of the text as being read orally by a reader who identifies with the audience. In such a situation, change of voice, gesture, and even scene accompanying the reading of the text can help account for this abrupt person and number change.

What can we learn about the community to which both the implied audience and the implied author of this text belong? Who are the "we" in these two verses? The sudden appearance of the "we" in the surrounding second person plural discourse indicates that the author-audience identifies itself over against another group in the community. The "we" understands itself to be distinct from a plural "you." Rather more explicitly, the "we" understands itself as a group of a "few survivors" (*śryd km't*), what might be described as a minority party in a larger group with whom it has shared an experience of disaster. In verse 10 the distinction from the "other" is further refined when the "we" makes the claim that the LORD is "our God," implying that he is not the god of the other group. Finally, these few survivors are distinguished from the other because they have something to offer the other — the "word" (*dbr*) and the "teaching" (*twrh*) of "the LORD our God."

Before discussing the relationship between the "we" and the "other," it will be helpful to look in more detail at the "we" portraying itself as a community of "a few survivors." Verses 7-8 present the situation in which the "we" speaks. The scene is one in which a land has been utterly destroyed by enemy invasion.[16]

> Your country lies desolate,
>   your cities are burned with fire;
> in your very presence
>   aliens devour your land;
>   it is desolate, as overthrown by aliens.
> And the daughter of Zion is left
>   like a booth in a vineyard,
> like a lodge in a cucumber field,
>   like a besieged city.

It is only because the LORD had left "a few survivors" that total and absolute annihilation, like that rained down on Sodom and

---

16. John E. A. Sawyer, *Isaiah,* 2 vols., DSB (Philadelphia: Westminster, 1984–86), 1:9.

Gomorrah, has been avoided.[17] The simile "like Sodom and Gomorrah" occurs only one other place in the Book of Isaiah. In 13:19 it is used to describe the total annihilation of Babylon, the nation that, as I argued in the last chapter, is used in Isaiah to exemplify the LORD's judgment against all the nations.[18]

> And Babylon, the glory of kingdoms,
>   the splendor and pride of the Chaldeans,
> will be like *Sodom and Gomorrah*
>   when God overthrew them.
> It will never be inhabited
>   or dwelt in for all generations;
> no Arab will pitch his tent there,
>   no shepherds will make their flocks lie down there.
> But wild beasts will lie down there,
>   and its houses will be full of howling creatures;
> there ostriches will dwell,
>   and there satyrs will dance.
> Hyenas will cry in its towers,
>   and jackals in the pleasant palaces;
> its time is close at hand
>   and its days will not be prolonged. (13:19-22)

The simile concerning Sodom and Gomorrah is significant for understanding the literary setting of the "we" speaking in chapter 1. The implied audience has experienced the fury of the LORD's plan to destroy "all the nations of the earth." This is not just a threat to the city's survival like that of Sennacherib's threatening Jerusalem in the days of Hezekiah.[19] This is a Sodom-and-Gomorrah situation. The community speaking in a first person voice in chapter 1 presents itself as experiencing the LORD's judgment against Babylon, against all the nations of the world.

17. See Gen. 19:24-25 for a portrayal of the total destruction of Sodom and Gomorrah: "Then the LORD rained on Sodom and Gomorrah brimstone and fire from the LORD out of heaven; and he overthrew those cities, and all the valley, and *all the inhabitants* of the cities, and what grew on [out of] the ground."
18. Concerning the significance of Babylon in the book, which occurs first in the oracles against the nations, Marvin A. Sweeney says, "Here Babylon is presented as the symbol of world power which is about to be overthrown as a major enemy of God" (*Isaiah 1-4 and the Post-Exilic Understanding of the Isaianic Tradition,* BZAW 171 [Berlin: de Gruyter, 1988], 11).
19. Most historical critics, who have looked for an eighth-century setting for what they understand to be the authentic words of Isaiah in chapters 1-39, interpret the historical background against which to read chapter 1 as that of Sennacherib's invasion. See, e.g., Sawyer, *Isaiah,* 1:7.

This observation is significant for understanding the struct̲re of the book. What the implied audience in chapter 1 experiences as a present reality is something that is announced as a future plan to destroy "the whole earth" (13:5) later on in the book (chaps. 1 -27). Just as the LORD's plan concerning Assyria reached partial fulfill-ment in the Hezekiah narrative, so the LORD's plan concerning Judah and Jerusalem is reaching partial fulfillment in the experience of the book's implied audience.

It was noted earlier that the book does not end with a narrative because the final completion of the LORD's plan has not occurred and needs to be envisioned. Similarly, the beginning of the book has no narrative introduction because the initial setting of the book is the present experience of its implied audience. The book thus begins with poetry concerned with the present experience of the LORD's judgment by its implied audience, moves to narratives that provide a setting in the past for the poetry announcing the LORD's plan for both past and future, and returns at the end of the book to the pres-ent and imminent fulfillment of the LORD's plan to institute a period of salvation for his people and for all the earth.

That the beginning and the end of the book are concerned with the present experience of the implied audience is evident in parallel references to the community. At the end of the book, the LORD speaks about the community as a community of survivors (66:18-21). At the beginning of the book, the community speaks of itself as a community of survivors (1:9-10). The word for "survivors" is differ-ent in the two passages; it is *śryd* in 1:9, and *plyṭ* in 66:19. Both of these words, however, are used for those who have escaped some disaster, most frequently the devastation of warfare. Both words also sometimes occur together with the same meaning (see Josh. 8:22; Jer. 42:17; 44:14, and Lam. 2:22).[20] It is not strange, therefore, that these two different but related words should be used to refer to the survivors,[21] one at the beginning and the other at the end of the book.

---

20. For a discussion of these two words and other related words, see G. F. Hasel, "Remnant," *ISBE*, vol. 4 (Grand Rapids: Eerdmans, 1988), 130–34; and his *Remnant* (Berrien Springs, Mich.: Andrews University, 1974).

21. Actually *śryd* occurs only in 1:9, and *plyṭ* occurs only in 66:19 and 45:20, where it is a plural construct form. The feminine noun *plyṭh* occurs in 4:2; 10:20; 15:9; 37:31, 32. The more common word in Isaiah is *š'r*.

A new piece of information concerning the survivors, however, is added in 66:18-21. The first chapter simply spoke about a few who managed to survive. In 66:18-21, survival means more than just hanging on. This chapter suggests that the survivors will participate in the LORD's restoration when he will gather all nations following his invasion of the world. The survivors will be sent to all the nations to declare the LORD's glory and to bring all "your brethren" (*'ḥykm*) to Jerusalem (v. 20).

To connect the survivors in 1:9 with those in 66:19 requires some additional explanation; the meaning of 66:19 is not unambiguous. As I will argue, however, some of these ambiguities have arisen in past commentary on this text because of the reading strategies of historical critics, which have led them to read this text in isolation from its larger literary context. Four problems are usually associated with this text.

1. Verse 18 begins with the pronoun *'nky* but lacks a verb that appears to be required in order for the sentence to make sense.

2. The antecedents for the pronominal suffixes in the words "their works" and "their thoughts" is not immediately clear. This is especially a problem for those who read verse 18 as if it had no relationship to verse 17.

3. The Hebrew in verse 18 has *b'h* "it (fem.) is coming," but the referent of "it" is not clear.

4. Most scholars are not clear about the meaning of the "sign" (*'wt*) in this passage (v. 19); the word is often thought to lack ample context for its interpretation.[22]

Problems 1 and 3 are usually resolved by following the Greek tradition, which adds the word "know" after the pronoun "I" and changes the verb to the first person singular "I am coming," as does the RSV. Most commentators, however, have found no clear solution to problems 2 and 4.[23]

---

22. For a list of these problems, see James Muilenburg, "The Book of Isaiah: Chapters 40-66," *IB*, (New York: Abingdon, 1956), 769-72; Sawyer, *Isaiah*, 2:221-23; and Claus Westermann, *Isaiah 40-66: A Commentary*, trans. D. M. G. Stalker, OTL (Philadelphia: Westminster, 1969), 424-26.
23. See, e.g., Muilenburg, "Isaiah," 770-71.

In the course of the discussion in this chapter, I will eventually deal with each of these problems. For the moment, however, I turn to the meaning of "sign" in this passage. To what does it refer? What is the sign that will be set among the nations? It is my contention that the meaning of the sign is ambiguous only if the passage is stripped from its literary context, the larger whole of Isaiah, and read in isolation. I have argued above that the Hezekiah narrative provides the narrative context for interpreting the poetry. It should not be surprising, therefore, to find that the Hezekiah narrative also speaks of survivors and also connects that survival with the granting of a sign.

After the taunt song against the Assyrian king (37:22-29) and before the announcement of the deliverance of the city of Jerusalem (vv. 33-35) as well as the demise of the Assyrian king (vv. 36-38), the LORD offers Hezekiah the following sign associated with his survival:

> And this shall be the sign (*h'wt*) for you: this year eat what grows of itself, and in the second year what springs of the same; then in the third year sow and reap, and plant vineyards, and eat their fruit. And the surviving remnant (*plytt*) of the house of Judah shall again take root downward, and bear fruit upward; for out of Jerusalem shall go forth a remnant (*š'ryt*), and out of Mount Zion a band of survivors (*plyth*). The zeal of the LORD of hosts will accomplish this. (37:30-32)

In this passage the sign will be the abundance of fruit, given both a literal and a figurative meaning. Not only will that which grows in the ground bear much fruit, but also the survivors in Zion-Jerusalem will produce an abundance of fruit (i.e., offspring). The fruit of the survivors will be so great that they, "a band of survivors,"[24] will go forth (*yṣ'*) from Mount Zion. This sign concerning the past band of survivors in Jerusalem provides the clue for understanding the sign associated with the survivors in 66:19. The sign refers to the present survivors of the nation in Jerusalem. It is these Jerusalemite survivors that the Lord will send to the nations.

The sign in chapter 66, like the sign in 37:30-32, is concerned with the enormous increase of the inhabitants in Jerusalem after the demise of the enemy. This meaning is evident from the preceding context. After the LORD announces the demise of his enemies (66:6),

---

24. In this passage the feminine form of the word *plyth* rather than the masculine form, as in 66:19, is used.

the chapter turns to imagery of new birth in Jerusalem. Birth will be so easy that Zion will bring forth sons without labor pains; so incredible will be the fruit of the womb, that it will be as if a nation were born in one day (vv. 7-8). Jerusalem's breasts will be full, and the bones of the inhabitants will flourish like grass (vv. 10-14).

These verses, then, along with the Hezekiah narrative, add to the reader's understanding of the community of survivors speaking in the first person plural in chapter 1. Although they are few in number, they will increase, as did the survivors in the days of Hezekiah. Their number will be so great that they, like the survivors of the Assyrian invasion who went out from Jerusalem, will be set as a sign among the nations. Furthermore, they will bring back all their brethren from the nations.

It might be objected by some that my interpretation does not do justice to the text. The text says, "I will set a sign among them (*bhm*). And from them (*mhm*) I will send survivors to the nations." The question could be raised, Does not the pronoun "them" in both instances refer to the nations? The verse would then be understood to mean the LORD will set his sign among the nations and from the nations will send survivors to the nations. This is the way the passage is sometimes understood.[25] Such an interpretation is problematic when the sign is understood to represent the survivors in Jerusalem. The LORD will send survivors not from the nations to the nations but from Jerusalem to the nations. To be sure, the phrase "from them" is still awkward. It might appear to make better grammatical sense for the text to read, "and from it (*mmnw*, i.e., from the sign) I will send survivors to the nations," that is, from a fruitful Zion.

We should note two points, however. First, the entire beginning of the pericope (66:18 and 19), as I have already indicated, is grammatically problematic. It is possible that these problems are not the result of supposed sloppy speech or sloppy transmission but are part of the text's design as it reaches its denouement and that the grammatical ambiguities relate to the oral delivery of the text. What is ambiguous to the silent reader may not be ambiguous to those to whom a text is performed. Second, whatever the explanation, the text creates a certain amount of ambiguity in the use of signs. As

25. See, e.g., Westermann, *Isaiah 40–66*, 425.

I have already pointed out, the text in which the LORD offers a sign to Ahaz has also raised questions. The identity of Immanuel is not clear from its context in chapter 7, in isolation from its larger literary context.[26] The identity of the sign as Hezekiah himself is evident only from the perspective of the Hezekiah narrative. Similarly, the meaning of the sign in 66:19 is evident only when it is read in light of the Hezekiah narrative. The text is structured so that the implied audience, those who are in the know, are able to resolve these apparent ambiguities. Ambiguity as a rhetorical technique presents insoluble problems only to those readers who choose to ignore the book as a whole.

What I am suggesting here, then, is that the text is structured to begin and end with poetry grounded in the experience of the implied audience. This implied audience is characterized as a community of survivors who has begun to experience the Sodom-and-Gomorrah judgment of the LORD against Babylon, which symbolizes the LORD's plan to destroy "the whole earth" (13:5). This community, as I indicated above, is waiting for the LORD to complete his plan and to create a future world peace for themselves and for all the nations of the earth.

THE SURVIVORS AND THEIR OPPONENTS

I noted above that the use of the first person plural in 1:9-10, as was the case in 42:24, indicates a division between the implied audience of survivors and another group in the community. For the sake of convenience, I will refer to this other group as the "opponents." The groups are portrayed as having shared a common heritage and a common identity as a social group. The opposition between the survivors and the opponents is internecine. The "other" is not alien, like the nations. Rather, the other is the enemy at home. This internal dissension, evident in 42:24 by the juxtaposition of "the LORD, against whom *we* have sinned" with "in whose ways *they*

---

26. For studies that survey discussion on this issue and that offer suggestions concerning the identity of Immanuel, see Herbert M. Wolff, "A Solution to the Immanuel Prophecy in Isaiah 7:14−8:22," *JBL* 91 (1972): 449–56; C. R. North, "Immanuel," *IDB,* vol. 2 (New York: Abingdon, 1962), 686–88; Joseph Jensen, "The Age of Immanuel," *CBQ* 41 (1979): 220–39; and Michael E. Thompson, "Isaiah's Ideal King," *JSOT* 24 (1982): 79–88.

would not walk / and whose law (*twrh*) they would not obey," is also found in 1:10 with the juxtaposition of "the teaching (*twrt*) of *our* God" with "*you* people." In 42:24 the survivors identify with their opponents in sharing corporate accountability for sin, but they do not identify with their opponents whose actions ignoring the law and ways of the LORD are the source of sin. In 1:10 the division within the community suggests different theological relationships. The opponents who have not obeyed the law of the LORD are a people cut off from the LORD, whom the survivors refer to as "our God."

Chapter 1 as a whole provides additional insight into the characterization of the opponents of the implied community. Significantly, the picture of the opponents in chapter 1 is reflected in the last two chapters in the book.[27] When read together, the following picture emerges: in both chapters the opponents are portrayed as carrying out sacrifices against the will of the LORD (1:10-14 and 66:3-4); in both passages those who practice sacrifice are linked with the shedding of blood, or murder. In chapter 1 the attack on sacrifice (vv. 10-14) is followed by an appeal to do justice (vv. 16-20). These two sections are linked by verse 15, quoting the LORD:

When you spread forth your hands,
  I will hide my eyes from you;
even though you make many prayers,
  I will not listen;
  your hands are full of blood.

The picture being drawn here (and by "picture" I suggest a product of the literary imagination and not necessarily a representation of an ancient reality) is that those who have stretched out their hands, covered with the blood of sacrifice, also have the blood of

27. Scholars in the past have noted the similarity between the first chapter of Isaiah and the last chapters of the book. Leon J. Liebreich has compiled a list of common vocabulary shared by chapters 1 and 66 ("The Compilation of the Book of Isaiah," *JQR* 46 [1956–57]: 276–77). The major argument of his work is that a redactor linked the major sections of the book by means of keywords common to the end of one section and the beginning of the following section. Other scholars have noted thematic relationships, for example, between chapter 1 and chapters 65–66 on the basis of the common portrayal of the group that I have been referring to as the opponents. See Joachim Becker, *Isaias—der Prophet und sein Buch,* Stuttgarter Bibelstudien 30 (Stuttgart: Verlag Katholisches Bibelwerk, 1968), 45–51; Rémi Lack, *La symbolique du Livre d'Isaïe: Essai sur l'image littéraire comme élément de structuration,* AnBib 59 (Rome: Biblical Institute, 1973), 139–41; and Sweeney, *Isaiah 1-4,* 21–24.

innocent victims on their hands. Those who practice sacrifice have committed social sins that are "like scarlet" and "red like crimson" (1:18). The linkage of sacrifice with abominable practices such as murder is also made in chapter 66. The equation is simply stated:

> He who slaughters an ox is one who kills a man;
>   he who sacrifices a lamb is one who breaks a dog's neck;
> he who presents a cereal offering is one who offers swine's blood;
>   he who makes a memorial offering of frankincense is one who blesses
>   an idol.
> These have chosen their own ways,
>   and their soul delights in their abominations. (66:3)[28]

This portrayal of the opponents suggests more than a friendly debate about liturgical practice. The enmity between the two groups is suggested to have resulted in murder.

Two further similarities unite the first and last chapters of the book. In both chapters the opponents are associated with idolatrous practices that take place in the gardens (*gnwt*). Compare 1:29 with 65:3 and 66:17.[29] Finally, both chapter 1 and chapter 66 end with the pronouncement of judgment on the opponents. In both places the judgment on the opponents is described as a fire that will not be quenched (*kbh*).[30] In chapter 1 the opponents are compared to a tree that will burn with an unquenchable fire.

> For you shall be like an oak
>   whose leaf withers,
>   and like a garden without water.
> And the strong shall become tow,
>   and his work a spark,
> and both of them shall burn together,
>   with none to quench (*mkbh*) them. (1:30-31)

In 66:24 the image of an unquenchable fire is even more gruesome. The survivors "shall go forth and look on the dead bodies of the men that have rebelled against me; for their worm shall not die, their fire

28. I have altered the RSV translation here. Where the RSV has "like him who" in the series, I have translated "is one who" because the MT does not have the preposition *k*. The text is equating sacrifice and abominable practices such as murder; it is not making comparisons.
29. For a more detailed discussion of the relationship between 1:29-31 and chapters 65-66, see Sweeney, Isaiah 1.4, 23-24.
30. See Liebreich, "Compilation," 277, who also calls attention to the similar use of the verb *kbh* at the end of both chapter 1 and chapter 66, which links them.

shall not be quenched (*tkbh*), and they shall be an abhorrence to all flesh." While the survivors look forward to salvation and peace, the future for the opponents is portrayed as one of grotesque and unceasing punishment.

HEAR THE WORD OF THE LORD

In one other significant way the beginning and the end of the book are linked in the chapters describing the survivors and their opponents. Both chapters contain an exhortation to hear the word of the LORD. In 1:10 the survivors exhort their opponents, alluding to Sodom and Gomorrah:

> Hear (*šm'w*) the word (*dbr*) of the LORD,
>   you rulers of Sodom!
> Give ear to the teaching of our God,
>   you people of Gomorrah!

The word of the LORD that follows concerns the opponents' sacrificial and cultic abuse. In 66:5 it is the LORD who exhorts the survivors, "Hear (*šm'w*) the word (*dbr*) of the LORD, you who tremble at his word (*dbrw*)." The word of the LORD that follows concerns the opponents, identified as "your brethren who hate you"; they will be put to shame.

> Your brethren who hate you
>   and cast you out for my name's sake
> have said, "Let the LORD be glorified,
>   that we may see your joy";
>   but it is they who shall be put to shame. (66:5)

Notice the emphasis on the "word" in 66:5. Those who "tremble at his *word*" are exhorted to hear "the *word* of the LORD." Notice also how the words of the opponents quoted here are a mockery of the words of the survivors. The phrase "hear the word of the LORD" is found in only two other places in the Book of Isaiah (28:14 and 39:5). The strategic location of this phrase at the beginning (1:10) and the end (66:5) of the book as well as in the Hezekiah narrative (39:5) suggests the importance of hearing the word of the LORD for understanding the design of the book.[31] In 39:5 the phrase "hear

---

31. In 28:14 the phrase is addressed to the opponents. In due course we consider this verse in the discussion.

(*šm'*) the word (*dbr*) of the LORD of hosts" is addressed to Hezekiah. In 1:10 and 66:5, however, whereas the word of the LORD is a negative word of judgment against the *opponents,* in 39:5 the word of the LORD is a negative word against Hezekiah and his house, that is, against the *survivors* of Assyrian invasion (39:6-7). This is the word that Hezekiah understands to be a short-term good because there would be peace and security in his days.

The significance of the phrase "hear the word of the Lord" at the end of the Hezekiah narrative, where it introduces the LORD's promise of the coming Babylonian judgment, requires some comment. In the last chapter, I argued that the transition between chapters 39 and 40 represented a dramatic change in scene. Chapter 39 ends with the announcement of a future Babylonian defeat of Judah and the promise of exile for the royal house. Chapter 40 begins with Babylonian judgment a reality. The quick and dramatic change, which historical critics argue is evidence for a different historical background reflected by the text,[32] is capable of a quite different interpretation. It can be seen as a formal or structural feature of the text that supports its content — namely, what it means to hear the word of the LORD. To hear the LORD's word is tantamount to the immediate fulfillment of that word. The coming to fulfillment of the LORD's word is like the creation by divine fiat in Genesis 1: "And God said. . . . And it was so." In 39:6-7 God said, and in 40:1 it was so!

This dramatic change after the end of the Hezekiah narrative is not without parallel elsewhere in the Book of Isaiah. The LORD's word against the Assyrian king and its fulfillment were similarly dramatic. In 37:33-35 God said,

> Therefore thus says the LORD concerning the king of Assyria: He shall not come into this city, or shoot an arrow there, or come before it with a shield, or cast up a siege mound against it. By the way that he came, by the same he shall return, and he shall not come into this city, says the LORD. For I will defend this city to save it, for my own sake and for the sake of my servant David.

In verses 36-38 it was so:

32. See, e.g., Bernhard W. Anderson, *Understanding the Old Testament,* 4th ed. (Englewood Cliffs, N.J.: Prentice-Hall, 1986), 322.

And the angel of the LORD went forth, and slew a hundred and eighty-five thousand in the camp of the Assyrians; and when men arose early in the morning, behold, these were all dead bodies. Then Sennacherib king of Assyria departed, and went home and dwelt at Nineveh. And as he was worshiping in the house of Nisroch his god, Adrammelech and Sharezer his sons, slew him with the sword, and escaped into the land of Ararat. And Esarhaddon his son reigned in his stead.

The speaking and hearing of God's word is tantamount to its fulfillment. The power of the word to reach sudden and immediate fulfillment explains why the survivors in 66:5 are described as those "who tremble at his word"; the survivors know the power of the LORD's word.

But the LORD's word does not only announce judgment and doom. As was argued in the last chapter, the plan of the LORD also concerns the establishment of world peace for the survivors. The Hezekiah narrative demonstrates how the LORD's word ensures survival. In the narrative, the speech of the Rabshakeh is introduced in such a way as to emphasize the orality of his message (an orality that the text of Isaiah can be seen to counter with its own audible words). "Then the Rabshakeh stood and called out in a loud voice in the language of Judah" (36:13). In the speech itself the arrogance of the Assyrian king is displayed by the Rabshakeh, whose exhortation to hear the words of Sennacherib is cast in the same style as the exhortation to hear the word of the LORD. "Hear (*šm'w*) the words of (*dbry*) the great king, the king of Assyria! Thus says the king . . ." (vv. 13-14a). As noted in the last chapter, the Rabshakeh calls into question the military strategy of Jerusalem, one he thinks is weak because it rests only on words. "Do you think that mere words are strategy and power for war?" (v. 5). The Rabshakeh later mockingly identifies the people's words, "We rely on the LORD our God" (v. 7). Note that the Rabshakeh quotes the people as saying they rely on the words of the LORD *our* God. The survivors also referred to the word of the LORD "our God" in 1:10. The strategy of relying on the words of the LORD our God in the Hezekiah narrative is also a strategy of the book's implied audience.

The irony of the narrative is that, while the Rabshakeh is mocking the people of Jerusalem for relying on words, he himself is fighting only with words. There is never any military action in Jerusalem.

The great Assyrian king returns home to die in the temple of his God without setting foot in Jerusalem. Because Sennacherib is absent, the Rabshakeh's purpose is to terrify the people of the city with words he speaks in the vernacular rather than in the official Aramaic (36:11-20). The reactions to the Rabshakeh are all concerned with words. The servants of Hezekiah do not respond to the Rabshakeh with a word (v. 21) but bring the words of the Rabshakeh to Hezekiah (v. 22). Hezekiah in turn sends his servants to Isaiah to see if the LORD may have heard the words of the Rabshakeh and might rebuke them. Isaiah answers that Hezekiah should not be afraid because of the words he has heard (37:5). The Rabshakeh returns and again attacks with a barrage of words, the main theme of which is that the gods of other nations have never delivered those nations, so that one should not rely on the LORD (vv. 8-13). This time in response Hezekiah himself prays to the LORD (vv. 14-20), imploring the LORD to see and hear the words of Sennacherib by which he has mocked "the living God" (v. 17). Significantly, in his prayer, Hezekiah makes a request in a first person plural voice: "So now, O LORD *our God,* save us from his hand, that all the kingdoms of the earth may know that thou alone art the LORD" (v. 20).

This first person plural voice is also paradigmatic for the survivors who speak in the book. They, like Hezekiah and unlike the opponents, are a people who know the LORD as "our God." Isaiah then gives Hezekiah the word of the LORD (37:22), in which the LORD heaps scorn on the arrogant boasting of the Assyrian king (vv. 22-29), offers a sign to Hezekiah (vv. 30-32), and gives him a final word of the LORD announcing the eventual demise of the king of Assyria (vv. 33-35).

The entire narrative, then, is dominated by a keen interest in words.[33] Survival is dependent on hearing the LORD's word (37:33-35). The survival of a past community, whose military strategy for survival was based on words, is paradigmatic for the implied audience, the survivors. The word of the LORD will ensure the salvation of the survivors and the demise of the opponents. The Rabshakeh had mocked a strategy of war that relied on "the LORD our God," but Hezekiah prayed for deliverance to "the LORD our

---

33. For a similar observation, see Danna Nolan Fewell, "Sennacherib's Defeat: Words at War in 2 Kings 18:13 — 19:37," *JSOT* 34 (1986): 79-90.

God," and the battle was won with a strategy that relied on words. The Rabshakeh's words were no match for those of the LORD. When the community in 1:10 exhorts the opponents to hear the word of the LORD our God, they, like Hezekiah and his community, are also following a strategy of war that relies on words.

A SUMMARY OF ISAIAH 1 AND 65-66

Before moving on, it will be helpful to summarize the discussion so far in this chapter. In 1:9 the implied audience speaks in a first person plural voice and describes itself as a community of survivors. At the end of the book, the LORD also speaks of the implied audience as a community of survivors (66:18-21). The beginning and end of the book, then, depict the present situation of the implied audience as one of calamity and destruction—a Sodom-and-Gomorrah-like judgment indicating that the LORD has already carried out his judgment against Babylon. The community is represented as waiting for the final manifestation of the LORD's plan to establish peace in all the world and to restore Zion to its promised glory. It is suggested that in such a situation the survivors encounter an opposition group who have abused cultic and social conventions—a group with the blood of innocent victims on its hands. The LORD's word announcing the demise of the opponents is given and threatens to put an end to the opponents as quickly and dramatically as the LORD's word manifested itself in the demise of the Assyrians and the coming of Babylonian exile. The book, therefore, is framed by a section of poetry concerned with the present situation of the implied community.

WAITING AND LOOKING FOR JUSTICE
AND RIGHTEOUSNESS

The implied audience speaks only briefly in a first person plural voice at the beginning of the book, but this voice speaks at length at the end of the book. When the LORD speaks about the community as survivors in chapters 65-66, he is answering the lament of the implied audience speaking in a first person plural voice in 63:7 – 64:12. The implied audience also makes a lament in a first person plural voice earlier, in 59:9-15. What the community says about itself in these two passages toward the end of the book is matched by the LORD's description of the community toward the beginning of the book (5:1-7). This is another link between the beginning and the end of the book and another clue to the structure of the larger whole.

We examine first the lament in 59:9-15. The setting for the first person plural voice here is like the "we-they" contrast in 42:24: "Was it not the LORD, against whom *we* have sinned (*ht'nw*), / in whose ways *they* would not walk (*l' 'bw bdrkyw hlwk*)?" Similarly in chapter 59 the social abuses of the opponents are detailed in verses 5-9, referred to in the third person plural, "they," while the lament of the implied audience (v. 12), the survivors, is that these are *"our transgressions"* (*pš'ynw*) and "our sins" (*ht'wtynw*). This contrast between a "we" who confesses that these are our sins and a "they" who did it suggests that the "we" is part of a larger group. As a part of that group, it takes responsibility for the consequences of the actions of the total group.

Actually, chapter 59 begins by addressing the opponents in the second person plural (vv. 1-3) and then referring to them in the third person plural (vv. 4-8) before the survivors speak in the first person plural (vv. 9-15). This similar change of person is found in chapter 1, where the opponents are referred to in the third person plural (v. 4) and then addressed in the second person plural (vv. 5-8) before the survivors speak in the first person plural (vv. 9-10).

In the beginning of chapter 59 the claim is made that, even though God can hear and save, the community has been cut off from the LORD:

> But your iniquities have made a separation
>   between you and your God,
> and your sins have hid his face from you
>   so that he does not hear. (59:2)

These sins and iniquities are understood as antisocial behavior that has led to social injustice. On two occasions these misdoings are associated with blood:

> For your hands are defiled with blood (*kpykm ng'lw bdm*)
>   and your fingers with iniquity. . . .
> Their feet run to evil,
>   and they make haste to shed innocent blood (*lšpk dm nqy*). (59:3, 7)

This imagery recalls the imagery of the shedding of innocent blood associated with the opponents in 1:15 and 66:3. This anti-social behavior, including the shedding of innocent blood, results in a society lacking justice and righteousness, as is evident in the two verses bracketing the third person plural language about the abuses of the opponents:

> No one enters suit justly (*sdq*),
>   no one goes to law honestly;
> they rely on empty pleas, they speak lies,
>   they conceive mischief and bring forth iniquity. . . .
> The way of peace they know not,
>   and there is no justice (*mšpt*)in their paths;
> they have made their roads crooked,
>   no one who goes in them knows peace. (59:4, 8)

The lack of justice and righteousness is a central motif in the lament of the implied audience in 59:9-15 and also echoes the lament of chapter 1:

> How the faithful city
>   has become a harlot,
>   she that was full of justice (*mšpt*)!
> Righteousness (*sdq*) lodged in her,
>   but now murderers. (1:21)

The survivors are in despair because they look for (*qwh*) justice (*mšpt*) and righteousness (*sdqh*),[34] but they are not to be found. In 59:9 justice and righteousness are paralleled by the metaphoric images of light and brightness, and their opposites, darkness and gloom.

> Therefore justice (*mšpt*) is far from us,
>   and righteousness (*sdqh*) does not overtake us;
> we look (*nqwh*) for light (*'wr*),
>   and behold, darkness (*hšk*),
>   and for brightness (*nghwt*), but we walk in gloom (*'plwt*).

In 59:11 "justice" is paralleled by "salvation." "We look (*nqwh*) for justice (*mšpt*), but there is none; / for salvation (*yšw'h*), but it is far from us."

---

34. For an important redactional-critical study emphasizing the importance of the terms "righteousness" and "justice" in the Book of Isaiah, see Rolf Rendtorff, "Zur Komposition des Buches Jesaja," *VT* 34 (1984): 305–14.

This lament of the implied audience parallels what the LORD says about the community at the beginning of the book. In the passage that has come to be known as the Song of the Vineyard (5:1-7), the community is understood metaphorically as a vineyard that the LORD planted on a fertile hill and planted with choice vines. The LORD looked for (*qwh*) the vineyard to produce fine grapes, but it produced only wild ones. This motif occurs twice, once in the third person (5:2) and once in the first person (5:4).

> And he looked for (*wyqw*) it to yield grapes,
>   but it yielded wild grapes. . . .
> When I looked for (*qwyty*) it to yield grapes,
>   why did it yield wild grapes?

The pun in verse 7 explains that the grapes, which the LORD looked for the community to produce, were justice and righteousness.

> And he looked for (*wyqw*) justice (*mšpṭ*),
>   but behold, bloodshed (*mśph*);
> for righteousness (*sdqh*),
>   but behold, a cry (*s'qh*)!

The lament of the implied audience toward the end of the book, that it is looking or hoping to no avail for justice and righteousness, is matched by the LORD's description of the community at the beginning of the book. The LORD looked for justice and righteousness but found in their stead bloodshed and a cry of distress.

The characterization of the community as an unproductive vineyard failing to yield justice and righteousness uses imagery associated with the portrayal of the survivors and their opponents in chapters 1 and 65–66. I have argued that the survivors will, as a sign among the nations (66:19), bear much fruit (cf. 37:30-32). Indeed, it is just such an image that occurs in the verses immediately preceding the Song of the Vineyard (4:2-6). These verses promise a glorious future, and verse 2 contains imagery about the survivors who will bear much fruit. "In that day the branch of the LORD shall be beautiful and glorious, and the fruit of the land shall be the pride and glory of the survivors of (*plyṭt*) Israel." The Song of the Vineyard is the negative side of this positive promise. It explains why such a promise is necessary — why the vineyard is nonproductive, leaving only survivors. The problem with the community is that it has abused social conventions, resulting in "bloodshed" (*mśph*) and a "cry of distress" (*ṣʿqh*) (5:7). Here the imagery of bloodshed recalls the imagery of the shedding of innocent blood associated with the opponents in 1:15, 21; 59:3, 7, and 66:3.

When Isaiah 5 is read in conjunction with chapter 59, the following picture emerges concerning the survivors and their opponents. The survivors and their opponents both make up the LORD's vineyard. The infertility of the vineyard occurs because of the wild grapes — the opponents whose social abuses have led to the disaster that the community now experiences. The "we" is part of a larger group and as a member of that larger group bears the consequences of the actions of the total group.

CUT OFF FROM THE PAST

When the "we" returns for the last time, it makes its longest statement in the book (63:7 – 64:12). The "we" is responding to the LORD's answer to two sets of rhetorical questions (63:1, 2). The rhetorical questions here, unlike the rhetorical questions posed in the announcement of the LORD's plan against the nations (chaps. 13–27 and 40–47), are readily answered by the LORD. The one who poses these questions is anonymous. The first question and answer occur in 63:1:

> Who is this that comes from Edom,
>   in crimsoned garments from Bozrah,
> he that is glorious in his apparel,
>   marching in the greatness of his strength?
> "It is I, announcing vindication,
>   mighty to save."

This question and answer suggest that the LORD has come to carry out his final victory in his plan to destroy all the peoples of the earth. In the second question and answer, the LORD is pictured as covered with the blood of warfare. The imagery of the garments stained red by the tramping of wine in the wine press recalls the imagery of the vineyard that the LORD threatened to destroy (5:5-6). Here the imagery is not the destruction of the vineyard but the crushing of grapes.

Why is thy apparel red,
   and thy garments like his that treads in the wine press?
"I have trodden the wine press alone,
   and from the peoples no one was with me;
I trod them in my anger
   and trampled them in my wrath;
their lifeblood is sprinkled upon my garments,
   and I have stained all my raiment.
For the day of vengeance was in my heart,
   and my year of redemption has come.
I looked (*w'byt*), but there was no one to help;
   I was appalled, but there was no one to uphold;
so my own arm brought me victory,
   and my wrath upheld me.
I trod down the peoples in my anger,
   I made them drunk in my wrath,
   and I poured out their lifeblood on the earth." (63:2-6)

These verses indicate that the LORD alone has carried out the battle against all the earth, as was announced in his plan (cf. 13:5) and argued in chapters 40–47.

To this portrayal of the LORD as a warrior who has come to destroy all the peoples of the earth, the implied audience responds in 63:7 – 64:12. Before looking specifically at what the implied audience says in the response, the form of address should be noted. The text begins with a first person singular "I" who identifies with the first person plural "us": "I will recount the steadfast love of the LORD . . . according to all that the LORD has granted us" (63:7). The passage goes on to speak about Israel in the third person plural (vv. 7-14) and concludes with a first person plural (63:15 – 64:12).[35] The passage does not specify who the "I" is who speaks other than to indicate that the "I" is one of the "us." In this chapter, as in chapter 59 and in 42:24, there is a "we-they" dichotomy. "They rebelled and grieved his holy Spirit" (63:10), and "we sinned" (*nht'*, 64:4). Again in this chapter there is the notion that the "we" accepts the consequences of the action of the larger group: we sinned, but they are responsible. There is a difference, however, in the way the "we" describes the "they" in this chapter. The LORD remembers the "they" as "my people." He "became their Savior." In "their affliction

---

35. There is a first person singular in 63:15.

he was afflicted," "in his love and in his pity he redeemed them," and "he lifted them up and carried them all the days of old" (63:8-9). This positive portrayal of the "they" redeemed by the LORD stands in sharp contrast to the judgment of the "they" noted in other sections of the book (cf. 1:28-31 and 66:24). The way the "they" is characterized here is similar to the way the nations are characterized. Just as the salvation for the nations (25:6-8) does not mean that the guilty will escape punishment (vv. 10-12), so the salvation of the "they" does not mean that the guilty will escape judgment. In the Book of Isaiah salvation does not mean that judgment will be ignored.

Having looked at the pronominal shifts in the text and the portrayal of the "they," I now consider more specifically what the "we" says in this passage. The lament of the implied audience speaking in a first person plural voice in this text concerns separation: from the LORD and from the past. As in 59:2, the sins or iniquities of the community have created a separation from the LORD. "For thou hast hid thy face from us, / and hast delivered us into the hand of our iniquities" (64:7). That the LORD has hidden his face from the community is also expressed in the petition, "Look down from heaven and see, / from thy holy and glorious habitation" (63:15). This petition continues, "Where are thy zeal (qn'tk) and thy might?" (v. 15). This yearning for the "zeal of the LORD" recalls the refrain "The zeal (qn't) of the Lord of hosts will do this," which occurs both in the promise of Hezekiah's kingship (9:7) and in conjunction with the deliverance of the survivors in the Hezekiah narrative (37:32). Here the survivors are requesting the LORD to intervene and deliver as he did in the days of Hezekiah.

The separation from the LORD is equated with a separation from the past: "the days of old" (ymy 'wlm) when the LORD redeemed and carried his people (63:9). The "days of old" are remembered as the days of Moses, when the LORD divided the waters and led his people through the depths (vv. 10-15). These days of the past are also the days of the patriarchs, but neither Abraham nor Israel knows this community that is cut off from its past (vv. 15-16). Yet the passage makes the claim that the community's salvation originates "from of old" (m'wlm).

> From of old no one has heard
> or perceived by the ear,

no eye has seen a God besides thee,
who works for those who wait (*mhkh*) for him. (64:3)

Salvation from the enemy is understood as waiting for the LORD. Those who wait for the LORD will be those who do "righteousness" (*ṣdq,* 64:5), that is, those who do what was lacking in the LORD's vineyard. To be separated from the past and to be separated from the LORD is to be in a time of waiting. Imagery stressing distance is countered in the passage by new imagery emphasizing closeness. The "our God" in passages such as 1:10 becomes "our Father" (63:16; 64:8) here. Furthermore, in both places this growing intimacy is associated with the "days of old." In 63:16 "our father" is associated with the fathers, Abraham and Israel. In 64:8 "our father" is also "our potter" (*yṣrnw*), evoking images of old at the time of Adam. The closeness between the survivors and the LORD is connoted by the use of the verb root *yṣr,* a word commonly used with the root *y'ṣ* to identify the LORD's activity as planner. The LORD's forming of the survivors has to do with his planning.[36]

Even though the LORD is confessed as "our Father," he has distanced himself from his people. Now the LORD fights against, not for, his people (63:10). Furthermore, according to this passage the LORD is actually responsible for the wayward actions of the people. "O LORD, why dost thou make us err from thy ways / and harden our heart so that we fear thee not?" (v. 17).

This last chapter, in which the implied audience speaks, provides a new perspective on the "we" in Isaiah. It suggests that to be cut off from the LORD is to be cut off from the past, from the days of old: the days of Moses, Abraham, and Israel. Even though the implied audience of survivors is "cut off" from the LORD and the past when he fought for his people, its "hope" (*qwh, ḥwh*) rests in the LORD, who has intervened in the past. Since that time no eye has seen nor ear heard of a god like the LORD, who works for those who wait for him. This hope and the closeness the implied audience feels to the

---

36. On the use of the verb *yṣr* as an important term for the LORD's imagining planning in the Old Testament, see Walter Brueggemann, "Imagination as a Mode of Fidelity," in *Understanding the Word: Essays in Honor of Bernhard W. Anderson,* ed. J. T. Butler, E. W. Conrad, and B. C. Ollenburger, JSOTSup 37 (Sheffield: JSOT, 1985): 15–19. The root *yṣr* is used in 43:1, 7, 21; 44:2, 21, 24; 45:9, 11; and 49:5 to indicate the LORD's relationship with Jacob-Israel.

LORD, whom it calls "our Father," persists, even though it is the LORD who has hardened the heart of the people and caused them to err from his ways.

ISAIAH, THE FIRST OF THE SURVIVORS

The imagery concerning the survivors and their opponents in chapters 59 and 63–64 confirms an observation made earlier in this chapter that the beginning and the end of the book concern the present experience of the implied community, divided and waiting the final triumph of the LORD, who is conducting a war against all the nations of the earth. These observations can be used to gain further insight into the structure of the beginning of the book. The narrative complex concerning Isaiah in chapters 6–8 has significant connections with the implied audience's self-portrayal in 59:9-15 and 63:7 − 64:12.

After the Song of the Vineyard, chapter 5 ends with the LORD's signaling "a nation afar off" to carry out his judgment.

> He will raise a signal for a nation afar off,
>   and whistle for it from the ends of the earth;
> and lo, swiftly, speedily it comes! (5:26)[37]

Since historical critics attempt to read chapters 1–39 against the background of the eighth century, the "nation afar off" is generally understood to be Assyria.[38] In light of my contention, however, that the beginning and end of the book represent the present background of the implied community, "nation afar off" would be better understood as the nation coming to overthrow Babylon, the nation that exemplifies all world powers.

Significantly, this passage announcing that the LORD will signal a nation from afar is followed by a passage that introduces the call of Isaiah, which had occurred in the past. "In the year that King Uzziah died I saw ($w'r'h$) the Lord sitting upon a throne, high and lifted up; and his train filled the temple" (6:1). This definite dating of Isaiah's call is important for understanding the structure of the book and the

37. Instead of "nation" in the first line, the MT actually reads "to the nations" (*lgwym*). Most emend the text to the singular (*lgwy*) to bring the text into harmony with the third singular in the rest of the verse.
38. See Sawyer, *Isaiah*, 1:63, who also argues that the "nation afar off" should not be restricted to Assyria.

place of the call of Isaiah (vv. 1-13) within that structure. The present experience of the implied audience is the context for understanding the call of Isaiah that took place at a precise time in the past ("the year that King Uzziah died"). The book is structured in such a way as to postpone "the vision of Isaiah" (*ḥzwn yš'yhw*), which he saw in the days of Uzziah, Jotham, Ahaz, and Hezekiah (1:1), until after the present experience of the survivors and their opponents is portrayed. According to the text's structure, the call of Isaiah is presented so that its audience will hear it as a past event in the light of the present experience of the implied community. As I will argue, Isaiah is presented as the first of the survivors, and his actions and words make the present meaningful for the book's implied audience.

Isaiah's description of his call (chap. 6) resembles in significant ways the experience of the survivors. First, Isaiah, like the survivors, understands that he dwells in the midst of a people who have strayed from the LORD. He understands himself to be part of a larger community with whom he identifies himself. "And I said: 'Woe is me! For I am lost; for I am a man of unclean lips, and I dwell in the midst of a people of unclean lips; for my eyes have seen the King, the LORD of hosts!' . . . And he touched my mouth, and said: "Behold, this has touched your lips; your guilt is taken away, and your sin (*wḥt'tk*) forgiven" (6:5-7). Verse 7 suggests that Isaiah, like the survivors (42:24; 59:12; 64:5), readily admits his sin.

Second, Isaiah hears (*šm'*) the word of God and obediently responds. "And I heard the voice of the Lord saying, 'Whom shall I send, and who will go for us?' Then I said, 'Here am I! Send me'" (6:8). Similarly, the obedience of the survivors in contrast to their opponents is implied in the LORD's comment that they tremble at his word (66:5). Furthermore, just as Isaiah was sent (*šlḥ*, 6:8) so the implied community with a task like Isaiah's — to be witnesses for the LORD — is sent (*šlḥ*, 66:19).

Third, Isaiah's message to exhort the people ("Hear and hear") has some similarity to the exhortation that the survivors use to address their opponents ("Hear the word of the LORD [1:10]).

Fourth, Isaiah is to make "the heart of this people fat" (6:10); this image is paralleled by a "heart" image in the lament of the "we" in

63:17. "O LORD, why dost thou make us err from thy ways / and harden our heart, so that we fear thee not?"

Finally, Isaiah is instructed to deliver his message:

> Until cites lie waste
>   without inhabitant,
> and houses without men,
>   and the land is utterly desolate,
> and the LORD removes men far away,
>   and the forsaken places are many in the midst of the land.
> And though a tenth remain in it,
>   it will be burned again,
> like a terebinth or an oak,
>   whose stump remains standing
>   when it is felled.
> The holy seed is its stump. (6:11-13)

This message of Isaiah applies to the present experience of the implied community at a time when "the land is utterly desolate" (v. 11; cf. 1:7). The implied community has experienced the full consequences of Isaiah's message of closing the eyes and ears of the people to the LORD. The desolation has come.

Furthermore, Isaiah and his disciples (8:16) represent the model for the "we" who are the present survivors. According to the book, the call of Isaiah had immediate effect. The narrative in chapter 7 indicates that Ahaz was not prepared to hear. There is a conflict, a division, between Isaiah and Ahaz. In response to this situation in which Ahaz and the people were not prepared to hear (cf. 8:6, 11), Isaiah gives the following instructions:

> Bind up the testimony, seal the teaching (*twrh*) among my disciples. I will wait (*whkyty*) for the LORD, who is hiding his face from the house of Jacob, and I will hope (*wqwyty*) in him. Behold, I and the children whom the LORD has given me are signs ('*twt*) and portents in Israel from the LORD of hosts, who dwells on Mount Zion. And when they say to you, "Consult the mediums and the wizards who chirp and mutter," should not a people consult their God? Should they consult the dead on behalf of the living? To the teaching (*twrh*) and to the testimony! Surely for this word which they speak there is no dawn. They will pass through the land, greatly distressed and hungry; and when they are hungry, they will be enraged and will curse their king and their God, and turn their faces upward; and they will look to the earth, but behold, distress and darkness, the gloom of anguish; and they will be thrust into thick darkness. (8:16-22)

What Isaiah says about himself in this passage closely resembles either what the "we" says about itself or what is said about the "we," as shown in the following examples:

1. Isaiah, like the survivors (59:9, 11; 64:3-4), finds himself in a community from which he feels separated, in a time of waiting or hoping (*ḥkh, qwh,* 8:17).
2. Isaiah's time is like that of the implied audience (59:2; 64:7), in that the LORD hides his face (*hmstyr pnyw,* 8:17).
3. Isaiah and his children are to be "signs and portents" (*'twt wmwptym*) in Israel (8:18), as the survivors are to be a sign (*'wt,* 66:19; cf. 37:30) to their brethren.
4. Isaiah's time, described in 8:22 as a time of "darkness" (*ḥškh*) and "gloom" (*'plh*), is like the time of the survivors, when there is no justice and righteousness, a time of "darkness and gloom."[39]
5. Isaiah orders that the testimony be bound up and the teaching (*twrh*) sealed (8:16, 20). The community, at the time when the message of Isaiah has reached fruition, exhorts the opponents to "give ear to the teaching (*twrt*) of our God" (1:10).

Because the narrative concerning Isaiah in chapters 6–8 is placed in the context of the present experience of the implied audience, and because Isaiah's words and actions in 6:1-13 and 8:16-22 resemble what the survivors say and what is said about them, it appears that the book is designed to present Isaiah as a paradigm for the present survivors. Just as the deliverance from the Assyrians in the Hezekiah narrative was paradigmatic for the survivors waiting deliverance from Babylonian oppression, so Isaiah's words and actions in the narratives in chapters 6–8 are paradigmatic for the community of survivors, who, like Isaiah, "dwell in the midst of a people of unclean lips."

THE SURVIVORS AND THE LORD'S PLAN
FOR THE FUTURE

The implied audience speaking with a first person plural voice at the beginning and end of the book has links not only with the past,

---

39. In 59:9 the masculine, *ḥšk,* is used, not the feminine noun as in 8:22.

with Isaiah, but also with the future, with the community that will experience the fruition of the LORD's plan (chaps. 24–27). An exploration of this connection will provide further insight into the overall structure of the book.

Chapter 24 reiterates the point made in this section of the book (chaps. 13–27) concerned with the announcement of the LORD's plan to lay waste to all the nations of the earth. The following chapters (25–27), also oriented toward the future, concern things that will happen in the day when the LORD accomplishes his plan. Among other things, these chapters indicate what a community, speaking in a first person plural voice, will say in that day. What this community will say foreshadows what the survivors say at length toward the end of the book. The implied audience of survivors is, therefore, associated not only with a voice of the past, with Isaiah, but also with what Isaiah in his vision describes as voices of the future, with those who will experience the final triumph of the LORD. The first person plural voice occurs for the first time in 25:9. "It will be said on that day, 'Lo, this is our God; we have waited (*qwynw*) for him, that he might save us. This is the LORD; we have waited (*qwynw*) for him; let us be glad and rejoice in his salvation." Just as Isaiah had waited for the LORD (8:17) and just as this future community will rejoice in the LORD, for whom they have waited and who has worked for their salvation, so the survivors recognize the LORD as a God "who works for those who wait for him" (64:4).

Chapter 26 is a song in the first person plural that will be sung in the future "in that day." Among other things, this song celebrates justice and righteousness (vv. 2, 7), namely, what was lacking in the days of the past, when the LORD destroyed his vineyard, and in the present, when the survivors lament the absence of justice and righteousness (59:9, 11; 64:6). Here again we find the motif of waiting for the LORD. To wait for the LORD is to experience the LORD's "judgments" (*mšptym*) which lead to "righteousness" (*sdq*).

In the path of thy judgments (*mšptyk*),
    O LORD, we wait for thee (*qwynwk*);
thy memorial name
    is the desire of our soul.
My soul yearns for thee in the night,
    my spirit within me earnestly seeks thee.

For when thy judgments (*mšptyk*) are in the earth,
the inhabitants of the world learn righteousness (*ṣdq*).
If favor is shown to the wicked,
he does not learn righteousness (*ṣdq*);
in the land of uprightness he deals perversely
and does not see the majesty of the LORD. (26:8-10)

According to this passage, those who wait for the LORD in that day will learn righteousness because of the LORD's judgments. Here the word *mšpt* is in the plural and refers to the acts of the LORD, as it does the only other time it appears in the plural in Isaiah (58:2). The LORD's justice is not accomplished by one act but by a series of acts against the nations. This observation confirms two points made earlier in the discussion. First, the LORD's plan against the nations concerns a series of acts against the nations (e.g., judgment was meted out against Assyria before it fell upon Babylon). Second, salvation in the Book of Isaiah does not mean that judgment will be ignored. Righteousness (victory, salvation) will come about only after justice is implemented.

In the context of the LORD's future establishment of justice and righteousness, there is a vision of a new vineyard, the restoration of what the LORD had destroyed in the past.

In that day:
"A pleasant vineyard, sing of it!
I, the LORD, am its keeper;
every morning I water it.
Lest any one harm it,
I guard it night and day;
I have no wrath.
Would that I had thorns and briers to battle!
I would set out against them,
I would burn them up together.
Or let them lay hold of my protection,
let them make peace with me,
let them make peace with me." (27:2-5)

Furthermore,

In days to come Jacob shall take root
Israel shall blossom and put forth shoots,
and fill the whole earth with fruit. (27:6)[40]

40. The Hebrew lacks the word for "days."

What is envisioned here is what is said about the survivors at the end of the book. Like the survivors in the days of Hezekiah, they will bear much fruit (37:30-32) and will be sent out to all the nations (66:19).

The survivors, then, are linked not only to Isaiah of the past but to Isaiah's vision of the future. This vision is of a new vineyard that will produce good grapes, so that righteousness and justice will prevail. This condition will occur, however, only after the LORD carries out his judgments against the whole earth.

SUMMARY AND CONCLUSION

In this chapter I have looked at a first person plural voice that speaks in both the beginning and the end of the book. I have understood this voice as a rhetorical device associated with the essential orality of the book. Through the first person plural voice the implied audience, a community of survivors, is incorporated into the world of the text. It emerges as a character with a speaking voice, as does Hezekiah. The beginning and end of the book are closely related because the "we," which speaks of itself in the beginning as a community of survivors having experienced the devastating judgment of the LORD, foreshadows the way the LORD speaks about the community of survivors at the end of the book.[41] This is an important observation for understanding the book's structure. Both the beginning and the end of the book present the situation of the implied audience, a community of survivors, thus framing the book. Furthermore, the first person plural voice that speaks toward the end of the book (59:9-15 and 63:7—64:12) is linked with both the past, the time of Isaiah (chaps. 6–8), and Isaiah's vision of the future, the judgment and salvation of the LORD (chaps. 24–27), experienced by the implied audience in the present. The midsection of the book, then, concerning both the past and the future, has its setting in the present experience of the implied community. The movement of the book is present—past/future—present. The middle segment links past and future because in the book the future is anchored in the past.

<hr />

41. For a study that argues for the primary importance of the present for defining past and future in older texts such as the Bible, see Bruce J. Malina, "Christ and Time: Swiss or Mediterranean?" *CBQ* 51 (1989): 1–31.

CHAPTER 5

Reading the Vision
of Isaiah

In this chapter I build on insights about the structure of the Book
of Isaiah suggested by the rhetorical techniques discussed in the
previous three chapters. The discussion thus far has highlighted the
point that the two narrative complexes,[1] Isaiah 6-8 and 36-39,
provide the narrative context for interpreting the poetry that sur-
rounds them.[2] The two narratives are set in the past. Both begin with
sentences that anchor them to a precise period of time. Isaiah 6
begins, "In the year that King Uzziah died I saw the Lord sitting
upon a throne. . . ." Isaiah 36 begins, "In the fourteenth year of
King Hezekiah, Sennacherib king of Assyria came up against all the
fortified cities of Judah and took them." The time frame is from
Uzziah to Hezekiah. But it is possible to be more precise than that.
The Hezekiah narrative closes with Isaiah saying to Hezekiah that
after his death (according to 38:5, Hezekiah had just been granted
fifteen years of additional life), his sons will be taken into Babylonian exile (39:5-8). Since Babylonian exile is the setting for the
beginning of chapter 40, the end of the narrative implies the death
of Hezekiah. A precise time frame — from the death of Uzziah to the
death of Hezekiah — applies to the part of the text from the beginning of chapter 6 to the end of chapter 39. This represents the very

---

1. By referring to these chapters as narrative, I am not suggesting that they do not
contain poetry. Indeed, both contain poetry, but the poetry is contained within what
is primarily the narrative presentation of a past event. In this sense they are narratives
like those of the Pentateuch, which also contains poetry in the narrative presentation.
2. On the narratives about Isaiah in the book as a setting for the poetry, see Christopher R. Seitz, "Isaiah 1-66: Making Sense of the Whole," in *Reading and Preaching the Book of Isaiah,* ed. C. R. Seitz (Philadelphia: Fortress Press, 1988), 118-19.

time period for the vision of Isaiah that is suggested by the superscription (or what critics are increasingly referring to as the title)[3] of
the book (1:1). "The vision of Isaiah the son of Amoz, which he saw
concerning Judah and Jerusalem in the days of Uzziah, Jothan,
Ahaz, and Hezekiah, kings of Judah."

It is a significant feature of the Book of Isaiah, however, that
while the narratives provide the framework for Isaiah's career as a
prophet, announced in the superscription, they do not provide the
framework for the beginning and the end of the book. A number of
scholars have noted that beginning with chapter 40, the Book of
Isaiah is nearly devoid of material suggesting a definitive historical
background.[4] But the same is also true for chapters 1-5.[5] Little indication of a historical setting is offered to the reader.[6] An essential
feature of the book's structure, then, is that the vision of Isaiah is
not to be equated with the book as a whole. Rather, it is presented
as part of the larger whole, that is, from the inaugural vision that
Isaiah had in the time of Uzziah's death (chap. 6) to the final words
of Isaiah in the book implying the death of Hezekiah (chap. 39).

In the last chapter it was argued that the beginning and the end
of the book concern the present situation of the implied audience.
The section of the book concerned with the past career of Isaiah
(chaps. 6-39) is framed by this present setting. Furthermore, the
announcement of the LORD's *future* plan to destroy all the nations
of the world (chaps. 13-27) appears in the section of the book
dealing with the *past* career of Isaiah. While this discussion has

3. See, e.g., John W. D. Watts, *Isaiah 1-33*, WBC 24 (Waco, Tex.: Word Books,
1985), 325; and Seitz, "Isaiah 1-66," 109.
4. According to Brevard Childs, "The original historical context of Second Isaiah—
whatever it was exactly—has been almost totally disregarded by those who trans-
mitted the material. What is left of the original context is, at best, scattered vestiges
which explains why the attempt to reconstruct it as a basis for exegesis has proven
so unsatisfactory and hypothetical" (*Introduction to the Old Testament as Scripture*
[Philadelphia: Fortress Press, 1979], 325). See also Seitz, "Isaiah 1-66," 117.
5. Seitz has argued that, in contrast to Jeremiah and Ezekiel, Isaiah fades into the
background; he makes no appearance in the book until chapter 6 ("Isaiah 1-66,"
119-21). It should also be pointed out that when Isaiah does appear in chapter 6, in
what seems to be an unambiguous reference, he is not mentioned by name.
6. The absence of the character of Isaiah in the book is evident in the historical-
critical attempt to separate the authentic words of Isaiah from the inauthentic ones.
Even with agreed interpretive strategies, there has been only limited agreement
among scholars on what constitutes the actual words of Isaiah. However one values
the information given about Isaiah in the book, there is very little data given.

begun to suggest a broad outline of the book's structure, three sections of the book have not been considered: (1) chapter 20, a third narrative about Isaiah; (2) chapters 28–35, a section that stands between the announcement of the LORD's plan to conduct warfare against the nations of the earth (chaps. 13–27) and the Hezekiah narrative (chaps. 36–39); and (3) material following chapter 47, about which little has been said apart from a discussion of 59:9-15 and 63:15 — 66:24. It will be necessary to say something about these three blocks of material before offering a more definitive analysis of the structure of the book.

NAKED AND BAREFOOT: ISAIAH 20

Isaiah 20 is a third narrative in the book presenting Isaiah as a character in the third person (the other two are Isaiah 7 and 36–39). This third narrative, along with the reference to the death of Ahaz in 14:28, is another pylon of the chronological structure to chapters 6–39. John Sawyer makes a similar point in the following comment on the function of Isaiah 20 in the book:

> There is a chronological sequence which runs through the book from "the year that King Uzziah died" (ch. 6) to "the year that King Ahaz died" (14:28), and from the year the Assyrians captured Ashdod (ch. 20) to "the fourteenth year of Hezekiah" (ch. 36). Not much biographical material on the prophet has been preserved, but what there is, has been arranged chronologically to root the prophecies in the life and times of Isaiah. The appearance of chapter 20 at this point, in the middle of a collection of, for the most part, undatable utterances, has the effect of reminding us of the important fiction that Isaiah the son of Amoz saw all these visions "concerning Judah and Jerusalem in the days of Uzziah, Jotham, Ahaz and Hezekiah, kings of Judah" (see commentary on 1:1).[7]

It is interesting to note how this chronology is related to the death of kings. The death of Uzziah (6:1) is associated with the invasion of Israel and Syria (7:1), and the death of Ahaz (14:28) is associated with the first mention in the book of the invasion of Assyria (chap. 20). Because the death of a king is associated with the rise of a new invading force, the Hezekiah narrative is concerned with Hezekiah's

---

7. John E. A. Sawyer, *Isaiah,* 2 vols., DSB (Philadelphia: Westminster, 1984–86), 1:178.

health (chap. 38). The death of Hezekiah will mean an invasion by
Babylon. There will be peace only for as long as Hezekiah lives. This
is evident in the last words attributed to Hezekiah in the narrative,
"For he thought, 'There will be peace and security in my days.'" This
concern for the death of kings suggests another reason that the
people have become king beginning in Isaiah 40 and are addressed
with war oracles, as was argued in chapter 2. Kings bring only a
fleeting and temporary peace. The peace envisioned in the book will
occur only through the reign of the people, who, as a community,
will never die but will have offspring of great abundance. The narrative of chapter 20 functions, then, along with chapters 6-8 and
36-39, to provide a historical setting for the poetry.

Chapter 20 provides a medial point in the chronology, linking two
type-scenes of kings being delivered from enemy invasion, but it also
provides thematic ties so tightly woven that even the same vocabulary is used. In 8:18, set in the time of Ahaz, Isaiah says that he and
his children will be "signs (*'twt*) and portents (*mwptym*) in Israel
from the LORD of hosts, who dwells on Mount Zion." At a later
time, after the death of Ahaz (14:28), Isaiah has already become a
sign and a portent in the time of Assyria's rise. "As my servant Isaiah
has walked naked and barefoot for three years as a sign (*'wt*) and
a portent (*mwpt*) against Egypt and Ethiopia, so shall the king of
Assyria lead away the Egyptians captives and the Ethiopians exiles,
both the young and the old, naked and barefoot, with buttocks un-
covered, to the shame of Egypt" (20:3-4).

In chapter 4 I argued that Isaiah as the first survivor was paradigmatic for the community of survivors who are the book's implied
audience. His words in 8:16-22, as I pointed out, are echoed by the
words of the survivors who speak in a first person plural voice in
59:9-15 and 63:7 – 64:12. Isaiah 20 indicates other ways in which
Isaiah is a paradigmatic survivor. He is a servant of the LORD (20:3),
like the survivors (see, e.g., 41:8). Like the survivors (66:19), he will
be a sign among the nations; in chapter 20 Isaiah is a sign and a
portent not to Judah or Jerusalem but to Ashdod, a "coastland" (*'y*,
20:6). Isaiah is a sign of the LORD's victory, as the survivors will be
a sign of the LORD's final victory "in that day" when all the nations
of the earth will be defeated and when salvation and peace will be
instituted for all the world.

As the names of Isaiah's children are also signs and portents, so is Isaiah's symbolic name. The names of Isaiah's children are *š'r yšwb,* meaning "a remnant will return" (7:3), and *mhr šll ḥš bz,* meaning "the spoil speeds, the prey hastens" (8:1). These major themes of survival and invasion appear throughout the book and also are meaningful aspects of the narratives in which the names occur. Isaiah's name, *yš'yhw,* meaning "the salvation of the LORD," is also a major theme of the book.[8]

One other point needs to be made about the function of chapter 20. Nowhere in the book is Isaiah explicitly introduced as a speaker who speaks in the first person singular voice. For example, the autobiographical accounts in chapters 6 and 8 do not specifically introduce Isaiah as a speaker. Nevertheless, the intervening narrative (chap. 7), in which Isaiah is portrayed in the third person, functions to suggest that it is Isaiah who speaks in a first person singular voice in chapters 6 and 8. In a similar way the third person narrative of Isaiah in chapter 20 suggests that it is Isaiah who speaks in a first person singular voice in chapter 21. The first person singular voice in chapters 21 and 8 quotes the LORD as speaking directly to the prophet (cf. 8:1, 5, 11 with 21:2, 6, 16). Emphasis seems to be placed on Isaiah as both the speaker and the direct recipient of divine communication. Such an emphasis undergirds Isaiah's authority in chapter 21, which contains Isaiah's final vision (v. 2) of the fall of Babylon (v. 9). The vision establishes that Isaiah had spoken long ago (vv. 1-10), in terms of the book's chronology, about what is to happen and thus forms the basis of the argument beginning in 40:1, concerning the present situation of the implied community and the immediate fall of Babylon (chaps. 40-47).

The prophet, whose vision about Assyria is announced and fulfilled in the book, has also spoken about the deliverance from Babylon. The implied audience's future hope in the deliverance from Babylon is firmly fixed in the past vision of Isaiah. Hence, the implied audience would be able to answer the questions in chapters

---

8. Peter Ackroyd has claimed that Isaiah 1–12 presents Isaiah as a prophet of salvation and that the symbolic significance of his name has contributed to this presentation ("Isaiah I–XII: Presentation of a Prophet," VTSup 29 [1978]: 16–48; reprinted in *Studies in the Religious Tradition of the Old Testament* [London: SCM, 1987], 79–104). What Ackroyd has claimed for chapters 1–12 could be claimed for the book as a whole.

40–47, which are unanswerable to the other nations and their gods —
questions such as those posed in 44:7-8.

> Who is like me? Let him proclaim it,
>   let him declare and set it forth before me.
> Who has announced from of old the things to come?
>   Let them tell us what is yet to be.
> Fear not, nor be afraid;
>   have I not told you from of old and declared it?
>   And you are my witnesses!
> Is there a God besides me?
>   There is no Rock; I know not any.[9]

A FAILED LEADERSHIP: ISAIAH 28–35 AND 1–5

In chapter 3 I focused my attention on how the Lord's plan
against all the nations of the earth, announced in chapters 13–27 and
partially fulfilled in the narrative about the demise of Assyria and
the deliverance of Zion-Jerusalem in chapters 36–39, served as the
basis for the Lord's argument against the nations and their gods in
chapters 40–47. Up to this point I have said nothing about chapters
28–35, but these chapters have an important role in the vision of
Isaiah and form a supporting member in the structure of the book.

Unlike chapters 13–27, these chapters center on local concerns of
Ephraim and Judah (see, e.g., 28:1, 14; 29:1). While chapters 13–27
contained Isaiah's vision concerning all the nations of the earth, on
whom the Lord will wage warfare, chapters 28–35 contain that part
of Isaiah's vision concerning the enemies of the Lord in the native
land.

In terms of the book's structure, these chapters are closely related
to the present situation of the implied community (the survivors and
their opponents) described in chapters 1–5 and in chapters 40–66,
the sections of the book framing the vision of Isaiah. Chapters
28–35 contain the past vision of Isaiah about the present situation
of the implied community.

Past historical-critical analysis has also linked chapters 28–35
with the beginning and end of the book: Chapters 28–33 have
frequently been associated with the early chapters of Isaiah (1–12),

---

9. In the third line the MT reads, "from my placing an eternal people and things to
come."

and chapters 34–35 with so-called Second Isaiah on the basis of an alleged common historical referent.[10] It is commonly maintained that, whereas the oracles against the nations contain much material that probably postdates Isaiah of Jerusalem, chapters 28–33, like the early chapters of the book, are more firmly set in the Jerusalem of the eighth century B.C.E. and are typical of the message of Isaiah.[11] John Sawyer says, for example, "In chapters 28–33 we return from the foreign nations (13–23) and the 'apocalypse' (24–27) to the mainstream of Isaianic prophecy. The form of the prophecies as well as their content immediately suggests that they go back to the eighth century B.C., like the bulk of chapters 1–12."[12]

While my understanding of the close relationship of chapters 28–33 with chapters 1–5 is consistent with the traditional historical-critical reading of these texts, my assessment of that relationship is significantly different. I understand both texts as depicting the present situation of the implied community and the rivalry that exists between the "survivors" and their "opponents"; I do not find these two sections to be related because they both provide an accumulation of reliable source material for reconstructing the message of Isaiah of Jerusalem in the eighth century B.C.E.

The historical background of chapters 34–35 is normally understood to be the sixth-century exilic setting of so-called Second Isaiah rather than the eighth-century B.C.E. setting of Isaiah of Jerusalem. B. W. Anderson's comment illustrates this position. "Chapters 34–35, the first a passage of doom and the second a passage of hope, are more like the poems of Second Isaiah than like the preceding material in the Book of Isaiah. Scholars generally agree that these two chapters, which deal with the end-time, do not come from the eighth century Isaiah."[13] While historical-critical scholars tend to argue that chapters 34–35 are related to chapters 40–55 because they presuppose a common exilic background, the relationship can be

10. See, e.g., Bernhard W. Anderson, *Understanding the Old Testament,* 4th ed. (Englewood Cliffs, N.J.: Prentice Hall, 1986), 322–23.
11. Chapters 34–35 are usually understood to postdate Isaiah and to approximate the material in Second Isaiah (chaps. 40–55).
12. Sawyer, *Isaiah,* 1:228.
13. Anderson, *Understanding the Old Testament,* 322. According to Georg Fohrer, "The eschatological discourses in 34–35" are "dependent on Deutero-Isaiah" (*Introduction to the Old Testament,* trans. D. E. Green [Nashville: Abingdon, 1965], 370).

seen as a literary, not a historical one. The separation of chapters 34-35 from 40-66 is structurally effective. According to the chronology of the book suggested by the location of the narratives concerning Isaiah, chapters 34-35 have their setting in the vision of Isaiah. In that setting they represent the words of Isaiah spoken in the past about the present situation of the implied community in chapters 40-66. The past vision of Isaiah (chaps. 6-39) is strategically located in the context of the present (chaps. 1-5 and 40-66). Isaiah's vision has anticipated the present and serves as the basis for the argument addressed to the implied community in 40-66.

The structural appropriateness of the placement of chapters 28-35 is reinforced by thematic relationships between these chapters and those that represent the framework of Isaiah's visions (chaps. 1-5 and 40-66). Both chapters 1-5 and 28-33 are concerned with the misguided and wrongheaded actions of the ruling elite within the community. In chapters 1-5 scattered reference is made to rulers (1:10), princes (1:23; 3:14), judges (1:26), counselors (1:26), and elders (3:14). A whole series of leaders is mentioned in 3:1-3 in a pericope suggesting that the total leadership of the community will be taken away by the LORD.

> For, behold, the Lord, the LORD of hosts,
>   is taking away from Jerusalem and from Judah
> stay and staff,
>   the whole stay of bread,
>   and the whole stay of water;
> the mighty man and the soldier,
>   the judge and the prophet,
>   the diviner and the elder,
> the captain of fifty
>   and the man of rank,
> the counselor and the skilful magician
>   the expert in charms.

The problem is not with select leaders within the community but with the total leadership. Leadership is characterized by pride and arrogance, as is eloquently stated in 2:12-17, with its series of metaphors of things lofty and superior.

> For the LORD of hosts has a day
>   against all that is proud and lofty,
>   against all that is lifted up and high;

against all the cedars of Lebanon,
  lofty and lifted up;
  and against all the oaks of Bashan;
against all the high mountains,
  and against all the lofty hills;
against every high tower,
  and against every fortified wall;
against all the ships of Tarshish,
  and against all the beautiful craft.
And the haughtiness of man shall be humbled,
  and the pride of men shall be brought low;
  and the LORD alone will be exalted in that day.

Associated with this imagery of the arrogance of leadership is the haughtiness of the proud daughters of Zion (3:16-17), which also has metaphorical significance.

The LORD said:
  Because the daughters of Zion are haughty
  and walk with outstretched necks,
  glancing wantonly with their eyes,
  mincing along as they go,
  tinkling with their feet;
the LORD will smite with a scab
  the heads of the daughters of Zion,
  and the LORD will lay bare their secret parts.

In chapters 28–35, the leaders are likewise presented as being wrongheaded and inept. The leaders specified here are the priests (28:7), prophets (28:7; 29:10), scoffers who rule Jerusalem (28:14), and seers (29:10). In these chapters the incompetence of the leaders is associated with drunkenness, as is evident from the opening image of the "proud crown of the drunkards of Ephraim" in 28:1. The teaching of the prophet and priest is likened to the gibberish of a staggering intoxicant (28:10). The theme of the haughtiness of this leadership recurs in this section in the image of the proud and easy-living women of Zion (32:9-12).

Significantly, chapters 1–5 and 28–35 are stylistically linked: each section contains six oracles beginning with "woe" (hwy).[14] These

14. The woes are found in 5:8, 11, 18, 20, 21, 22 and 28:1; 29:15; 30:1; 31:1; 33:1. In his important two-part article ("The Compilation of the Book of Isaiah" (JQR 46 [1955-56]: 259-77; 47 [1956-57]: 114-38), L. J. Liebreich also identifies chapters 1–5 and 28–35 as two important divisions within the book. He points out the close

twelve woes (with the exception of 33:1) are directed against the misguided leadership within the community.[15] A motif that occurs in
the woes both in chapters 1-5 and in 28-35 is that of faulty planning.
This common element is important because it helps clarify the relationship of chapters 28-35 with chapters 13-27, in which the LORD's
plan is enunciated. The problem with the leaders is that they do not
consider seriously the LORD's plan to wage war against all the
nations of the world.

In chapters 1-5 the planner (yw'ṣ, 3:3) is listed with the inventory
of leadership that the LORD will oust (3:1-3), and it is planners
(y'ṣym) that the LORD will restore in the future (1:26) (RSV: counselor[s]). The woe oracle delivered against the leaders shows them
to be impatient, demanding immediate disclosure and fulfillment of
the divine plan in 5:18-19.

> Woe to those who draw iniquity with cords of falsehood,
>   who draw sin as with cart ropes,
> who say: "Let him make haste,
>   let him speed his work (m'śhw)
>   that we may see it;
> let the plan of ('ṣt) the Holy One of Israel draw near,
>   and let it come, that we may know it!"[16]

The attitude of the failed leadership is that the LORD, the Holy
One of Israel, should "make haste" (mhr) and "speed (ḥwš) his
work" so that his "plan" ('ṣh) will come (bw') and be made known
(nd'h). This attitude is in sharp contrast to the attitude of the
survivors discussed in chapter 4. The confession of the survivors is
that they will wait (qwh, ḥkh) for the LORD (see, e.g., 64:4). In the
vision of Isaiah the community is to assume the posture of waiting
until the day when the LORD will carry out his judgment against the
nations (see 25:9), and the theme of waiting also appears in the part
of Isaiah's vision concerning the immediate situation of the implied
community.

---

relationship between these divisions, each of which contains six woes. To explain the
structure of the book, Liebreich proposes a theory of *Stichworte,* the means the final
redactor used to compile the book.
15. The woe oracle in 33:1 is directed against Babylon, as discussed below at the end
of this section.
16. The RSV translates 'ṣt as "purpose."

O Lord, be gracious to us; we wait (*qwynw*) for thee.
Be our arm every morning,
our salvation in the time of trouble. (33:2)

Here Isaiah speaks in a first person plural voice paradigmatic of the implied community's voice. The appearance of the first person plural voice in the vision of Isaiah strengthens the link between the present community and the vision of Isaiah by blurring the distinction and narrowing the distance between the vision of the past and the reception of that vision in the present.

Woes directed against unsatisfactory planning in the community are also contained in the vision of Isaiah. In 28:23-29 a positive statement is made about the planning of the Lord. Here agricultural imagery is used to describe the wonder of the Lord's planning:

Give ear, and hear my voice;
    hearken, and hear my speech.
Does he who plows for sowing plow continually?
    Does he continually open and harrow his ground?
When he has leveled its surface,
    does he not scatter dill, sow cummin
and put in wheat in rows
    and barley in its proper place,
    and spelt as the border?
For he is instructed aright;
    his God teaches him.
Dill is not threshed with a threshing sledge,
    nor is a cart wheel rolled over cummin;
but dill is beaten out with a stick,
    and cummin with a rod.
Does one crush bread grain?
    No, he does not thresh it for ever;
when he drives his cart wheel over it
    with his horses, he does not crush it.
This also comes from the Lord of hosts;
    he is wonderful in counsel (*'sh*),
    and excellent in wisdom.

The agricultural imagery recalls the imagery describing the Lord's failed vineyard, which went astray because it produced wild grapes (5:4) rather than the good grapes that the Lord had planned for it (vv. 1-2). The Lord's planning is wonderful, and plowing and threshing are done the way they are because the Lord planned them

that way. The connection of the LORD's wise and wonderful planning also points forward to the argument beginning in chapter 40
that connects the LORD's plan with the created order of things (cf.
40:12-17).

In chapter 29 a woe oracle is directed against those who disregard
the LORD's plan. They are confused because they think they can
devise their own plan and hide it from the LORD. Such a thing is as
mistaken as misconstruing the potter and the clay.

> Woe to those who hide deep from the LORD their counsel ('*sh*),
>   whose deeds are in the dark,
>   and who say, "Who sees us? Who knows us?"
> You turn things upside down!
>   Shall the potter be regarded as the clay;
> that the thing made should say of its maker,
>   "He did not make me";
> or the thing formed say of him who formed it,
>   "He has no understanding"? (29:15-16)

This confusion resulting in the inversion of the order of things
recalls a similar theme of a woe oracle in chapter 5.

> Woe to those who call evil good
>   and good evil,
> who put darkness for light
>   and light for darkness,
> who put bitter for sweet
>   and sweet for bitter! (5:20)

The notion that plans of one's own making can be concealed from
the LORD in the dark (hidden "deep from the LORD" by those whose
"deeds are in the dark," who ask, "who sees us?") echoes visual
imagery in another woe oracle in chapter 5. "Woe to those who are
wise in their own eyes, / and shrewd in their own sight!" (v. 21). The
woe in Isaiah's vision directed at those who have misconstrued the
order of things anticipates a woe oracle in the argument beginning
in chapter 40, where potter-and-clay imagery is used.

> Woe to him who strives with his Maker,
>   an earthen vessel with the potter!
> Does the clay say to him who fashions it, "What are you making"?
>   or "Your work has no handles"? (45:9)

While the first woe oracle in Isaiah's vision is directed against those who would rely on themselves for laying out plans, a second woe oracle is directed against those who, ignoring the LORD's plan, would look elsewhere for a plan to follow.

> "Woe to the rebellious children," says the LORD,
>   "who carry out a plan (*'ṣh*), but not mine;
> and who make a league, but not of my spirit (*rwḥy*),
>   that they may add sin to sin;
> who set out to go down to Egypt,
>   without asking for my counsel,
> to take refuge in the protection of Pharaoh,
>   and to seek shelter in the shadow of Egypt!" (30:1-2)

This oracle recalls the denunciation of the Egyptian planners earlier in Isaiah's vision (chap. 19), where the LORD confused the plans of the Egyptians by emptying out their spirit. It also anticipates the argument in 40:13 that good planning is connected with the spirit of the LORD.

It will be helpful to summarize the discussion of chapters 28–35 and their relationship to the larger structure of the book. I have argued that these chapters are the part of Isaiah's vision concerned with a failed and inept leadership. Woe oracles addressed to this failed leadership concern its failure to regard the LORD's plans by following its own plans or by looking at the plans of foreigners such as the Egyptians. In this sense chapters 28–35 are concerned with issues that typify the present situation of the implied community depicted in 1–5. Isaiah's vision, which the structure of the book situates in the past, confirms the view of the present depicted in chapters 1–5.

This past vision of Isaiah, however, also functions within the book to create a vision of the future beyond that of a society with a bumbling and bungling leadership. The woe oracles in chapters 28–33 not only point back to chapters 1–5 but also anticipate the argument about an imminent new age in chapters 40–66. While the first five woe oracles in chapters 28–33 point back (in the book) to the inept leadership of the present community to which the implied audience belongs, the last woe oracle (33:1) is directed against Babylon the destroyer.[17] This woe oracle anticipates the downfall of

17. Babylon is referred to as the destroyer in 21:2.

Babylon, which is symbolic of all present inept and unjust power structures. Furthermore, just as the oracles of judgment against the nations (chaps. 13–23) close with a vision of future peace, so the pronouncements of woe against the enemies within the community (chaps. 28–33) end with a vision of world peace (chaps. 34–35).[18] The LORD's victory against the pride and aggression of foreign powers will also bring victory against the aggressive arrogance of the leaders within the local community. Israel's vision, then, functions within the structure of the book to open the vista of the implied audience so that it can see beyond the present situation of destruction and doom (chaps. 1–5) to a new world with a new social order, a world without arrogant leaders either domestic or foreign—a world where, as I argued in chapter 2, the people will be king and there will be noble rather than wicked plans (see 32:7-8).

I have shown how chapters 28–35 are related to the present situation of the implied community as presented in chapters 1–5. It is also important to consider in more detail how chapters 28–35 are related to the present situation of the implied community as presented in chapters 40–66.

READ THIS!

A significant clue to the structure of the Book of Isaiah appears in the motif of the reading of books that occurs within chapters 28–35. What is said about reading in these chapters may also suggest how contemporary readers of the Book of Isaiah might envisage the reception of the book as a whole. I first consider 29:11-12. "And the vision (*hzwt*) of all this has become to you like the words of the book (*hspr*)[19] that is sealed (*hhtwm*). When men give it to one who can read ([*h*]*spr*),[20] saying, 'Read (*qr'*) this,' he says, 'I cannot, for it is sealed (*htwm*).' And when they give the book to one who cannot read, saying, 'Read (*qr'*) this,' he says, 'I cannot read.'" I contend

---

18. See Otto Kaiser, *Isaiah 13–39,* trans. R. A. Wilson, OTL (Philadelphia: Westminster, 1974), 353.

19. The RSV translates *hspr* as indefinite, "a book." The use of the definite article, however, suggests a definite translation.

20. Here the RSV follows the Qere (*spr*), translating it as an infinitive construct. Some follow the Kethib (*hspr*), translating the form as a noun ("the book" or "the scripture"). The latter is the suggestion of Watts (*Isaiah,* 1:384) and Hans Wildberger (*Jesaja,* vol. 3, BKAT [Neukirchen-Vluyn: Neukirchener Verlag, 1982], 1112–13).

that the vision (*ḥzwt*)[21] referred to here is the vision of Isaiah, that is, chapters 6–39.[22] These words that come toward the end of Isaiah's vision echo in significant ways what Isaiah says about his vision in the autobiographical narratives (chaps. 6 and 8) at the beginning of his vision. That this vision has become like a book that cannot be read because it is sealed (*ḥtwm*) reflects what Isaiah said about his vision toward the end of the autobiographical narrative, "Bind up the testimony, seal (*ḥtwm*) the teaching among my disciples" (8:16). Furthermore, a vision that cannot be seen is one that cannot be heard. The inability to hear and see the words of Isaiah is a significant theme of Isaiah's call. Isaiah is commanded to say to the people, "Hear and hear, but do not understand; / see and see, but do not perceive" (6:9).

The surrounding context of 29:11-12 echoes vocabulary and imagery from the beginning of the account of Isaiah's vision in chapters 6 and 8. The opaqueness of Isaiah's message to an audience that cannot hear or see (6:9-11) recurs in 29:9-10 in the images of the prophets and seers who, because they are "blind drunk," are oblivious to sight and sound. More significant, however, are the verses following the passage about the sealed book that is unreadable (29:11-13). The LORD is then quoted as saying,[23]

> Because this people (*hʿm hzh*) draw near with their mouth (*bpyw*)
>   and honor me with their lips (*bśptyw*),
>   while their hearts (*lbw*) are far from me,
> and their fear of me is a commandment of men learned by rote;
> therefore, behold, I will again
>   do marvelous things with this people (*hʿm hzh*),
>   wonderful and marvelous;
> and the wisdom of their wise men shall perish,
>   and the discernment of their discerning men shall be hid. (29:13-14)

21. The word for vision that occurs here is the same word for vision that occurs in 21:2 in the phrase "a stern vision is told me." Since I have argued earlier in this chapter that the first person language in chapter 21 is that of Isaiah, 21:2 is another instance in which the word *ḥzwt* is used with reference to the vision of Isaiah. The word for vision that occurs in the superscription (1:1) is *ḥzwn*. That this word is not a technical term reserved for the vision of Isaiah is clear from its use in 29:7, where it is equated with the "dream" (*ḥlwm*), understood to be fleeting (v. 8).
22. On this point, see Watts, *Isaiah*, 1:386. "The book of the vision (*spr ḥzwn*) of Nahum of Elkosh" (Nah. 1:1) provides another instance where the vision of a prophet can be seen as a book within a book.
23. Actually, *'dny* rather than the tetragrammaton is used.

In these verses in which the LORD is speaker, the "you" (pl.) of verses 11-12 has become a third person "this people" (*h'm hzh*). The change from the second to the third person connotes a distancing of the LORD from the community. Similarly, when the LORD is quoted as speaking in chapters 6 and 8, the implication is that the LORD has detached himself from the community. He refers to the community as "this people" (*h'm hzh*):[24]

> And he [the LORD] said, "Go, and say to this people (*h'm hzh*):
> 'Hear and hear, but do not understand;
> see and see, but do not perceive.'
> Make the heart (*lb*) of this people (*h'm hzh*) fat,
>   and their ears heavy,
>   and shut their eyes;
> lest they see with their eyes,
>   and hear with their ears,
> and understand with their hearts (*lbbw*),
>   and turn and be healed." (6:9-10)

See also 8:11: "For the LORD spoke thus to me [Isaiah] with his strong hand upon me, and warned me not to walk in the way of this people (*h'm hzh*)." Both in the autobiographical material concerning Isaiah's call as well as in the words near the end of Isaiah's vision, the community incapable of receiving the vision of Isaiah is referred to as "this people," a form of reference that suggests separation.

The vocabulary concerned with the mouth, lips, and heart of the people in 29:13-14 also recalls the autobiographical narratives at the beginning of Isaiah's vision. That the *hearts* of the people "are far from me" (29:13) echoes the directive given to Isaiah "to make the *heart* of this people fat" (6:10). Furthermore, the couplet "this people draw near with their mouth / and honor me with their lips" (29:13) recalls Isaiah's encounter with the LORD, which required that Isaiah's mouth and lips be cleansed with a burning coal. "Then flew one of the seraphim to me, having in his hand a burning coal which he had taken with tongs from the altar. And he touched my mouth (*py*), and said: 'Behold, this has touched your lips (*sptyk*); your guilt is taken away, and your sin is forgiven'" (6:6-7).

Another passage associating Isaiah's vision with a book is

---

24. See Watts, *Isaiah*, 1:386, who also sees a relationship between the address of the community as "this people" in 29:13-14 and 6:10 and 8:11.

30:8-11. Vocabulary and imagery in Isaiah's autobiographical accounts in chapters 6 and 8 reverberate in this passage, as in 29:11-12:

> And now, go, write it (*ktbh*) before them on a tablet (*lwḥ*),
>   and inscribe it (*ḥqh*) in a book (*spr*),
> that it may be for a day to come (*ywm 'ḥrwn*)
>   as a witness ('*d*) for ever ('*d* '*wlm*).
> For they are a rebellious people,
>   lying sons,
> sons who will not hear (*šmw'*)
>   the instruction of (*twrt*) the LORD;
> who say to the seers, "See (*tr'w*) not";
>   and to the prophets, "Prophesy not to us what is right;
> speak to us smooth things,
>   prophesy illusions,
> leave the way, turn aside from the path,
>   let us hear (*hšbytw*) no more of the Holy One of Israel."[25]

If isolated from the larger literary context of Isaiah as a whole, the command "write it . . . inscribe it" appears ambiguous because there is no clear antecedent for the object of the imperative verbs. It is my contention that this object of the verb refers to the vision (*ḥzwt*) of Isaiah; and vision is a motif in the previous chapter (29:11). This contention is based not only on the observation that the objects of the verb are feminine, as is *ḥzwt,* but also on the observation that the language of 30:8-11 shares similar imagery with other passages in the book (8:16-20 and 29:11-12) concerning the perpetuation of Isaiah's vision.[26] The command to "write it" on a tablet and

25. The RSV translates *ywm 'ḥrwn* in line 3 as "for the time to come." In the fourth line, the MT points *l'd* to read as two prepositions: *l* and '*d.* As Watts suggests, "since a second '*d* follows it makes no sense" (Watts, *Isaiah,* 1:393). Many translations, including the RSV, therefore point the word to read "for a witness." This is the suggested reading by BHS and has the support of the Targum and the Vulgate as well as Aquila, Theodotion, and Symmachus.
26. The imagery of a prophet commanded to write a vision on a tablet is an image found elsewhere in the prophetic corpus of material in the Old Testament In Hab. 2:2-3 the LORD commands the prophet in a way similar to the command in Isa. 30:8-11:

> And the LORD answered me:
> Write (*ktwb*) the vision (*ḥzwn*);
>   make it plain upon tablets (*hlḥwt*),
>   so he may run who reads (*qwr'*) it.
> For still the vision (*ḥzwn*) awaits its time;
>   it hastens to the end—it will not lie.

"inscribe it" in a book that it may be a "witness forever" recalls Isaiah's command in the earlier autobiographical narrative: "Bind up (*ṣwr*) the testimony (*t'wdh*), seal (*ḥtwm*) the teaching (*twrh*) among my disciples" (8:16). The verbs referring to the preservation of the vision in these two passages— "write" (*ktb*), "inscribe" (*ḥqq*), "bind" (*ṣrr*), and "seal" (*ḥtm*)—connote authority and permanence. Some commentators have suggested that the verbs in 30:8 seem to be confused.[27] "To inscribe on a tablet" and "to write in a book" would make better sense than "to write in a tablet" and "to inscribe on a book," since "tablet" (*lwḥ*) refers chiefly to something hard such as stone on which inscriptions are made, and since "book" (*spr*) refers to a scroll on which one writes.[28] This seeming confusion, however, becomes problematic only if one understands the language referentially rather than figuratively, that is, if one attempts to read this language as evidence for the actual production of the Book of Isaiah or some other book or inscription. The noun "tablet" in one phrase and the verb "inscribe" in the other, each of which connotes durability, force longevity upon the impermanence of writing and the perishable scroll respectively. This imagery is reinforced by the following line of poetry: "that it may be for a day to come (*lywm 'ḥrwn*) / as a witness for ever ('*d 'wlm*)."

The word "witness" ('*d*) in 30:8 and its counterpart "testimony" (*t'wdh*) in 8:16 (cf. 8:20), both of which connote legal proceedings and the official and weighty status given to legal transactions,[29] add the undertone of authority to the imagery of permanence. The forensic ambience is augmented by the verb "to seal" (8:16; cf. 29:11), which can also be used in the sense of "to attest by sealing" a legal document.[30]

> If it seem slow, wait (*ḥkh*) for it;
> it will surely come, it will not delay.

Writing a vision on a tablet to be read later by those who wait for it is an image of the preservation of a prophet's vision that is like that of the image of the preservation of Isaiah's vision in 8:16-20 and 29:11-12.

27. Kaiser, *Isaiah 13–39*, 293–94.

28. This is the meaning, for example, in 34:4, where the metaphor suggests that *spr* be translated as "scroll."

29. See, e.g., Ruth 4:7-10, where both words occur in the same context of a legal transaction.

30. See, e.g., Jer. 32:10-11, where it is used with a deed of purchase. Notice also here that the transaction took place in the presence of "witnesses" ('*dym*). See also Esther 3:12 and 8:8, where the word "seal" is used in connection with a royal edict.

The preservation of the vision of Isaiah as a "testimony" and a "witness" for the time to come suggests a relationship between the past vision of Isaiah in chapters 6–39 and the present setting of the implied community in 40–66. In chapter 3 I argued that the LORD's plan to wage war against all the nations of the earth (chaps. 13–27) is used as the basis for the LORD's argument against the nations in chapters 40–47. In those chapters the nations are often addressed as if they were on trial, as for example in 41:1-5, 21-29; 43:8-15; 44:6-8; 45:11-13, 20-25.[31] The argument in these trial scenes is that the LORD, unlike the gods of the other nations, has long ago announced beforehand what is about to occur: his final victory over Babylon. The other nations have no witnesses to declare that their gods proclaimed long ago what was and what will be.

> Let all the nations gather together,
>   and let the peoples assemble.
> Who among them can declare this,
>   and show us the former things?
> Let them bring their witnesses ('*dyhm*) to justify them,
>   and let them hear and say, It is true. (43:9)

But the LORD does have witnesses, as he announces in 43:10-12:

> "You are my witnesses ('*dy*)," says the LORD,
>   "and my servant whom I have chosen,
> that you may know and believe me
>   and understand that I am He.
> Before me no god was formed,
>   nor shall there be any after me.
> I, I am the LORD,
>   and besides me there is no savior.
> I declared and saved and proclaimed,
>   when there was no strange god among you;
> and you are my witnesses," says the LORD.

He makes the same point in 44:6-8:

> Thus says the LORD, the King of Israel
>   and his Redeemer, the LORD of hosts:
> "I am the first and I am the last;
>   besides me there is no God.

---

31. For a discussion of the trial speeches against the foreign nations, see Claus Westermann, *Isaiah 40-66: A Commentary,* trans. D. M. G. Stalker, OTL (Philadelphia: Westminster, 1969), 15–17.

Who is like me? Let him proclaim it,
    let him declare and set it forth before me.
Who has announced from of old the things to come?
    Let them tell us what is yet to be.
Fear not, nor be afraid;
    have I not told you from of old and declared it?
    And you are my witnesses (*'dy*)!
Is there a God besides me?
    There is no Rock; I know not any."[32]

According to the trial scenes, then, the LORD's case against the nations of the earth will be proven by an appeal to his witnesses: the community Jacob-Israel. Interestingly, these two trial scenes (43:8-15 and 44:6-8) in which the LORD claims that Jacob-Israel will be his witnesses are preceded by war oracles (43:1-7 and 44:1-5) addressed to the community Jacob-Israel as king. It is as royalty that the community will bear witness in the world of nations — a role that was formerly performed by Davidic kings.

Incline your ear, and come to me;
    hear, that your soul may live;
and I will make with you an everlasting covenant,
    my steadfast, sure love for David.
Behold, I made him a witness (*'d*) to the peoples,
    a leader and commander for the peoples.
Behold, you shall call nations that you know not,
    and nations that knew you not shall run to you,
because of the LORD your God, and of the Holy One of Israel,
    for he has glorified you. (55:3-5)

In the vision of Isaiah, the vision itself will be preserved as a witness or testimony, that is, as legal attestation of what the LORD proclaimed long ago to Isaiah. In the trial scenes, however, the implied audience will be the LORD's witnesses. The question this arrangement raises is: How does the vision of Isaiah as witness become a community of witnesses? The answer to this question is suggestive for the structural relationship between the vision of Isaiah (chaps. 6-39) and the address to the present community, the implied audience in 40-66.

---

32. The Hebrew of the line "Who has announced from of old the things to come?" is difficult here. It could be rendered literally, "from my placing an eternal people and things to come," as the RSV indicates in a footnote. In the next line, "let them tell us" in the MT is *ygydw lmw,* "let them tell them."

For an answer to the question, we need to turn to a third passage in Isaiah's vision. It begins with the phrase "in that day," suggesting the imminent fulfillment of the LORD's plan to wage his final war against all the haughty of the earth.

In that day the deaf shall hear
   the words of a book,
and out of their gloom and darkness
   the eyes of the blind shall see. (29:18)

The vision of Isaiah originally addressed to an audience that could neither see nor hear (6:9-10) — the vision containing words sealed in a book (8:16; 29:11) that could not be read and therefore could not be heard (29:11-12) — will, in that day, be "words of a book" that will be heard by the deaf and seen by the eyes of the blind. The Book of Isaiah thus describes the occasion when Isaiah's vision will be read aloud — when the words that had become like a sealed book will be proclaimed. The command to read the vision in 29:11, which could not be obeyed by either the literate or the illiterate, is issued again immediately after the close of Isaiah's vision. With the close of the vision the scene changes from the past days of Isaiah and Hezekiah to "that day" when Israel's warfare has ended and Babylon, the symbol of foreign oppression, is facing imminent overthrow.

In 40:6 a voice reiterates the command to read (*qr'*), a command that reflects the command to read in 29:11. The usual translation of the imperative in 40:6 is "cry," as in the RSV. "A voice says, 'Cry!' / And I said, 'What shall I cry?'" There is nothing wrong with this translation, but in light of the close connection that I have suggested between Isaiah's vision (chaps. 6–39) and chapters 40–66, the full connotations of *qr'* should be considered. What is to be called out aloud here is what is to be read out aloud. To read is also to cry or call.[33]

---

33. The RSV does not follow the MT *'mr,* "and he said," but follows Qª, LXX, and Vulgate, and translates the verb as first person singular, "and I said." The first person singular translation supports those who find a prophetic call in Isaiah 40. My thesis is not altered by the adoption of either position. Whether the reader reports his own speech or whether someone else is reporting the speech of the reader is of no consequence for my argument. For an important discussion of Isa. 40:1-8, see Christopher R. Seitz, "The Divine Council: Temporal Transition and New Prophecy in the Book of Isaiah," *JBL* 109 (1990): 229–47. The Old Testament contains other references

Reading, then, implies sight and audition. The blind will see, and the deaf will hear. The disclosure of Isaiah's vision by reading means that the "witness" or "testimony" sealed up in a book will be borne by living witnesses who now can see and hear.

The response of the reader (in the sense of a voice contained within the book) who asks, "What shall I read?" is the following declarative lines of poetry:

> All flesh is grass,
>   and all its beauty is like the flower of the field.
> The grass withers, the flower fades,
>   when the breath of the LORD blows upon it;
>   surely the people is grass.
> The grass withers, the flower fades;
>   but the word (*dbr*) of *our God* (*'lhynw*) will stand for ever. (40:6b-8)

These words suggest that all flesh, the whole of humankind, is mortal and cannot stand the breath of God. This fact is just what has been announced in Isaiah's vision of destruction and demonstrated in the fading of the Assyrian king. The imagery of a humanity before the power of the LORD recalls a similar image in 24:4-7.

> The earth mourns and withers,
>   the world languishes and withers;
>   the heavens languish together with the earth.
> The earth lies polluted
>   under its inhabitants;
> for they have transgressed the laws,
>   violated the statutes,
>   broken the everlasting covenant.
> Therefore a curse devours the earth,
>   and its inhabitants suffer for their guilt;
> therefore the inhabitants of the earth are scorched
>   and few men are left.
> The wine mourns,
>   the vine languishes
>   all the merry-hearted sigh.

Another observation about the reader in 40:8 that is important for understanding the larger structure of the book is that the reader

to a prophet's writing his words in order that they be read (*qr'*) aloud (see Jer. 36:6, 8, 14, 15, 21). That literature was written in order to be read aloud (*qr'*) to an assembled audience is clear in Neh. 8:3, 8, 18.

identifies with the implied audience in a first person plural voice: the word is the "word of *our* God." This phrase reflects the first person plural address in the first chapter of the book:

> Hear the *word* of the LORD,
>   you rulers of Sodom!
> Give ear to the teaching of (*twrt*) *our God,*
>   you people of Gomorrah! (1:10)

Chapters 1 and 40, then, each open a section of the book concerned with the present situation of the implied community, and in each section the reader identifies with the audience in a first person plural reference to "the word" as the word of "our God."

The role of the reader in the book will be discussed later in the next chapter, but I now want to consider in more detail what is meant by "the word of the LORD." This phrase refers to that which is contained in the vision of Isaiah, to be read out, as the book suggests, in that day to Jacob-Israel, who will be witnesses to the nations. There are a number of reasons for such an interpretation. In the passages concerned with the preservation of Isaiah's vision, just discussed, the vision is understood to contain the "teaching" (*twrh*) of the LORD. In 8:16 and 20, that which is to be bound up and sealed as "testimony" (*t'wdh*) is also understood to be "teaching" (*twrh*). In a number of passages in the Book of Isaiah, "teaching" (*twrh*) and "word" (*dbr*) parallel each other in the poetry, indicating a similar meaning. This is the case in 1:10, where the opponents are commanded to hear the "word-teaching" of "our God." The two words also occur in parallel in 2:3, a passage concerning what will take place in that day. "For out of Zion shall go forth the teaching (*twrh*), / and the word (*dbr*) of the LORD from Jerusalem."[34]

More significant, however, is the way the two words are used in 30:8-14, one of the passages cited above concerning the preservation of Isaiah's vision. After the command is given to write the vision on a tablet and to inscribe it in a book (30:8), the reason for taking such an action is given.

---

34. RSV translates *twrh* as "law." I have rendered it as "teaching" here for clarity of presentation in the argument. In 5:24 *twrh* parallels *'mrh,* another word for "word" in a context that suggests an equivalent meaning to the use of *twrh* and *dbr*.

For they are a rebellious people,
  lying sons,
sons who will not hear
  the teaching (*twrh*) of the LORD. (30:9)[35]

The consequences for the rebellious people who will not hear (30:9)
and see (vv. 10-11) are stated in verses 12-14.

Therefore thus says the Holy One of Israel,
"Because you despise this word (*dbr*),
  and trust in oppression and perverseness
  and rely on them;
therefore this iniquity shall be to you. (30:12-13a)

Notice that what was "inscribed-written" in a "tablet-book" in 30:8
is "teaching" in 30:9 and "word" in 30:12. These passages in which
"teaching" and "word" are used as synonyms for that which is contained in Isaiah's vision lend weight to my argument that what the
reader is to read in 40:8 is the vision of Isaiah, containing the
"teaching-word" of the LORD.[36] Just as the preserved vision will be
a witness "forever" (*'d 'wlm*, 30:8), so the reader in 40:8 testifies that
"the word of our God" will stand "for ever" (*l'wlm*).

That "the word of our God" refers to the contents of Isaiah's
vision is also evident from the way the LORD refers to his word in
45:22-23. Although in chapters 40-66 it is the LORD who does most
of the talking, the LORD refers in 45:22-23 to his word as something
past. In this passage he addresses the nations:

Turn to me and be saved,
  all the ends of the earth!
For I am God, and there is no other.
By myself I have sworn,
  from my mouth has gone forth (*yṣ'*) in righteousness
  a word (*dbr*) that shall not return;
"To me every knee shall bow,
  every tongue shall swear."

The LORD is addressing the nations concerning a word that has
gone forth. The use of the perfect verb "has gone forth" indicates

35. The RSV translates *twrh* here as "instruction."
36. For a study of "torah" in Isaiah, see Joseph Jensen, *The Use of tôrâ by Isaiah:
His Debate with the Wisdom Tradition,* CBQMS 3 (Washington, D.C.: Catholic
Biblical Association, 1973). Jensen seeks to locate the meaning of torah in a context
external to the book.

that this is a past event. According to my analysis of the structure of the Book of Isaiah, the setting for that past word concerning the nations, announced long ago, is to be found in the vision of Isaiah. The LORD's word that has gone forth is his plan to wage war against all the nations. This word is the basis of the LORD's case when he puts the nations on trial. While the LORD has witnesses who can testify to his word about his plan, the nations do not have the word of a planner like the LORD. The LORD declares in 41:28,

> But when I look there is no one;
> among these there is no planner
> who, when I ask returns a word.[37]

In the Book of Isaiah, then, the *vision* of Isaiah contains the LORD's word concerning all the nations.[38] That word the reader in 40:8 declares is everlasting, unlike the human word, which in time withers away. This insight further clarifies the division within the implied community between the survivors and their opponents. In the last chapter I argued that in 1:10 the opponents are invited to hear the word and to give ear to the teaching of our God, while in 66:2 and 5, the survivors are described as those who tremble at the LORD's word. It is the word of the LORD contained in the LORD's vision that the opponents are invited to hear and at which the survivors tremble. The rift in the community concerns the respective attitudes of the survivors and the opponents to the LORD's word.

The opponents despise the word of the LORD (30:12). More important, 28:10 and 13 suggest that to the opponents the word of the LORD has become incomprehensible. In 28:13 the following comment is made about the leadership within the community:

> Therefore the word (*dbr*) of the LORD will be to them,
> *ṣw lṣw ṣw lṣw*
> *qw lqw qw lqw*
> *z'yr šm z'yr šm*

The words I have left untranslated, which repeat words from verse 10, have been a source of considerable debate. All sorts of

---

37. RSV renders "counselor" for "planner" and "gives an answer" for "returns a word."

38. In the vision of Isaiah *dbr* is used to identify the pronouncements of the LORD. See 9:8; 16:3; 24:3; 28:13, 14.

suggestions have been offered for rendering what appears to be gibberish.[39] To try to make sense of gibberish, however, is to miss the point. To the opponents the word of the LORD has become nonsensical. This has happened, as the end of verse 13 indicates, "in order that they will go, and stumble (*wkšlw*) backward, / and be broken (*wnšbrw*), and be snared (*wnwqšw*), and be captured (*wnlkdw*)."[40] These consequences for those who have recognized the word of the LORD only as gibberish repeat vocabulary indicating similar consequences for the opponents of Isaiah in 8:15. "And many shall stumble (*wkšlw*) thereon; they shall fall and be broken (*wnšbrw*); they shall be snared (*wnwqšw*) and taken (*wnlkdw*)." Significantly, these words in 8:15 occur just before the command is given in 8:16, "Bind up the testimony, seal the teaching among my disciples." It is because the LORD's word or teaching has become nonsensical to the opposition that it will be sealed up in a book. The word that they are unable to make sense of will become the source of their demise.

It will be helpful to summarize the main points I have made in this section about reading the vision of Isaiah. I have argued that vocabulary and imagery in the autobiographical accounts of Isaiah in chapters 6 and 8 concerning how his vision contains the "word" or the "teaching" of the LORD are reiterated in chapters 28–35. In both places the point is made that the vision of Isaiah has not been favorably received and should be bound or sealed up in a book. A sealed book cannot be read; therefore, the community has become blind and deaf to the teaching of the LORD about the course of historical events to culminate in the defeat of Babylon. This closed book, however, is understood to be a "testimony" or a "witness" forever. This closed book is the vision of Isaiah, contained within the Book of Isaiah. Metaphorically speaking, the vision is itself sealed within the Book of Isaiah, specifically, between chapters 1–5 and 40–66.

The vision serves as the basis for the LORD's argument beginning in chapter 40 about his own superiority (indeed, incomparability) among the gods of the nations at the time of Babylonian downfall.

---

39. For suggestions as to a possible meaning for these words, see Kaiser, *Isaiah 13–39*, 245–46; and Watts, *Isaiah*, 1:362–64.
40. This is my own, rather literal translation.

Only the LORD had announced long ago what now comes to pass. He has witnesses to prove his point. His witnesses are Jacob-Israel, who, as a community with royal status, will have the role of witness among the nations, a role once reserved for kings such as David (55:4). The community of survivors within Jacob-Israel will become witnesses in the day of the imminent fall of Babylon, when the community will hear the words of a book and the eyes of the blind will see (29:18). Such is the occasion and setting of chapter 40:6, when the voice of a reader asks, "What shall I read?" The answer is implied in his comment that "the word of our God will stand forever" (40:8). The LORD's word or teaching preserved in the vision of Isaiah will again be made known to a deaf and blind community. The word of the LORD contained in Isaiah's vision, treated as mere gibberish by the opponents in Isaiah's day, is at the root of the division of the survivors and the opponents in the present day. Some in the present community addressed as Jacob-Israel beginning in chapter 40 will remain blind and deaf to the teaching contained within the vision of Isaiah.

The Book of Isaiah, then, contains within it another book — the vision of Isaiah contained in chapters 6–39. My thesis may appear to resemble traditional source analysis, which also understood that the Book of Isaiah, while appearing to be one book, actually contained several books. Traditional critical analysis, however, attempted to locate books within the book for a different purpose: to assign blocks of source material to different periods of history, ranging from the eighth to the sixth centuries or later. My identification of a book within the book, however, does not call into question the integrity of the book as a single book. In my analysis, Isaiah's vision, the book within the book, has its appropriate setting within the Book of Isaiah itself; its setting is not some supposed historical setting that makes its present literary setting irrelevant. The book within the book that I have located is an integral part of its structural wholeness and not an indication of its disunity.

COMMUNITY AND COMMUNITIES IN ISAIAH

An interesting feature of the vision of Isaiah, which constitutes a book within the Book of Isaiah, is its chronology. As suggested earlier, Isaiah's vision, at its beginning, its middle, and its end, is associated with the death of kings. The inauguration of the vision occurs "in the year that King Uzziah died" (6:1). In the middle of Isaiah's career, the oracle against Philistia comes "in the year that King Ahaz died" (14:28). The final narrative account of the interaction between Isaiah and King Hezekiah has to do with Hezekiah's death and what will happen at his demise. There came days when "Hezekiah became sick and was at the point of death" (38:1). Hezekiah prays to the LORD, and Isaiah delivers an oracle to him in which the LORD says, "I have heard your prayer, I have seen your tears; behold, I will add fifteen years to your life" (38:5). The last oracle that Isaiah delivers to Hezekiah is that after his death his sons will be taken into Babylonian exile (39:5-7).[41]

That Isaiah's vision is measured by the death of kings implies a negative valuation of kingship based on the mortality of kings and the ominous corollary that royal death presages enemy invasion. With Uzziah's death comes Syro-Ephraimite invasion; with Ahaz's death comes Assyrian invasion; and with Hezekiah's death will come Babylonian invasion. This structuring of Isaiah's vision indicates the failure of kingship to bring lasting peace and security. This is the case even when kings are good and faithful, as was Hezekiah. Hezekiah's near-death and recovery, when the LORD granted him fifteen years of additional life, only underscores the thought that security dependent on kings is fleeting. This seems to be the point of the narrator's inclusion of Hezekiah's unspoken thoughts after hearing the word of the LORD. "Then said Hezekiah to Isaiah, 'The word of the LORD which you have spoken is good.' For he thought, 'There will be peace and security *in my days*'" (39:8).

The implied death of Hezekiah in the Book of Isaiah suggests the death of the Davidic kingship itself. To be sure, the book acknowledges that the LORD continues to wage war in the world arena by raising up and dethroning foreign kings, and according to the book,

---

41. On the significance of the death of Hezekiah in Old Testament texts, see Peter R. Ackroyd, "The Death of Hezekiah—a Pointer to the Future?" in *De la Tôrah au Messie. Mélanges Henri Cazelles. Études d'exégèse et d'herméneutique bibliques offertes à Henri Cazelles pour ses 25 années d'enseignement à l'Institut Catholique de Paris (Octobre 1979)*, ed. M. Carrez et al. (Paris: Desclée, 1982), 219–26, reprinted in *Studies in the Religious Tradition of the Old Testament* (London: SCM, 1987), 172–80.

at the time of the imminent demise of Babylonian sovereignty (chap. 47), Cyrus is the new foreign Messiah on the scene (44:28 and 45:1). For the LORD's people who dwell in Zion, however, there will be no new Uzziahs, Ahazes, or Hezekiahs. The last reference in the book to a conventional Davidic king is in 37:35, where the LORD says to Hezekiah, the Davidic king, "I will defend this city to save it, for my own sake and for the sake of my servant David."[42]

The movement in the book from Hezekiah to Babylon, from the past vision of Isaiah to the present experience of the implied community, is a movement from the conventional to the unconventional portrayal of Judean royalty. The vocation of Davidic kingship, once the function of individuals such as Ahaz and Hezekiah, has become the vocation of the community, Jacob-Israel. In the days of the Syro-Israelite threat and later the Assyrian threat, royal war oracles were delivered to conventional Davidic kings assuring them of deliverance — to Ahaz in 7:4-9 and to Hezekiah in 36:6-7. In the days of Babylonian oppression royal war oracles are now delivered to Jacob-Israel (41:8-13, 14-15; 43:1-4, 5-7; 44:1-5). Where once an everlasting covenant (*bryt 'wlm*) was made with David, who would be a witness (*'d*) to the nations, this covenant is now to be made with the community (55:3-5), who will be the LORD's witnesses (*'dym*) to the nations (43:10 and 44:8). In 37:35 the LORD referred to Hezekiah, the Davidic king, as "my servant" (*'bdy*),[43] but after the vision of Isaiah it is the community Jacob-Israel who is addressed in the royal war oracles (41:8, 9; 44:1, 2) and elsewhere (42:1, 19; 44:21; 45:4; 49:3; 52:13, and 53:11) as "my servant" (*'bdy*) and as "my chosen one" (*bhyry,* in 42:1; 43:20; 45:4), a title used in other places in the Old Testament for the Davidic king.[44] In Psalm 89, a royal psalm, the LORD is quoted as referring to the Davidic king, with

---

42. The LORD is identified as the God of David in 38:5.
43. In 20:3 the LORD refers to the prophet Isaiah as "my servant" (*'bdy*). The term "servant" does not automatically connote kingship. When it is used in conjunction with other vocabulary, images, and ideas associated with kingship, one can understand its royal implications.
44. On the use of *bhyr* in a title for royalty, see Edgar W. Conrad, "Patriarchal Traditions in Second Isaiah" (Ph.D. diss., Princeton Theological Seminary, 1974), 154–64; and Hans Wildberger, "Die Neuinterpretation des Erwählungsglaubens Israel in der Krise der Exilzeit," in *Wort — Gebot — Glaube: Beiträge zur Theologie des Alten Testaments,* ed. Joachim Stoebe, Abhandlungen zur Theologie des Alten und Neuen Testament, 59 (Zürich: Zwingli, 1970), 319–20.

whom an everlasting covenant has been made, as "chosen one" in parallel with "servant." The Davidic king quotes the LORD as follows:

> Thou has said, "I have made a covenant (*bryt*) with my chosen one (*bhyry*),
> I have sworn to David my servant (*'bdy*):
> 'I will establish your descendants for ever (*'d 'wlm*)
> and build your throne for all generations.'" (Ps. 89:3-4)

The movement from the end of Isaiah's vision in 39:8 to the present situation of the implied community in 40:1 is a movement from the death of the old (the location of power in the persons of conventional kings) to the birth of the new (the democratization of power, or the location of power in the people as king).[45] Although Isaiah's vision comes to an end as a literary unit, a book within a book, this does not mean the end of Isaiah's vision in terms of its reception. On the contrary, Isaiah's vision had not been received in the old days of kingship. People had been blind and deaf to its teaching and word, perceived as merely gibberish. The movement from the old age to the new age is a movement to a time when the deaf will hear and the blind will see. It is a time when the words of Isaiah's vision, which have been sealed up as a testimony and a witness, will be read aloud to what is hoped will be a receptive audience: an audience without a king, an audience whose land lies desolate (1:7), an audience whose warfare has ended (40:2).

The identification of the new age as an Isaian version of "people power" should not be understood as spiritualizing. This is a point effectively argued by Brueggemann in his study on the unity of Isaiah.[46] The new age, in which the vision of Isaiah is to be read aloud, with its promise of a new heaven and a new earth (chaps. 24-27), is clearly depicted as the real world. The text suggests division within the community, as I have already noted in the last chapter in the discussion of the survivors and their opponents. The opposition and conflict in the community is also evident in chapters 1-5 and 28-33, where a series of woes are directed against the leadership in the present community. Who those opponents were, although

45. See Hans Wildberger, "Neuinterpretation," 285-90.
46. Walter Brueggemann, "Unity and Dynamic in the Isaiah Tradition," *JSOT* 29 (1984): 89-107; see esp. 100-101.

undoubtedly known to the original audience of the book, are unknown to us as contemporary readers. It is possible to imagine them, however, as those who grasp for power even in times of desolation in war-torn lands. Although the book envisions a new experiment with shared royalty amid the desolation, it suggests that some will grasp for power to rebuild the old, blinding themselves again to the vision of Isaiah.

That the vision of a democratized throne on which all the people will sit is not an unbroken throne is evident in the way the book develops after chapter 40. There is a movement toward pluralization that represents a movement also toward disintegration and diversity. The community that the LORD addresses in the singular becomes a community addressed in the plural. The LORD's reference to the community as "servant" and "chosen one" eventually becomes pluralized to "servants" (54:17; 65:8, 9, 14, 15; 66:14)[47] and "chosen ones" (65:9, 15, 22).[48] There is also a comparable development in the community's own voice after chapter 40. The community's first person singular voice (40:6, 27; 48:16; 50:4-9; 57:21; 61:1, 10; 63:7, 15) by the end of the book has become a first person plural (59:9-13; 63:16 – 64:12).[49]

That democratization leads to disruption and division is evident in other ways in the book. For example, old boundaries dissolve and are subject to redefinition. Foreigners will join themselves to the LORD and become his servants (56:6). Such times of dramatic change bring suffering, and a path into suffering can be traced in the accounts of the servant in the so-called suffering servant songs (42:1-4; 49:1-6; 50:4-11, and 52:13 – 53:12). The opposition between the survivors and their opponents, as I noted in the last chapter, is depicted as having been violent, involving the shedding of blood.

---

47. The community, speaking in a first person plural voice, identifies itself in the plural as "your servants" in 63:17.
48. Liebreich, "Compilation," 274.
49. The first person plural voice does make brief appearances throughout the book, as I have already noted in the discussion of 1:10 and 42:24. The phrase "our God" (*'lhynw*) occurs with relative frequency (1:10; 25:9; 26:12; 35:2; 36:7; 37:20; 40:3, 8; 52:10; 55:7). Note that when this phrase occurs in the vision of Isaiah outside the Hezekiah narrative, it refers to what the community will say "in that day," i.e., in the day when Isaiah's vision will be read. In 42:17 "our gods" is the voice of the idolaters referring to their idols.

The vision of an imagined new social order also results in a distancing from the past. A sharp break from the past is implied by the book's structure. There is no smooth transition between the end of the old age of kingship (39:8) and the new age of people power (40:1). The movement from 39:8 to 40:1 means more than the movement from the death of conventional kingship to the birth of a new kind of royalty. It also means a movement from old traditions to new ones.

It has frequently been argued by traditional historical-critical scholarship that so-called Second Isaiah looks to the deliverance from Babylon as a new exodus implying a break with the past.[50] Such an interpretation is clearly justified, for example, by 43:14-21. In this passage the LORD alludes to the former exodus from Egypt, where he made a way through the sea, vanquishing the chariot and horse, the army and the warrior (43:16-17) — in contrast to the new deliverance, where he will make a way through the wilderness (43:19). The new exodus will be as nonconventional as the new kingship. Whereas the old exodus conquered the water by making a way through the sea, this new exodus will make a way in the desert by providing water "to give drink" to the "chosen people" of the LORD (43:20). Water, which in the old exodus was a threat because it represented entrapment and impending death, in the new exodus represents liberation and a life support.[51]

The traditions concerning the ancestors will likewise reappear in a new and nonconventional way. In 51:1-2 the community is directed to look to Abraham and Sarah, whom the LORD blessed by increasing their number. The new feature of the blessing given to the descendants of Abraham and Sarah appears in the following verse.

> For the LORD will comfort Zion;
>   he will comfort all her waste places,
> and will make her wilderness like Eden,
>   her desert like the garden of the LORD;

---

50. The Babylonian exodus is understood as the new thing that the LORD is doing that has a typological relationship with the former exodus from Egypt. See the thesis of Bernhard W. Anderson in his well-received article "Exodus Typology in Second Isaiah," in *Israel's Prophetic Heritage: Essays in Honor of James Muilenburg*, ed. B. W. Anderson and W. Harrelson (New York: Harper and Row, 1962), 177–95.
51. In his vision Isaiah spoke of deliverance from Assyria in a nonconventional way also; see 11:15-16 and 19:23-25.

joy and gladness will be found in her,
thanksgiving and the voice of song. (51:3)

Whereas Abraham and Sarah were blessed with posterity in a land promised to them but always beyond their grasp in a story that continued the tale of human banishment from Eden, the new community is promised posterity and a return to a land like the garden of Eden itself.

The radical separation between the present and the past is also evident in the words of the implied community in their extended last speech in the book (63:7 – 64:12). The community says that although the LORD "remembered the days of old, / of Moses his servant" (63:11), it questions whether the LORD is at present acting as he did in the days of old.

Where is he who brought up out of the sea
the shepherds of his flock?
Where is he who put in the midst of them
his holy Spirit,
who caused his glorious arm
to go at the right hand of Moses,
who divided the waters before them
to make for himself an everlasting name,
who led them through the depths? (63:11b-13a)

Although the LORD had promised a new exodus (43:14-21), there is no present evidence of his intervention in the life of the community. Because the LORD has not yet intervened, the separation from the past, from the days of Moses, is also seen as a spatial separation from the LORD himself. "Look down from heaven and see, / from thy holy and glorious habitation" (63:15a). As suggested earlier, while the community acknowledges their temporal separation from Moses and their spatial separation from the LORD, they acknowledge the LORD as "our Father"; in making that acknowledgement, however, they indicate another kind of radical separation.

For thou art our Father,
though Abraham does not know us (yd'nw)
and Israel does not acknowledge us (ykyrnw);
thou, O LORD, art our Father,
our Redeemer from of old is thy name. (63:16)

This verse undergirds the theme of the rupture with the past. Because the ancestors Abraham and Israel have passed from the scene, they do not know, and could not know, the present community. The verse may also indicate that the community is separated from the normal identification markers of the LORD's people. That Abraham does not "know" (*yd'*) this community implies that it is not properly descended from him; and that Israel does not acknowledge this community suggests that it is not regarded as legitimate. The blurring of boundaries here recalls 56:6, where foreigners are referred to as the servants of the LORD.

The democratization of kingship, the envisioned new exodus, and a new period of patriarchal blessing in an Eden-like land imply a radical separation from the past. With the separation from the past comes disintegration of the traditional community and a radical reconstitution of community boundaries. That this new community will encompass foreigners recalls Isaiah's vision of a new community that will include foreigners as, for example, 14:1 ("The LORD will have compassion on Jacob and will again choose Israel, and will set them in their own land, and aliens will join them and will cleave to the house of Jacob") or 19:24-25 ("In that day Israel will be the third with Egypt and Assyria, a blessing in the midst of the earth, whom the LORD of hosts has blessed, saying, 'Blessed be Egypt my people, and Assyria the work of my hands, and Israel my heritage'"). The vision of Isaiah spoken in the days of old about the present situation of the implied community manifests itself in the present community of the LORD's servants, which includes foreigners among its ranks.

To move from 39:8 to 40:1 is to move into a new world. This new world was understood by traditional historical critics as reflecting a time gap and the merging of once-independent sources coming from different centuries. I am suggesting an aesthetic, rather than a historical, explanation for the gap. The gap can be explained synchronically suggesting the text's wholeness rather than diachronically questioning its integrity. Chapters 40–66 represent the "in that day" about which Isaiah's vision speaks. It is that day when his vision will be read to the blind and deaf, who now can see and hear. It is that day when the vision will provide the testimony of and a witness to the LORD's work in the world. It is that day when the LORD will have witnesses to his plan announced long ago in Isaiah's vision. It is that day that is about to occur and that constitutes the present experience of the implied community. It is that day when there will be a deliverance from Babylon, a far more magnificent deliverance than that from Assyria. It will be a day when the people will reign. It will be that day when even foreigners will refer to the LORD as our Father. It will be a day of peace and security that will be far more enduring than the peace and security in the days of Hezekiah.

The setting for reading the vision of Isaiah beginning in chapter 40 is portrayed as a "now" that lacks smooth links with the past — a past that, according to the book's chronology, ends with the implied death of Hezekiah. In fact, the "former things" and the "things to come" confirm thematically the break from the past evident in the book's structure.[52] Recent suggestions that the "former things" should refer to the prophecies of First Isaiah and not to the past history of Israel deflect the full impact of this phrase.[53] A more appropriate interpretation of the phrase would be that the "former things" — the old social, political, and theological conventions typical of Israel's past history — have come to an end, signaled by the new thing that was first declared long ago in Isaiah's vision, one that can now be read out again in the days of the imminent downfall of Babylon. That the LORD first announced his plan in Isaiah's vision, as I argued in chapter 3, is underscored, for example, in 41:21-29, in a setting where the nations are put on trial. In the course of the trial the LORD raises the following questions:

> Who declared it from the beginning, that we might know,
>   and beforetime, that we might say, "He is right"?
> There was none who declared it, none who proclaimed,
>   none who heard your words.
> I first declared it to Zion,
>   and I gave to Jerusalem a herald of good tidings.
> But when I look there is no one;
>   among these there is no planner (yw's)
>   who, when I ask, gives an answer. (41:26-28)[54]

The vision containing the LORD's announcement of his plan has been preserved as testimony for the LORD's witnesses at trials such

---

52. The passages usually cited are 41:21-29; 42:6-9; 43:8-21; 44:6-8; 45:20-21; 46:8-11; 48:3-8, 14-16.
53. See, e.g., Childs, Introduction, 329-30.
54. The RSV translates yw's as "counselor."

as this, where the gods cannot defend themselves. Unlike the LORD, the group of other gods do not have a "planner" (*yw's*) among them. Both Isaiah's vision (his prophecies) and the conventional notions of kingship and community are past (former things); what is now occurring is the institution of a new era with a new kingship, a new exodus, and a new blessing in a return to Eden (the things to come). The new era is "that day" anticipated by Isaiah's vision.

SUMMARY AND CONCLUSION

In this chapter I have looked at those sections of the Book of Isaiah that were not considered in previous discussions: the narrative about Isaiah in chapter 20, the section of Isaiah's vision concerning the internal affairs of the implied community in chapters 28-35, and the latter chapters of the book concerning the disintegration that has emerged in a radically redefined community. A number of points have emerged in the discussion that are of fundamental importance for understanding the book's structure.

The narrative about Isaiah in chapter 20 serves with the other two narrative complexes (chaps. 6-8 and 36-39) to create a past setting for the vision of Isaiah. The narratives are not so much surviving documents from an actual historical period placed loosely or coincidentally with the poetry of another period as they are part of a literary construct ("the vision") consisting of poetry and narratives that suggest a setting for the poetry. This setting in the days of Uzziah, Ahaz, and Hezekiah[55] (possibly based on historical events) has the effect of giving authority to the poetry in a time (the "present") when it is being received.[56]

The key moments in the chronology of events concern the death of Davidic kings. Since the narratives begin with the death of one king (6:1) and end with the implied death of another (39:8), the book suggests the death of Davidic kingship as an institution. This thesis is confirmed in the poetry beginning in 40:1, where kingship has become democratized—the people have become king. Isaiah's vision, which has come to an end in 39:8, is set in the past. In the

---

55. While Jotham is mentioned in the title, he is not mentioned in the narrative settings for the poetry.
56. For a study that argues for the importance of the present in the conception of time in biblical literature, see Bruce J. Malina, "Christ and Time: Swiss or Mediterranean?" *CBQ* 51 (1989): 1-31.

book it closes a period of time when the former things have come to an end, for the LORD is about to do a new thing — bring about the plan announced in the vision of Isaiah.

In contrast to the vision of Isaiah, the new time is given no clear context or setting.[57] That is so because the movement from 39:8 to 40:1 is a movement from the past to the present situation of the implied community. The audience brings to the text its own context, one that needs no elaboration.

It is a context, however, that is illuminated by the vision of Isaiah: a time when cities lie desolate (1:7), that is, when the time that the community was to remain deaf and blind to the vision of Isaiah has elapsed (6:11). While the beginning (8:16-20) and end (30:8) of the vision indicate that provisions have been made for sealing up the testimony in a book so that it may be a witness and a testimony forever, the time of the implied community is the occasion for reading out the vision of Isaiah (40:6). In the former times the book could not be read (29:11-12), but this is that day when the deaf and blind will hear the words of the book of Isaiah's vision (v. 18).

The reception of this message, with its radical redefinitions of kingship and community, does not take place at a time of hegemony. As the book moves toward its conclusion, there are indications that the implied audience has opponents who are hostile to the vision of Isaiah read in a context of positive regard for fundamental change. This division is reflected in the motif of the servant who suffers. Rejection of those who call for social change results in persecution by those who are reactionary and seek to preserve the status quo. Rejection also results in the pluralization of a unified community. Since the whole community does not understand itself as a servant or chosen one, it becomes necessary to refer to members of a sub-group of the community as servants and chosen ones. Since the community cannot speak as a unified "I," it becomes a "we," a plurality of individuals.

The woes delivered against the opponents in the vision of Isaiah (chaps. 28–33) and anticipated in the description of the implied community in chapter 5 suggest that the opposition is an official one. The part of the community that disregards the teaching and word of "the LORD our God" is characterized as the leaders who are so confused as to mistake evil for good.

57. There are only tantalizing hints, e.g., 44:28 and 45:1.

CHAPTER 6

Reading the Book
of Isaiah

The Book of Isaiah stands in the modern world as a literary monument from the ancient past. We know nothing about its real author(s) or the original audience for which it was written. This lack of information about the book's inception and original reception is the major problem encountered by contemporary readers. How is the reader to read the Book of Isaiah? The answer to the question is vitally important for determining meaning. As contemporary readers, we do know how to read contemporary texts because our reading skills have been shaped by the same conventions that shaped the production of the contemporary texts we read. To read Isaiah, however, is to read an alien text. Because the book has been separated from its moorings in its original space and time and has had a life of its own in Western culture, the foreignness of the Book of Isaiah has often been overlooked. It stands in Western culture as both familiar and foreign—like other remains from the past, a textual Stonehenge.

Contemporary historical-critical reading of Isaiah has sought to overcome the distance the text has traveled from its past by journeying back in a kind of literary time machine to the days of its origin. The aim of the historical-critical approach has been to read the text in the context of its original historical background and in terms of its original authors' intentions. Contemporary historical-critical readers attempt to bridge the gulf between the past and the present by reconstructing the text and in that sense returning to the time of the text's inception. But the past is not something to which we can journey; we are locked in a fleeting present. It is no more possible to reconstruct the developmental history of the text of Isaiah and uncover the intentions of its authors than it is to relive the construction of other stone monuments that are now part of our present. This does not mean that we have no links with the past. The gap with the past has been bridged, but the text, not the reader, does the traveling. As past text, the Book of Isaiah is present to contemporary readers. It is precisely because the text has made the journey from the past that I have made the text the object of my study. The text, not its authors or original audience, is available to the contemporary reader for critical study. This does not mean that the text is to be contemporized and read as if it were a modern production.[1] In this study I have endeavored to examine the text of Isaiah itself for clues about its structure and its implied audience in order to gain insight into how to read it. In doing that, I am keenly aware of my own involvement as a reader in constructing meaning. We cannot escape the fact that Isaiah must always be read as a present, although alien, text.

ISAIAH: ITS STRUCTURE

According to my analysis, the Book of Isaiah (chaps. 1-66) provides the context and occasion for reading another book, the book of Isaiah's vision (chaps. 6-39). The book is structured in such a way as to provide a present context as the framework (chaps. 1-5 and 40-66) for the reception of the ancient vision of Isaiah (chaps. 6-39). According to the vision of Isaiah, the original audience of the vision was unreceptive; the community of Isaiah's time was deaf and blind to his vision (6:9-10). It was bound up and sealed (8:16-20) — written/ inscribed on a book/tablet (30:8) — so that the vision was unreadable (29:11). In his own time the vision of Isaiah was an alien text. Although I have suggested that the Book of Isaiah is an alien text in the twentieth century, the Book of Isaiah presents the vision of Isaiah as an alien text at the time of its inception because in its own

---

1. Ironically, that has often been the case with much historical-critical reading of texts such as Isaiah because contemporary assumptions about the nature of authorship (prophecy) and unity have been applied to alien genres. On this point, see John Barton, "Reading the Bible as Literature: Two Questions for Biblical Critics," *Journal of Literature and Theology* 1 (1987): 135-53.

time it was a book written for another time, a future time. Only after Isaiah's time could the vision of Isaiah be read with understanding.

> In that day the deaf shall hear
>   the words of a book,
> and out of their gloom and darkness
>   the eyes of the blind shall see. (29:18)

The occasion for reading the vision of Isaiah is the renewed command to read in 40:6, when the vision of Isaiah can be read aloud to a receptive audience.

The Book of Isaiah, then, presents the vision of Isaiah as the antithesis of what is normally expected of ancient books. While it is usual to understand books written long ago as hard to read because they reflect the social conventions of a forgotten past, the Book of Isaiah understands the vision of Isaiah as an old book that has become easy to read because it reflects the social conventions of an age posterior to its inception. It is an age when Davidic kingship has died and a new democratized kingship has emerged. It is an age when the old boundaries of the Israelite community have broken down and the LORD's servants and chosen ones include foreigners. It is an age that would not be known or acknowledged by the ancestors. It is an age when warfare has ended for the LORD's people and a time when the LORD is already engaged to overthrow all the nations of the world in order to establish world peace.

ISAIAH: ITS AUDIENCE

Who was the audience of the Book of Isaiah? It is impossible to identify precisely the original audience of the book that was written as the context for the reception of another book, Isaiah's vision. All that remains is the Book of Isaiah itself. While the book contains no hard evidence for locating itself in a specific place and time, it does imply an audience whose ideological features can be deduced from the text.[2] Since the Book of Isaiah was written for oral delivery, the first person plural language offers some clues. I have argued above that the audience of the book is a community of survivors with minority status. That this community is powerless is

---

2. On this point, see Giovanni Garbini, *History and Ideology in Ancient Israel,* trans. John Bowden (London: SCM, 1986), 1–20.

indicated by the characterization of its opponents as leaders who are corrupt and inept. The community as royal servant is a community that suffers and is threatened by murder and bloodshed.

The community perceives the legal and religious institutions to be morally bankrupt. It waits for justice and righteousness, but there is only bloodshed and a murderous cry (5:7 and 59:9-15). It sees empty religious ritual performed by those who will not hear the word of the LORD or tremble at his teaching (1:10-17 and 66:3-5). It is a people whose critique of ideology and whose embrace of suffering and pain have led to what Walter Brueggemann has called the "release of social imagination," by which he means the "energy and courage to envision the world alternatively arranged."[3] It is a community that imagines a society where the people will be king, so that the future peace and security will no longer be dependent on frail and mortal individual kings. It will be a community without borders. There will be a highway from Assyria to Egypt, and even foreigners will be servants of the LORD. The vision of Isaiah about an international community of world peace is summarized in 2:1-4.

The word which Isaiah the son of Amoz saw concerning Judah and Jerusalem.
It shall come to pass in the latter days
    that the mountain of the house of the LORD
shall be established as the highest of the mountains,
    and shall be raised above the hills;
and all the nations shall flow to it,
    and many peoples shall come, and say:
"Come, let us go up to the mountain of the LORD,
    to the house of the God of Jacob;
that he may teach us his ways
    and that we may walk in his paths."
For out of Zion shall go forth the law,
    and the word of the LORD from Jerusalem.
He shall judge between the nations,
    and shall decide for many peoples;
and they shall beat their swords into plowshares,
    and their spears into pruning hooks;

---

3. Walter Brueggemann, "Unity and Dynamic in the Isaiah Tradition," *JSOT* 29 (1984): 99. What Brueggemann describes as the social imagination of Third Isaiah, I understand to be characteristic of the part of the book that presents the setting for Isaiah's vision—chapters 1-5 and 40-66.

nation shall not lift up sword against nation,
neither shall they learn war any more.

This word of Isaiah occurs in the context of the portrayal of the
present community (chaps. 1–5) and anticipates and summarizes
Isaiah's vision. It suggests the importance of Isaiah's vision for this
implied present community. The vision of a radical new age to come
is grounded in the past vision of Isaiah. Isaiah, "the salvation of the
Lord," is himself a sign and portent (8:18) of the salvation the
implied present community sees in its own time — a time when the
vision of Isaiah can be read out with clarity. His message, unconventional for his own time, now reaches receptive ears. The implied
present community hears about its own future in the past vision of
Isaiah. Hearing about the future helps the community to make sense
of its present.

THE BOOK OF ISAIAH AND ITS
CONTEMPORARY READERS

The Book of Isaiah, as a significant part of the canon of Judeo-
Christian literature, has become familiar. As contemporary readers
of that book, however, we must never overlook its being an alien
book as well. Although it is present as a testimonial from the past,
there is much about the book that we do not know and never will
know. In chapter 4, I argued that as contemporary readers we often
overlook the orality of Isaiah; like other ancient books, it was
written for oral presentation to a community. To be aware of the
orality of Isaiah makes us alert to rhetorical features of the text
utilized for spoken delivery. Yet much about that oral delivery is
lost. It is not clear how the text was read aloud. It may have been
as simple as an individual reading to a group, or it may have been
as complex as the dramatic performance with a cast of different
voices, as recently suggested by John D. W. Watts.[4] In the present
study I have assumed a single reader who is a representative of the
implied community and who speaks, at times, for that community
in a first person plural voice. Yet, I suspect the situation was more

---

4. John D. W. Watts, *Isaiah 1–33,* and *Isaiah 34–66,* WBC 24 and 25 (Waco, Tex.:
Word Books, 1985 and 1987). See especially *Isaiah 1–33,* xliv–liv. The thesis is more
of a suggestion than an argument in the commentary proper.

complex than that. Often the reader speaks in a first person singular voice that modulates into a first person plural voice, as in 63:7 – 64:12. What is to be made of the first person singular? Is the reader claiming some kind of authoritative status over the community?[5] The answers to these questions are not readily apparent.

Because the Book of Isaiah is a present text that had its inception in the distant past, it is a text that is both near and far. The interpretive strategies that have characterized the academic reading of Isaiah by scholars in mainline Protestant, Catholic, and Jewish traditions have emphasized its remoteness. The strategy has been to read Isaiah as a source of information about the past. This historical-critical approach has analyzed the Book of Isaiah in order to locate and discover the intentions of authors in historical settings that have had to be reconstructed. Reading strategies have become so complex that the Book of Isaiah has become virtually inaccessible to the nonspecialist,[6] available primarily through the *secondary* texts of the specialist.[7]

Historical criticism has re-created the gulf between the past and the present that the text itself has spanned. Because the text has been made remote, it has threatened to make the Bible irrelevant as a canonical text for the present life of communities of faith. The biblical theology movement that was at its zenith in the middle of this century was intended to bridge this gulf. It represented an attempt to overcome the historical distance of the Bible by making history itself the arena of divine activity linking the present with the past. It failed to meet its goal primarily because history and God's activity in it were never clearly defined.[8] Childs's canonical approach has been offered more recently as an alternative to the

---

5. The reader might perhaps be seen as a poetic variation of a narrative voice of authority such as that suggested by Robert Polzin, *Moses and the Deuteronomist: A Literary Study of the Deuteronomic History* (New York: Seabury, 1980).
6. On this point, see the discussion of James Barr, "Reading the Bible as Literature," *BJRL* 56 (1973): 19–20.
7. See Edgar W. Conrad, "Changing Context: The Bible and the Study of Religion," in *Perspectives on Language and Text: Essays in Honor of Francis I. Andersen's Sixtieth Birthday, July 28, 1985,* ed. E. W. Conrad and T. G. Newing (Winona Lake: Eisenbrauns, 1986), 399–401.
8. This was the challenge posed by Langdon B. Gilkey, "Cosmology, Ontology, and the Travail of Biblical Language," *JR* 41 (1961): 194–205, reprinted in *God's Activity in the World: The Contemporary Problem,* ed. Owen C. Thomas, Studies in Religion 31 (Chico, Calif.: Scholars Press, 1983), 29–43.

biblical theological movement. It has the major weakness, however, of dehistoricizing the Bible completely, so that the Bible as a canonical witness of the community of faith has been decontextualized.[9]

Fundamentalism has also attempted to overcome the distance of the text created by historical criticism. This attempt has been less academically honest than the biblical theology movement or the canonical approach of Childs. Fundamentalism has had popular appeal in part because it has denied the remoteness of the Bible. It has embraced the Bible as a familiar text that can be situated easily in the late twentieth century and treated as though it were thoroughly modern. Here the Bible is treated as if it were a twentieth-century document containing scientific data. A book like Isaiah may be read by fundamentalists as if it contained contemporary political commentary on the world scene or described imminent events.[10] This mistaken view of the Bible denies the Bible's alien character, leading many to think that the Bible is as easily accessible to its readers as literature that has had its inception in the twentieth century.

My strategy as an interpreter in this study has been to preserve both the presence and remoteness of the Book of Isaiah. Seeing Isaiah as an alien book, one must be more reflective about what it is as a book. How to read the Book of Isaiah is not obvious because it had its inception in the remote past in a society with literary conventions different from our own. Those conventions are available to contemporary readers only in the text itself. Although we cannot discover who the original authors were or in what historical context they wrote, one thing clearly accessible to us is the text itself as it has been preserved. My reading of Isaiah has therefore concentrated on the existing book as we have received it: its structure, its rhetorical features, and its suggestions about the audience it addresses.

The interpretive strategies I am using have links with the hermeneutic that, as Regina M. Schwartz has proposed, is suggested by the Old Testament itself in its portrayal of texts as lost and found, tablets broken and rewritten. As she remarks, "The Book itself is imperiled, lost over and over. And so it must be remembered,

9. Brueggemann, "Unity and Dynamic," 91.
10. See James Barr, *Fundamentalism* (London: SCM, 1977), 90–103, 123–24, 253–55.

recovered, rewritten, and rediscovered over and over, in a perpetual activity that defies the grand designs of fulfillment constructed by typology."[11]

Although recognizing the remoteness of the text of Isaiah, I have not read it as if its language reflected only a dim and distant past. The fact that the Book of Isaiah describes itself as a vision suggests that its language is not used primarily for descriptive or mimetic purposes. Indeed, as I have shown, the setting that the book provides for the reception of the vision of Isaiah is an imagined world in which the conventional ideologies of kingship and community have been replaced, a world that never was but that is filled with the possibility of what might be. To enter into that world does not require a journey into the past but contemplation of a future.

The world of democratized kingship in which the people are addressed as kings and informed that their warfare has ended is not a world that is remote from the experiences of twentieth-century survivors. Our century has seen the emergence of "people power," which has effected change in some countries and holds out the hope of change in others. To read this alien text from the past is to share in a vision of the future. As a text that calls into question the fleeting security of regimes that do not look beyond themselves in pursuit of

---

11. Regina M. Schwartz, "Joseph's Bones and the Resurrection of the Text: Remembering in the Bible," *Publications of the Modern Language Association of America* 103 (1988): 117. She argues that the Joseph story in Genesis suggests "re-membering" as a hermeneutic. With regard to the larger Old Testament writings, she says, "A dialectic of forgetting and remembering, loss and recovery, is so frequently depicted in the text and enacted by the text that it informs each of the 'scenes of writing' the Bible offers. Deuteronomy tells the story of the exodus with a second Moses repeatedly enjoining his hearers to remember and retell the story themselves. But the injunctions of Deuteronomy are forgotten. The text is lost. Even the reminder to remember is forgotten. During a religious reform that included the restoration of the Temple, the lost book is found amid debris, according to the account in 2 Kings, and with the recovery of the book, the contents — to remember and what to remember — are remembered. The lost-and-found phenomenon recurs for another text: the scroll of Jeremiah. After reading the first twenty-five chapters of Jeremiah, we are told how they came to be, and not to be, and to be again. As each page is read to the king, it is torn off and burned in the fire of his winter apartments. Despite this destruction Jeremiah and his scribe begin all over again. The text persists. When Moses receives the tablets of the law, before he even begins to promulgate it, he dashes the tables to pieces. The Torah is rewritten; thus, all we have from the beginning is a copy, one that proliferates further copies." To Schwartz's list of "lost-and-found" texts the "vision of Isaiah" can be added as a text lost to a deaf and blind audience in Isaiah's time but one found and read out in a later period to restore the memory of the LORD's witnesses.

security and peace in their own days, the Book of Isaiah ceases to be remote. A world as envisioned by Isaiah — where the boundaries that separated the great powers of the ancient world were disappearing — is a world not so strange to our own shrinking world, where direct routes link once-enemy powers. A world cut off from past nationalisms so as to become unrecognizable to the ancestors is a world like our own.

Like readers of other canonized literary works, we can find in the Book of Isaiah shared insights as we face our own future. Although we can read the book as speaking to our age, it cannot be domesticated and tamed. Because the text has originated in another time, it will always remain "other." To contemporary readers who are horrified by the Jewish holocaust, the killing fields of Cambodia, and Tiananmen Square in China, some of the imagery of the book is horrifying. Although the reader has read the imagery of the cruel demise of Babylon (13:17-22) and the horrible fate of the Moabites (25:10-12), the final verse in the Book of Isaiah (66:24), is jolting. "And they shall go forth and look on the dead bodies of the men that have rebelled against me; for their worm shall not die, their fire shall not be quenched, and they shall be an abhorrence to all flesh." As a contemporary reader, I do not know what to do with this verse. I want to delete it as well as others of its kind. To do so, however, would be to engage in the process of remaking Isaiah in the refinishing school of Western good taste. It would be to eliminate its distance. Strategies for reading Isaiah must assert both the text's presence and its distance.

IMPLICATIONS FOR BIBLICAL THEOLOGY

Biblical studies such as this one that acknowledge the central role of the reader for ascertaining a text's meaning have important implications for determining the aims of biblical theology. Unlike the present study, the so-called biblical theology movement that flourished at the middle of this century stressed the inception and not the reception of the text.[12] The classic formulation of the task of biblical

---

12. The phrase "biblical theology movement" was first suggested by Brevard S. Childs in his *Biblical Theology in Crisis* (Philadelphia: Fortress Press, 1970), 9. For a critical survey of this movement in addition to that of Childs, see James Barr, "Biblical Theology," *IDBS* (Nashville: Abingdon, 1976), 104–11.

studies for the biblical theology movement was made by Krister Stendahl in his article on biblical theology in the *Interpreter's Dictionary of the Bible*. According to Stendahl, the task of biblical study was primarily a descriptive one. To use his terminology, the biblical scholar was to be concerned with "What *did* it mean?" and the constructive theologian with "What *does* it mean?"[13] While many in the biblical theology movement may not have stated this dichotomy so boldly, Stendahl was describing what was indeed happening in biblical theology. The biblical theology movement advocated the interpretive strategies of historical criticism that emphasized the identification of the intentions of the author in the original historical context in which the author wrote.[14]

Why did the biblical theology movement, which wanted to affirm the relevance of the Bible for the contemporary world, stress interpretive strategies that were historical and descriptive? Why did it place such a heavy emphasis on authorial intention and the location of the text in the past? The answers to these questions can be associated with Johann Philipp Gabler, often recognized as the initiator of the discipline of biblical theology.[15] In his inaugural lecture for his professorship in theology at the University of Altdorf in 1787, entitled "Oratio de iusto discrimine theologiae biblicae et dogmaticae regundisque recte utriusque finibus," he argued that biblical theology is "historical in character and sets forth what the sacred writers thought about divine matters; dogmatic theology, on the contrary, is didactic in character, and teaches what a particular theologian philosophically and rationally decides about divine matters, in accordance with his character, time, age, place, sect or school, and other similar influences."[16] Distinguishing biblical theology from dogmatic theology, Gabler emphasized biblical studies as a historical discipline allowing the Bible "to speak for

13. Krister Stendahl, "Biblical Theology, Contemporary," *IDB*, vol. 1 (New York: Abingdon, 1962), 418–32.
14. Childs, *Biblical Theology in Crisis*, 79, 35.
15. See Robert C. Dentan, *Preface to Old Testament Theology*, rev. ed. (New York: Seabury, 1963), 22–23.
16. Cited in ibid., 23. For a discussion of biblical theology and the place of Gabler in the field, see Ben. C. Ollenburger, "Biblical Theology: Situating the Discipline," in *Understanding the Word: Essays in Honor of Bernhard W. Anderson* ed. James T. Butler, Edgar W. Conrad, and Ben. C. Ollenburger, JSOTSup 37 (Sheffield: JSOT, 1985), 37–62.

itself" rather than to speak the alien ideas of a dogmatics that originated in an age posterior to the Bible's inception. The continuing appeal of historical-critical reading strategies, I think, is associated with the assumption that such strategies free the text from the subjective input of readers intent on making the text say whatever the reader wants it to say.[17]

In this study, however, I have argued that all interpretive strategies, even historical-critical ones, are reader dependent. There can be no detached interpretation of the biblical text, no textual meaning independent of the present reception of the biblical text. There can be no assured reconstruction of authorial intention or of the historical development of the biblical text. The recognition of the inevitable subjectivity of the interpreter poses again, in a different way, the question that the biblical theology movement, using historical-critical interpretive strategies, thought it had resolved: Can the biblical text mean anything a reader wishes it to mean?

The problem of the indeterminacy of meaning has been posed not only for the biblical text but for all texts by the reader-oriented literary theories known as deconstruction, commonly associated with the name of Jacques Derrida.[18] This is an issue taken up recently by Michael LaFargue, who focuses "specifically on the question of determinacy: whether there is something definite and determinate which is the object of textual interpretation, or whether texts are subject to an infinite number of incompatible, but equally valid, readings."[19] The issue LaFargue raises suggests that biblical scholars interested in biblical theology find themselves again in a situation not unlike that before Gabler, where the biblical text was made to say what a dogmatic theology wanted it to say. Does not the recognition of the role of the reader in the construction of meaning deny the status of the text as "other"?

According to LaFargue, the notion of the indeterminacy of textual

17. The assumption that historical criticism allows the text to speak for itself rather to be dictated to by the ideas of its readers is at the basis of Brian Rice McCarthy's comment cited in chap. 1 above (n. 2).

18. For an introduction to Derrida's thought and its relation to biblical studies, see Robert Detweiler, ed., *Derrida and Biblical Studies,* Semeia 23 (Chico, Calif.: Scholars, 1982).

19. Michael LaFargue, "Are Texts Determinate? Derrida, Barth, and the Role of the Biblical Scholar," *HTR* 81 (1988): 341.

interpretation is associated with Derrida's notion of all reality as a differential system—a model drawn from Saussure's analysis of language.

> For Derrida, "the world" (the experienced world of any individual) is a differential system. Each "thing" in the world is experienced as it is because of the particular relation it bears to the experienced character of all other "things" in the same world. We cannot make a distinction between the nature of texts and the nature of things. (As his context makes clear, this is the best way of interpreting Derrida's famous hyperbole: "There is nothing outside the text" [*Il n'y a pas de hors-texte*]). . . . Moreover, there is no privileged view of things "as they really are."[20]

This position has affinities with the one I argued in the first chapter concerning the nonreferentiality of language. Unlike the historical critics, I suggested that language is to be understood as constructing reality and not as referring to realities external to it (e.g., authorial intention, ideas, or historical events).

While not denying this basic assumption of Derrida that all reality is a differential system of culture-bound experience, LaFargue argues that it does not follow from this assumption that textual interpretation is indeterminate. It is the differential system that provides the basis on which one can speak of how the elements of a text receive their determinate character, or what he calls their "substantive content."

> What I mean [by the determinate "substantive content" of a given text] can be illustrated by the case of a joke: "Did you hear the one about the Texan who was involved in a ten-car accident before he left his garage?"
>
> We can speak of "getting" or "not getting" this joke. This means that there is something definite to get or not to get. If we had to explain what this is, we could point to some key relationships that have to shape one's reading, most importantly, (1) the contrast in normal circumstances between "ten-car accident" and "garage," and (2) the evocation of wealth in the term "Texan" that explains the contrast. If one gave some other relationships a central role in one's reading—say the relationship between "one" in the first part and "ten" in the second—one would fail to get the joke. We would also speak of a certain "mode of engagement" necessary to fully get the joke: one has

20. Ibid., 344–46 (quotation on p. 346).

to expect the ten-car accident to occur in traffic, and then be surprised to hear that it occurred in a garage. One who implicitly perceives these relationships, and engages in the words in this way, "gets" the joke. What she "gets" is what I call the "substantive content" of the joke.

The substantive content is not something one can extract from the joke, something one can tell instead of telling the joke. The only reason for distinguishing the substantive content from the words themselves is that (in the case of a foreigner, say) someone can hear and understand these same words individually, and still not "get" the joke. My thesis is that any given biblical text has a determinate content, which ought to be the primary focus of biblical research.

This formulation avoids one of the most frequent objections of textual determinacy: the implication that we can capture a text's meaning in a neat formulation which invites no more thought. The above formulation of determinacy contains no such implications. It accepts the fact that the best texts have an endless depth of meaning. It then attributes this thought-provoking property to a text to the very particular character of its substantive context — not capturable in paraphrase — rather than to its mere vagueness.[21]

LaFargue's understanding of textual determinacy helps clarify a literary approach to a text such as Isaiah that acknowledges both the central role of the reader in the production of a text's meaning and the engagement with the text as "other." In my reading of Isaiah above I have attempted to acknowledge the alien character of Isaiah by paying careful attention to the text of Isaiah as a whole. Both fundamentalism and historical criticism engage in interpretive activities that ignore a text's otherness. Fundamentalism's proof-texting and historical-criticism's analysis of the text into bits and pieces ignore the differential system, the substantive content, whereby the parts of a text are seen to have meaning in relationship to the whole.

Biblical studies, then, must be concerned with the whole of a biblical text because, if the whole is ignored, one will not "get" the text. Biblical texts such as the sixty-six chapters of Isaiah, however, are far more complicated than LaFargue's joke, which means that getting the text is a far more intricate affair. But the getting of a biblical text is only the beginning of meaning; the getting can never be complete or definitive. A myriad of readers may engage with the text, which has an endless depth of meaning.

21. Ibid., 341–42.

All of this has important implications for the role of biblical scholarship and the practice of biblical theology. The professional biblical scholar should focus his or her attention on exploring the determinative substantive content of biblical texts.[22] In this way the biblical scholar invites and facilitates the reading of biblical texts by larger communities both within and outside communities of faith.[23] Just as the linguist examines languages as differential systems, so the biblical scholar should examine biblical texts as differential systems, facilitating their reading by larger communities.

As I argued in the first chapter, the interpretive strategies of historical criticism, concerned with probing for meaning behind the text, had the opposite effect to that of facilitating reading. Textual analysis became so complex that the practice of historical criticism created a gulf between its practitioners and ordinary readers. Rather than facilitate reading, historical criticism with its prolific production of larger and larger commentaries, had the effect of convincing ordinary readers that they could not read the text meaningfully. The biblical text was available only through the secondary works of the biblical scholars themselves.

The practice of biblical theology should not be something that biblical scholars reserve for themselves. Biblical scholarship (even in secular university departments of religion) should be concerned with exploring the "otherness" of the biblical text.[24] Otherness is not here to be understood as synonymous with "transcendent otherness."[25] The practice of biblical theology needs to be carried out by its readers in communities of faith, readers whose faith does clearly link the Bible with transcendence.[26] In such communities the Bible

22. LaFargue also makes this point: "The role of the biblical scholar, as scholar, is to be a servant of the biblical text, to guard its otherness, to help make its substantive content something modern people can in some way experience and understand, its particularity and its otherness" (ibid., 355).
23. The biblical scholar may of course also be part of other communities, including communities of faith.
24. For a discussion of poetry and art as the source of otherness, see George Steiner, *Real Presences: Is There Anything in What We Say?* (London: Faber and Faber, 1989), 200–32. Steiner refers to this otherness as "alterity" (p. 211).
25. Many, such as the fundamentalists, who associate the Bible with transcendence, do not respect the text as "other."
26. In making this point, I am following in the footsteps of my mentor, Bernhard W. Anderson, who has argued that biblical theology should not be separated from the

as other can provide a wealth of meanings. The Bible has a myriad of presences in the contemporary world. All its readers should be heard. Biblical theology needs to be pluralized. To continue to speak of biblical theology in the singular as if it had a grand design around a center is to deny the Bible's plurality of meanings.[27] Biblical theology cannot, as I have shown, continue to focus on what the Bible referred to at the time of its inception. The importance of reader reception and the plurality of meaning can be recognized in readings of the Bible that have led, for example, to feminist and third-world theologies. Books such as Isaiah present their readers with a vision from the past. Because such books can be received as "other," they create visions of new possibilities.

context of worship. See, e.g., his "Crisis in Biblical Theology," *Theology Today* 28 (1976): 321-37.

27. Barr shows that the search for a "center" characterized the biblical theology movement ("Biblical Theology," 109-10).

Bibliography

Abrams, M. H. *The Mirror and the Lamp: Romantic Theory and Critical Tradition.* New York: Oxford University Press, 1953.

Achtemeier, Elizabeth. "Isaiah of Jerusalem: Themes and Preaching Possibilities." In *Reading and Preaching the Book of Isaiah,* ed. Christopher R. Seitz. Philadelphia: Fortress Press, 1988.

Achtemeier, Paul J., and Tucker, Gene M. "Biblical Studies: The State of the Discipline." *BCSR* 11 (1980): 72–76.

Ackroyd, Peter R. "The Biblical Interpretation of the Reigns of Ahaz and Hezekiah." In *In the Shelter of Elyon: Essays on Ancient Palestinian Life and Literature in Honor of G. W. Ahlström,* ed. W. Boyd Barrick and John R. Spencer. JSOTSup 31. Sheffield: JSOT, 1984. Reprinted in *Studies in the Religious Tradition of the Old Testament.* London: SCM, 1987.

———. "The Death of Hezekiah – a Pointer to the Future?" In *De la Tôrah au Messie. Mélanges Henri Cazelles. Études d'exégèse et d'herméneutique bibliques offertes à Henri Cazelles pour ses 25 années d'enseignement à l'Institut Catholique de Paris (Octobre 1979),* ed. M. Carrez et al. Paris: Desclée, 1982. Reprinted in *Studies in the Religious Tradition of the Old Testament.* London: SCM, 1987.

———. "Isaiah I–XII: Presentation of a Prophet." VTSup 29 (1978): 16–48. Reprinted in *Studies in the Religious Tradition of the Old Testament.* London: SCM, 1987.

———. "Isaiah 36–39: Structure and Function." In *Von Kanaan bis Kerala: Festschrift für Prof. Mag. Dr. Dr. J. P. M. van der Ploeg OP zur Vollendung des siebzigsten Lebenjahres am 4 Juli 1979,*

169

ed. W. C. Delsman et al. Alter Orient und Altes Testament 211. Neukirchen-Vluyn: Neukirchener Verlag, 1982. Reprinted in *Studies in the Religious Tradition of the Old Testament*. London: SCM, 1987.

Alter, Robert. *The Art of Biblical Narrative*. London: George Allen and Unwin, 1981.

——. "Biblical Type-scenes and the Uses of Convention." *Critical Inquiry* 5 (1978): 355–68.

Anderson, Bernhard W. "The Crisis in Biblical Theology." *Theology Today* 28 (1976): 321–37.

——. "Exodus Typology in Second Isaiah." In *Israel's Prophetic Heritage: Essays in Honor of James Muilenburg*, ed. B. W. Anderson and W. Harrelson. New York: Harper and Row, 1962.

——. *Understanding the Old Testament*. 4th ed. Englewood Cliffs, N.J.: Prentice-Hall, 1986.

Auld, A. Graeme. "Poetry, Prophecy, Hermeneutic: Recent Studies in Isaiah." *SJT* 33 (1980): 567–81.

Barr, James. "Biblical Theology." *IDBS*. Nashville: Abingdon, 1976.

——. *Fundamentalism*. London: SCM, 1977.

——. "Reading the Bible as Literature." *BJRL* 56 (1973): 10–33.

Barth, Hermann. *Die Jesaja-Worte in der Josiazeit: Israel und Assur als Thema einer produktiven Neuinterpretation der Jesaja-überlieferung*. WMANT 48. Neukirchen-Vluyn: Neukirchener Verlag, 1977.

Barton, John. "Classifying Biblical Criticism." *JSOT* 29 (1984): 19–35.

——. *Oracles of God: Perception of Ancient Prophecy in Israel after the Exile*. London: Darton, Longman and Todd, 1986.

——. "Reading the Bible as Literature: Two Questions for Biblical Critics." *Journal of Literature and Theology* 1 (1987): 135–53.

——. *Reading the Old Testament: Method in Biblical Study*. London: Darton, Longman and Todd, 1984.

Becker, Joachim. *Isaias – der Prophet und sein Buch*. Stuttgarter Bibelstudien 30. Stuttgart: Verlag Katholisches Bibelwerk, 1968.

Begrich, Joachim, "Das priesterliche Heilsorakel." *ZAW* 52 (1934): 81–92. Reprinted in *Gesammelte Studien zum Alten Testament*. Theologische Bücherei 21. Munich: Chr. Kaiser, 1964.

Berlin, Adele. *Poetics and Interpretation of Biblical Narrative.* Bible and Literature Series 9. Sheffield: Almond, 1983.

Blenkinsopp, Joseph. *A History of Prophecy in Israel: From the Settlement in the Land to the Hellenistic Period.* Philadelphia: Westminster, 1983.

Boling, Robert G. *Joshua: A New Translation with Notes and Commentary.* Introduction by G. E. Wright. AB. Garden City, N.Y.: Doubleday, 1982.

Boomershine, Thomas E. "Peter's Denial as Polemic or Confession: The Implications of Media Criticism for Biblical Hermeneutics." In *Orality, Aurality, and Biblical Narrative,* ed. Lou H. Silberman, 47–68. Semeia 39. Decatur, Ga.: Scholars, 1987.

Brodie, Louis. "The Children and the Prince: The Structure, Nature, and Date of Isaiah 6–12." *BTB* 9 (1979): 27–31.

Brueggemann, Walter. "The Book of Jeremiah: The Portrait of the Prophet." *Int* 37 (1983): 130–45.

———. *Hopeful Imagination: Prophetic Voices in Exile.* Philadelphia: Fortress, 1986.

———. "Imagination as a Mode of Fidelity." In *Understanding the Word: Essays in Honor of Bernhard W. Anderson,* ed. J. T. Butler, E. W. Conrad, and B. C. Ollenburger. JSOTSup 37. Sheffield: JSOT, 1985.

———. "Unity and Dynamic in the Isaiah Tradition." *JSOT* 29 (1984): 89–107.

Brunner, Emil. *The Divine-Human Encounter.* Trans. A. W. Loos. Philadelphia: Westminster, 1943.

Burrow, J. A. *Medieval Writers and Their Work: Middle English Literature and Its Background, 1100–1500.* Oxford: Oxford University Press, 1982.

Childs, B. S. *Biblical Theology in Crisis.* Philadelphia: Fortress Press, 1970.

———. "The Canonical Shape of the Prophetic Literature." *Int* 32 (1978): 46–55.

———. *Introduction to the Old Testament as Scripture.* Philadelphia: Fortress Press, 1979.

Clements, R. E. "Beyond Tradition History: Deutero-Isaianic Development of First Isaiah's Themes." *JSOT* 31 (1985): 95–113.

———. *Isaiah 1–39.* NCB. Grand Rapids: Eerdmans; London: Marshall, Morgan and Scott, 1980.

———. *Isaiah and the Deliverance of Jerusalem.* JSOTSup 13. Sheffield: JSOT, 1980.

———. "Patterns in the Prophetic Canon." In *Canon and Authority,* ed. George W. Coats and Burke O. Long. Philadelphia: Fortress Press, 1977.

———. "The Unity of the Book of Isaiah." *Int* 36 (1982): 117–29.

Clifford, Richard J. "The Function of Idol Passages in Second Isaiah." *CBQ* 42 (1980): 450–64.

Clines, David J. A. "Story and Poem: The Old Testament as Literature and as Scripture." *Int* 34 (1980): 115–27.

Conrad, Edgar W. "Changing Context: The Bible and the Study of Religion." In *Perspectives on Language and Text: Essays in Honor of Francis I. Andersen's Sixtieth Birthday, July 28, 1985,* ed. E. W. Conrad and E. G. Newing. Winona Lake, Ind.: Eisenbrauns, 1987.

———. "The Fear Not Oracles in Second Isaiah." *VT* 34 (1984): 126–52.

———. *Fear Not Warrior: A Study of 'al tira' Pericopes in the Hebrew Scriptures.* Brown Judaic Studies 75. Chico, Calif.: Scholars, 1985.

———. "Patriarchal Traditions in Second Isaiah." Ph.D. diss., Princeton Theological Seminary, 1974.

———. "The Community as King in Second Isaiah." In *Understanding the Word: Essays in Honor of Bernhard W. Anderson,* ed. James T. Butler, Edgar W. Conrad, and Ben C. Ollenburger. JSOTSup 37. Sheffield: JSOT, 1985.

———. "The Royal Narratives and the Structure of the Book of Isaiah." *JSOT* 41 (1988): 67–81.

———. "Second Isaiah and the Priestly Oracle of Salvation." *ZAW* 93 (1981): 234–46.

Cornill, C. H. "Die Composition des Buches Jesaja." *ZAW* 4 (1884): 83–105.

Dentan, Robert C. *Preface to Old Testament Theology.* Rev. ed. New York: Seabury, 1963.

Detweiler, Robert, ed. *Derrida and Biblical Studies.* Semeia 23. Chico, Calif.: Scholars, 1982.

Dumbrell, William J. "The Purpose of the Book of Isaiah." *Tyndale Bulletin* 36 (1985): 111–28.

Eaton, J. H. "The Origin of the Book of Isaiah." *VT* 9 (1959): 138–57.

Eissfeldt, Otto. *The Old Testament: An Introduction*. Trans. Peter R. Ackroyd. New York: Harper and Row, 1965.

Evans, Craig. "The Unity and Parallel Structure of Isaiah." *VT* 38 (1988): 129–47.

Fewell, Danna Nolan. "Sennacherib's Defeat: Words at War in 2 Kings 18:13 – 19:37." *JSOT* 34 (1986): 79–90.

Fichtner, J. "Jahves Plan in der Botschaft des Jesaja." *ZAW* 63 (1951): 16–33.

Fish, Stanley. *Is There a Text in This Class? The Authority of Interpretive Communities*. Cambridge: Harvard University Press, 1980.

Fohrer, Georg. *Das Buch Jesaja*. 3 vols. Zürcher Bibelkommentare. Stuttgart: Zwingli, 1962–64.

———. "Entstehung, Komposition, und Überlieferung von Jesaja 1–39." *BZAW* 99 (1967): 113–47.

———. *Introduction to the Old Testament*. Trans. David E. Green. Nashville: Abingdon, 1965.

———. "Jesaja 1 als Zusammenfassung der Verkündigung Jesajas." *BZAW* 99 (1967): 148–67.

Fowler, Robert M. "Who Is 'the Reader' in Reader Response Criticism?" In *Reader Response Approaches to Biblical and Secular Texts*. Semeia 31. Decatur, Ga.: Scholars, 1985.

Friedländer, M., ed. *The Commentary of Ibn Ezra on Isaiah: Edited from MSS. and Translated, with Notes, Introductions, and Indexes*. London, 1873. Reprint. New York: Philip Feldheim, 1948.

Garbini, Giovanni. *History and Ideology in Ancient Israel*. Trans. John Bowden. London: SCM, 1986.

Gilkey, Langdon. "Cosmology, Ontology, and the Travail of Biblical Language." *JR* 41 (1961): 194–205. Reprinted in *God's Activity in the World: The Contemporary Problem*, ed. Owen C. Thomas. Studies in Religion 31. Chico, Calif.: Scholars, 1983.

Gitay, Yehoshua. "Deutero-Isaiah: Oral or Written?" *JBL* 99 (1980): 185–97.

——. *Prophecy and Persuasion: A Study of Isaiah 40—48.* Forum Theologiae Linguisticae 14. Bonn: Linguistica Biblica, 1981.

Goody, J., ed. *Literacy in Traditional Societies.* Cambridge: Cambridge University Press, 1968.

Grimm, Werner. *Fürchte dich nicht: Ein exegetischer Zugang zum Seelsorgepotential einer deuterojesajanischen Gattung.* European University Studies 23. Frankfurt: Peter Lang, 1986.

Gunkel, Hermann. *The Psalms: A Form-Critical Introduction.* Trans. Thomas Horner. Facet Books Biblical Series 19. Philadelphia: Fortress Press, 1967.

Gunn, David. "New Directions in the Study of the Hebrew Narrative." *JSOT* 39 (1987): 65–75.

Hasel, G. F. "Remnant." *ISBE,* vol. 4. Grand Rapids: Eerdmans, 1988.

——. *The Remnant.* Berrien Springs, Mich.: Andrews University, 1974.

Hirsch, E. D. *The Aims of Interpretation.* Chicago: University of Chicago Press, 1976.

——. *Validity in Interpretation.* New Haven: Yale University Press, 1967.

Holub, Robert C. *Reception Theory: A Critical Introduction.* New Accents. London: Methuen, 1984.

Iser, Wolfgang. *The Act of Reading: A Theory of Aesthetic Response.* London: Routledge and Kegan Paul, 1978.

Jauss, Hans Robert. *Aesthetic Experience and Literary Hermeneutics.* Trans. Michael Shaw. History and Theory of Literature 3. Minneapolis: University of Minnesota Press, 1982.

——. "Literary History as a Challenge to Literary Theory." *New Literary History* 2 (1970): 7–37.

——. *Toward an Aesthetic of Reception.* Trans. Timothy Bali. Theory and History of Literature 2. Minneapolis: University of Minnesota Press, 1982.

Jeanrond, Werner G. *Text and Interpretation as Categories of Theological Thinking.* Trans. Thomas J. Wilson. New York: Crossroad, 1988.

Jensen, Joseph. "The Age of Immanuel." *CBQ* 41 (1979): 220–39.

———. *The Use of tôrâ by Isaiah: His Debate with the Wisdom Tradition*. CBQMS 3. Washington, D.C.: Catholic Biblical Association, 1973.

———. "Weal and Woe in Isaiah: Consistency and Continuity." *CBQ* 43 (1981): 167–87.

———. "Yahweh's Plan in Isaiah and in the Rest of the Old Testament." *CBQ* 48 (1986): 443–55.

Jones, D. R. "The Traditio of the Oracles of Isaiah of Jerusalem." *ZAW* 67 (1955): 226–46.

Kaiser, Otto. *Isaiah 1–12*. 2d ed. Trans. John Bowden. OTL. Philadelphia: Westminster, 1983.

———. *Isaiah 13–39*. Trans. R. A. Wilson. OTL. Philadelphia: Westminster, 1974.

Koch, Klaus. *The Growth of the Biblical Tradition: The Form-Critical Method*. Trans. S. M. Cupitt. New York: Charles Scribner's Sons, 1969.

Kolodny, Annette. "Dancing through the Minefield: Some Observations on the Theory, Practice, and Politics of Feminist Literary Criticism." In *Men's Studies Modified: The Impact of Feminism on the Academic Disciplines,* ed. Dale Spender. The Athene Series. Oxford: Pergamon, 1981.

LaCapra, Dominick. *History and Criticism*. Ithaca: Cornell University Press, 1985.

Lack, Rémi. *La symbolique du Livre d'Isaïe: Essai sur l'image littéraire comme élément de structuration*. AnBib 59. Rome: Biblical Institute, 1973.

LaFargue, Michael. "Are Texts Determinate? Derrida, Barth, and the Role of the Biblical Scholar." *HTR* 81 (1988): 341–57.

Liebreich, Leon J. "The Compilation of the Book of Isaiah." *JQR* 46 (1955–56): 259–77; and 47 (1956–57): 114–38.

Long, Burke O. "On Finding Hidden Premises." *JSOT* 39 (1987): 10–14.

Luther, Martin. "The Babylonian Captivity of the Church." In *Three Treatises,* trans. A. T. W. Steinhäuser and rev. F. C. Ahrens and A. R. Wentz. Philadelphia: Fortress Press, 1960.

McCarthy, Brian Rice. "Reforming the Church's Self-Understanding: The Role of Historical-Critical Studies." *JES* 24 (1987): 232–53.

176   *BIBLIOGRAPHY*

McKnight, Edgar V. *The Bible and the Reader: An Introduction to Literary Criticism.* Philadelphia: Fortress Press, 1985.

Malina, Bruce J. "Christ and Time: Swiss or Mediterranean?" *CBQ* 51 (1989): 1–31.

Melugin, Roy F. *The Formation of Isaiah 40–55.* BZAW 141. Berlin: de Gruyter, 1976.

Moore, Stephen D. "Negative Hermeneutics, Insubstantial Texts: Stanley Fish and the Biblical Interpreter." *JAAR* 54 (1986): 707–19.

Morgan, Robert, with John Barton. *Biblical Interpretation.* Oxford Bible Series. Oxford: Oxford University Press, 1988.

Muilenburg, James. "The Book of Isaiah: Chapters 40–66." *IB,* vol. 5. New York: Abingdon, 1956.

Naidoff, Bruce D. "The Rhetoric of Encouragement in Isaiah 40:12-31: A Form Critical Study." *ZAW* 93 (1981): 62–76.

North, Christopher R. "Immanuel." *IDB,* vol 2. New York: Abingdon, 1962.

Ollenburger, Ben. C. "Biblical Theology: Situating the Discipline." In *Understanding the Word: Essays in Honor of Bernhard W. Anderson,* ed. James T. Butler, Edgar W. Conrad, and Ben. C. Ollenburger. JSOTSup 37. Sheffield: JSOT, 1985.

Patrick, Dale. *The Rendering of God in the Old Testament.* OBT. Philadelphia: Fortress Press, 1981.

Pfeiffer, R. H. *Introduction to the Old Testament.* New York: Harper and Brothers, 1941.

Polk, Timothy. *The Prophetic Persona: Jeremiah and the Language of the Self.* JSOTSup 32. Sheffield: JSOT, 1984.

Polzin, Robert M. *Moses and the Deuteronomist: A Literary Study of the Deuteronomic History.* New York: Seabury, 1980.

Rendtorff, Rolf. "Zur Komposition des Buches Jesaja." *VT* 34 (1984): 295–320.

Rimmon-Kenan, Shlomith. *Narrative Fiction: Contemporary Poetics.* New Accents. London: Methuen, 1983.

Sawyer, John E. A. *Isaiah.* 2 vols. DSB. Philadelphia: Westminster, 1984–86.

Schmitt, John J. *Isaiah and His Interpreters.* New York: Paulist, 1986.

Schoors, Antoon. *I Am God Your Saviour: A Form Critical Study of the Main Genres in Is. XL–LV.* VTSup 24. Leiden: Brill, 1973.

Schwartz, Regina M. "Joseph's Bones and the Resurrection of the Text: Remembering in the Bible." *Publications of the Modern Language Association of America* 104 (1988): 114–24.

Seitz, Christopher R. "The Divine Council: Temporary Transition and New Prophecy in the Book of Isaiah." *JBL* 109 (1990): 229–47.

———. "Isaiah 1–66: Making Sense of the Whole." In *Reading and Preaching the Book of Isaiah,* ed. C. R. Seitz. Philadelphia: Fortress Press, 1988.

Sheppard, Gerald T. "The Anti-Assyrian Redaction and the Canonical Context of Isaiah 1–39." *JBL* 104 (1985): 193–216.

Simon, Uriel. "Ibn Ezra between Medievalism and Modernism: The Case of Isaiah XL–LXVI." VTSup 36 (1985): 257–71.

Spykerboer, H. C. *The Structure and Composition of Deutero-Isaiah: With Special Reference to the Polemics against Idolatry.* Rijksuniversiteit te Groningen. Franeker, Netherlands: T. Wever, 1976.

Steiner, George. *Real Presences: Is There Anything in What We Say?* London: Faber and Faber, 1989.

Stendahl, Krister. "Biblical Theology, Contemporary." *IDB,* vol. 1. New York: Abingdon, 1962.

Sternberg, Meir. *The Poetics of Biblical Narrative: Ideological Literature and the Drama of Reading.* Indiana Studies in Biblical Literature. Bloomington: Indiana University Press, 1985.

Suleiman, Susan, and Crosman, Inge, eds. *The Reader in the Text: Essays on Audience and Interpretation.* Princeton: Princeton University Press, 1980.

Sweeney, Marvin A. *Isaiah 1–4 and the Post-Exilic Understanding of the Isaianic Tradition.* BZAW 171. Berlin: de Gruyter, 1988.

Thompson, Michael E. "Isaiah's Ideal King." *JSOT* 24 (1982): 79–88.

Tompkins, Jane P., ed. *Reader Response Criticism: From Formalism to Post-Structuralism.* Baltimore: Johns Hopkins University Press, 1980.

Vermeylen, J. *Du prophète Isaïe à l'apocalyptique. Isaïe i-xxxv, miroir d'un démi-millénaire d'expérience religieuse en Israël.* 2 vols. Paris: J. Gabalda, 1977.

Vorster, Willem S. "Readings, Readers, and the Succession Narrative: An Essay on Reception." *ZAW* 98 (1986): 351-62.

Watts, John D. W. *Isaiah 1-33.* WBC 24. Waco, Tex.: Word Books, 1985.

——. *Isaiah 34-66.* WBC 25. Waco, Tex.: Word Books, 1987.

Weippert, Manfred. "Assyrische Propheten der Zeit Asarhaddons und Assurbanipals." In *Assyrian Royal Inscriptions: New Horizons in Literary, Ideological, and Historical Analysis,* ed. F. M. Fales. Orientis Antiqui Collectio 17. Rome: Istituto per l'Oriente, 1981.

Westermann, Claus. *Isaiah 40-66: A Commentary.* Trans. D. M. G. Stalker. OTL. Philadelphia: Westminster, 1969.

Wiklander, Bertil. *Prophecy as Literature: A Text Linguistic and Rhetorical Approach to Isaiah 2-4.* ConB OT 22. Stockholm: Liber Tryck, 1984.

Wildberger, Hans. *Jesaja.* Vol. 3. BKAT. Neukirchen-Vluyn: Neukirchener Verlag, 1982.

——. "Jesajas Verständnis der Geschichte." *VTSup* 9 (1962): 83-117.

——. "Die Neuinterpretation des Erwählungsglaubens Israel in der Krise der Exilzeit." In *Wort — Gebot — Glaube: Beiträge zur Theologie des Alten Testaments,* ed. Joachim Stoebe. Abhandlungen zur Theologie des Alten und Neuen Testament, 59. Zürich: Zwingli, 1970.

Wolff, Herbert W. "A Solution to the Immanuel Prophecy in Isaiah 7:14 — 8:22." *JBL* 91 (1972): 449-56.

Index of

Biblical Passages

Index of
Authors